OPINION AND EVIDENCE

Harry P. Kerr HARVARD UNIVERSITY

OPINION *and* EVIDENCE

CASES FOR ARGUMENT AND DISCUSSION

HARCOURT, BRACE & WORLD, *Inc.*

NEW YORK · CHICAGO · SAN FRANCISCO · ATLANTA

64276

CONTENTS

PREFACE

ARGUMENT, persuasion, and discussion are widely employed outside the classroom to settle questions dealing with past events, but within the classroom these methods of oral discourse are usually confined to questions of future policy. The emphasis is not capricious. Policy questions tend to be inherently more worthy of the student's time. Attempting to determine the most suitable method of rehabilitating a criminal, for example, might well contribute more to a student's understanding of the world in which he lives than would close consideration of the probably bizarre circumstances which led to the criminal's incarceration.

If the value of investigating past events is in some ways more limited, of course, it is by no means inconsequential. Judges, legislators and historians, among others, are much concerned with interpreting the pronouncements of earlier ages, with eliciting and evaluating testimony, and with inferring the probable from the certain. Investigation of policy questions normally provides only limited and indirect experience with these undertakings.

That such important areas of human activity are touched upon lightly in schools is no doubt due less to unwillingness than to the difficulty of securing adequate information about a sufficient variety of questions. A reasonable amount of research in books and periodicals available to the general public would produce much information concerning the rehabilitation of criminals, but the essential facts which led to a man's imprisonment might well have to be winnowed from a thousand-page transcript of his trial—if the transcript could be secured. Rehabilitation raises certain considerations, moreover, and foreign trade clearly raises others. Frequently it is not obvious that a murder trial and a congressional investigation confront the student with identical tasks in evaluating expert testimony, while two ostensibly similar trials for grand larceny may hinge on the quite different problems of interpreting a statute and evaluating eyewitness testimony.

Opinion and Evidence represents an effort to minimize the difficulties of access and selection by presenting condensed statements of twenty-six problems in interpreting past events. The essential information in some cases can be mastered in a few minutes; none requires more than a few hours. Most of the student's time can therefore be devoted to the characteristic difficulties encountered in asking questions about the past. He will find that emphasis has been placed on the necessity of discovering the point at issue and the considerations which are relevant to it. He will find also that there are many problems in handling documentary and physical evidence, expert and eyewitness testimony, and interpretation and application of statutes.

The cases can be employed in a variety of ways. Those in Part I are particularly well suited to impromptu speaking and group discussion. "The Speluncean Explorers" furnishes admirable material for an introduction to one phase of legal advocacy, and the cases in Part II challenge the student's ability to formulate a coherent argument from a mass of conflicting evidence. The latter cases also provide material for exercises in briefing, as illustrated by the student papers which follow *The People v. Lucas.*

With the exception of "The Speluncean Explorers," each case is based on an actual incident. Names have often been changed to avoid unnecessary embarrassment, and in some cases, notably the first eight in Part II, the facts have been altered to provide a closer balance among several possible interpretations. Nothing here is unreal or improbable, however, except as human conduct sometimes strains credulity. "The Greasy Carving Knife" may, for example, seem to be the product of an energetic imagination, but in fact the story was reported in the New York *Times* for June 17, 1960.

Herbert A. Wichelns of Cornell University composed the Lucas case and taught the present writer most of what he knows about the preparation and use of such material. The seven cases which follow Lucas (Harvey, Ingram, Marman-Nielsen, Giordano, McCollum, Dempsey, and Tower) were written by the late Russel H. Wagner while he was a member of the Cornell faculty. Four short cases (Miller, Koppell, Watson, and Lowenthal) were taken from a collection of anonymous materials compiled at Cornell. These twelve cases are published with the permission of Professor Wichelns, Mrs. Helen F. Wagner, and Cornell's Department of Speech and Drama.

The late James A. Winans is the probable adaptor of the Blaisdell and Weeks cases for student use. Winans' lifelong interest in the Knapp-White murder is well known. He seems also to have been chiefly responsible for introducing Wichelns, Wagner, and others to classroom use of cases. I am indebted to Clarence S. Angell of the University of Massachusetts, Wilbur S. Howell of Princeton, and Almon B. Ives of Dartmouth for bringing the Blaisdell and Weeks cases to my attention and for telling me something of Winans' early work.

In response to the suggestions of colleagues and students over a period of years, I have made changes in most of the cases mentioned above and consequently should be charged with any shortcomings in them as well as with deficiencies in the remaining eleven. It is a pleasure to acknowledge the advice that users of the cases have given me, and to thank those who have graciously granted permission to publish their work. To my wife, Roslyn M. Kerr, who never admitted she was tired of listening, I offer my deepest appreciation.

H. P. K.

Cambridge, Massachusetts
August 1962

Part I

INTERPRETATION AND IMAGINATION

THE ABILITY to perceive many sides of a question is essential to successful argument. Without it, only chance determines whether the line of argument that occurs to one first is the strongest available, or merely a feeble imitation which he would abandon instantly if given a choice. Without it, he is blind to the strengths and weaknesses of his own position as an opponent might see them, and is consequently at a serious disadvantage in anticipating and preparing for the opponent's attacks.

Professor Fuller's entertaining and instructive "Speluncean Explorers" illustrates the varying complexion a given set of circumstances can assume when viewed from different perspectives. The intent of the case, as the author points out in a postscript, is to bring "into a common focus certain divergent philosophies of law and government [which] presented men with live questions of choice in the days of Plato and Aristotle [and which] perhaps . . . will continue to do so when our era has had its say about them."

These divergent philosophies emerge in opinions expressed by the five justices of the "Supreme Court of Newgarth" who must rule on the applicability to a simple but bizarre situation of the statute forbidding murder. No member of the court wishes to send the defendants to the gallows, but each finds it difficult to square his understanding of the law with his sentiments toward the prisoners.

Chief Justice Truepenny is the staunch advocate of literal interpretation. He finds the defendants guilty within the letter of the law, but salves his conscience with the belief that executive clemency will save them from the death penalty. Justice Foster neither denies his conscience nor takes comfort in the likelihood of outside intervention. He discovers two independent lines of argument, either of which in his opinion will free the alleged murderers. One is a rather uncommon notion concerning the limits of the sphere to which man-made law should be applied. Foster's second position is an extreme one, the counterpart to Truepenny's equally extreme attachment to the letter of the law. Foster would interpret the statute in terms of its spirit or intent. Justice Tatting wrestles with Foster's contentions in an effort to refute them, but ends as a model of judicial indecision. He is unable to form an opinion regarding the case and withdraws. Justice Keen dispatches Foster's arguments with greater vigor and apparently greater personal satisfaction than Tatting. No advocate of halfway measures, Keen says firmly that the defendants are guilty under the law, that the law is badly drawn, and that the legislature should write more precise laws which judges can apply with both logic and equity. Justice Handy, finally, rejects Keen's recourse to the lawmakers. Government, says Handy, cannot be a government of laws, but must be a government of men who sensibly employ law as an instrument for regulating society. But even as Handy writes, his opinion inadvertently suggests some of the problems that arise when lines of authority are blurred and courts undertake to play the role of legislatures.

No summary of "The Speluncean Explorers" can adequately portray the many additional problems which Professor Fuller suggests through humor and innuendo. But we should not pass silently over the final irony. Tatting's indecision and consequent withdrawal results in an evenly divided court, and this automatically affirms the lower court's verdict of guilty. Tatting's inability to act appropriately makes him the instrument for the very act from which he shrank.

One or more of the philosophies exemplified in this case underlies most decisions rendered from the bench and the jurors' box. One or more of these philosophies governs the strategy employed by advocates in virtually every case argued in court. Their significance is not limited to the courtroom, however. What Justice Handy summarizes in his opinion as "learned disquisitions on the distinction between positive law and the law of nature, the language of the statute and the purpose of the statute, judicial functions and executive functions, judicial legislation and legislative legislation" have their counterparts in the attitudes of those who judge and those who argue in all areas of man's activities.

Viewpoints of such wide currency are well worth becoming familiar with, but the utility of "The Speluncean Explorers" to the student of argument goes beyond merely illustrating some common ways of interpreting laws and actions, as valuable as that may be. The case depicts vividly why it is important to be able to consider a problem from many viewpoints. If one is first attracted to the position of Truepenny, then Foster, then Tatting, then Keen, then Handy, and is finally somewhat confused about the whole matter, he will perceive that his convictions rested on shallow roots and will realize that any man's convictions must be shallow until he comprehends, examines, and rejects opposing convictions.

"The Speluncean Explorers" will be of greater profit, both as an approach to the interpretation of rules and as an exercise in broadening one's perspective on problems, if one undertakes to defend what he considers to be the soundest solution to the case. The ten remaining cases in Part I offer further opportunities to strengthen and test one's powers of interpretation and imagination on problems which are less bizarre, but not less demanding, than that which confronted the Supreme Court of Newgarth.

THE SPELUNCEAN EXPLORERS *by* Lon L. Fuller

Carter Professor of General Jurisprudence, Harvard Law School

IN THE SUPREME COURT OF NEWGARTH, 4300

THE DEFENDANTS, having been indicted for the crime of murder, were convicted and sentenced to be hanged by the Court of General Instances of the County of Stowfield. They bring a petition of error before this Court. The facts sufficiently appear in the opinion of the Chief Justice.

TRUEPENNY, C. J. The four defendants are members of the Speluncean Society, an organization of amateurs interested in the exploration of caves. Early in May of 4299 they, in the company of Roger Whetmore, then also a member of the Society, penetrated into the interior of a limestone cavern of the type found in the Central Plateau of this Commonwealth. While they were in a position remote from the entrance to the cave, a landslide occurred. Heavy boulders fell in such a manner as to block completely the only known opening to the cave. When the men discovered their predicament they settled themselves near the obstructed entrance to wait until a rescue party should remove the detritus that prevented them from leaving their underground prison. On the failure of Whetmore and the defendants to return to their homes, the Secretary of the Society was notified by their families. It appears that the explorers had left indications at the headquarters of the Society concerning the location of the cave they proposed to visit. A rescue party was promptly dispatched to the spot.

The task of rescue proved one of overwhelming difficulty. It was necessary to supplement the forces of the original party by repeated increments of men and machines, which had to be conveyed at great expense to the remote and isolated region in which the cave was located. A huge temporary camp of workmen, engineers, geologists, and other experts was established. The work of removing the obstruction was several times frustrated by fresh landslides. In one of these, ten of the workmen engaged in clearing the entrance were killed. The treasury of the Speluncean Society was soon exhausted in the rescue effort, and the sum of eight hundred thousand frelars, raised partly by popular subscription and partly by legislative grant, was expended before the imprisoned men were rescued. Success was finally achieved on the thirty-second day after the men entered the cave.

Since it was known that the explorers had carried with them only scant provisions, and since it was also known that there was no animal or vegetable matter within the cave on which they might subsist, anxiety was early felt that they might meet death by starvation before access to them could be obtained. On the twentieth day of their imprisonment it was learned for the first time that they had taken with them into the cave a portable wireless machine capable of both sending and receiving messages. A similar machine was promptly installed in the rescue camp and oral communication established with the unfortunate men within the mountain. They asked to be informed how long a time would be required to release them. The engineers in charge of the project answered that at least ten days would be required even if no new landslides occurred. The explorers then asked if any physicians were present, and were placed in communication with a committee of medical experts. The imprisoned men described their condition and the rations they had taken with them, and asked for a medical opinion whether they would be likely to live without food for ten days longer. The chairman of the committee of physicians told them that there was little possibility of this. The wireless machine within the cave then remained silent for eight hours. When communication was re-established the men asked to speak again with the physicians. The chairman of the physicians' committee was placed before the apparatus, and Whetmore, speaking on behalf of himself and the defendants, asked whether they would be able to survive for ten days longer if they consumed the flesh of one of their number. The physicians' chairman reluctantly answered this question in the affirmative. Whetmore asked whether it would be advisable for them to cast lots to determine which of them should be eaten. None of the physicians present was willing to answer the question. Whetmore then asked if there were among the party a judge or other official of the government who would answer this question. None of those attached to the rescue camp was willing to assume the role of advisor in this matter. He then asked if any minister or priest would answer their question, and none was found who would do so. Thereafter no further messages were received from within the cave, and it was assumed (erroneously, it later appeared) that the electric batteries of the explorers' wireless machine had become exhausted. When the imprisoned men were finally released it was learned that on the twenty-third day after their entrance into the cave Whetmore had been killed and eaten by his companions.

From the testimony of the defendants, which was accepted by the jury, it appears that it was Whetmore who first proposed that they might find the nutriment without which survival was impossible in the flesh of one of their own number. It was also Whetmore who first proposed the use of some method of casting lots, calling the attention of the defendants to a pair of dice he happened to have with him. The defendants were at first reluctant to adopt so desperate a procedure, but after the conversations by wireless related above, they finally agreed on the plan proposed by Whetmore. After much discussion of the mathematical problems involved, agreement was finally reached on a method of determining the issue by the use of the dice.

Before the dice were cast, however, Whetmore declared that he withdrew from the arrangement, as he had decided on reflection to wait for another week before embracing an expedient so frightful and odious. The others charged him with a breach of faith and proceeded to cast the dice. When it came Whetmore's turn, the dice were cast for him by one of the defendants, and he was asked to declare any objections he might have to the fairness of the throw. He stated that he had no such objections. The throw went against him, and he was then put to death and eaten by his companions.

After the rescue of the defendants, and after they had completed a stay in a hospital where they underwent a course of treatment for malnutrition and shock, they were indicted for the murder of Roger Whetmore. At the trial, after the testimony had been concluded, the foreman of the jury (a lawyer by profession) inquired of the court whether the jury might not find a special verdict, leaving it to the court to say whether on the facts as found the defendants were guilty. After some discussion, both the Prosecutor and counsel for the defendants indicated their acceptance of this procedure, and it was adopted by the court. In a lengthy special verdict the jury found the facts as I have related them above, and found further that if on these facts the defendants were guilty of the crime charged against them, then they found the defendants guilty. On the basis of this verdict, the trial judge ruled that the defendants were guilty of murdering Roger Whetmore. The judge then sentenced them to be hanged, the law of our Commonwealth permitting him no discretion with respect to the penalty to be imposed. After the release of the jury, its members joined in a communication to the Chief Executive asking that the sentence be commuted to an imprisonment of six months. The trial judge addressed a similar communication to the Chief Executive. As yet no action with respect to these pleas has been taken, as the Chief Executive is apparently awaiting our disposition of this petition of error.

It seems to me that in dealing with this extraordinary case the jury and the trial judge followed a course that was not only fair and wise, but the only course that was open to them under the law. The language of our statute is well known: "Whoever shall willfully take the life of another shall be punished by death." N.C.S.A. (N.S.) § 12-A. This statute permits of no exception applicable to this case, however our sympathies may incline us to make allowance for the tragic situation in which these men found themselves.

In a case like this the principle of executive clemency seems admirably suited to mitigate the rigors of the law, and I propose to my colleagues that we follow the example of the jury and the trial judge by joining in the communications they have addressed to the Chief Executive. There is every reason to believe that these requests for clemency will be heeded, coming as they do from those who have studied the case and had an opportunity to become thoroughly acquainted with all its circumstances. It is highly improbable that the Chief Executive would deny these requests unless he were himself to hold hearings at least as extensive as those involved in the trial below, which lasted for three months. The holding of such hearings (which would virtually amount to a retrial of the case) would scarcely be compatible with the function of the Executive as it is usually conceived. I think we may therefore assume that some form of clemency will be extended to these defendants. If this is done, then justice will be accomplished without impairing either the letter or spirit of our statutes and without offering any encouragement for the disregard of law.

FOSTER, J. I am shocked that the Chief Justice, in an effort to escape the embarrassments of this tragic case, should have adopted, and should have proposed to his colleagues, an expedient at once so sordid and so obvious. I believe something more is on trial in this case than the fate of these unfortunate explorers; that is, the law of our Commonwealth. If this Court declares that under our law these men have committed a crime, then our law is itself convicted in the tribunal of common sense, no matter what happens to the individuals involved in this petition of error. For us to assert that the law we uphold and expound compels us to a conclusion we are ashamed of, and from which we can only escape by appealing to a dispensation resting within the personal whim of the Executive, seems to me to amount to an admission that the law of this Commonwealth no longer pretends to incorporate justice.

For myself, I do not believe that our law compels the monstrous conclusion that these men are murderers. I believe, on the contrary, that it declares them to be innocent of any crime. I rest this conclusion on two independent grounds, either of which is of itself sufficient to justify the acquittal of these defendants.

The first of these grounds rests on a premise that may arouse opposition until it has been examined candidly. I take the view that the enacted or positive law of this Commonwealth, including all of its statutes and precedents, is inapplicable to this case, and that the case is governed instead by what ancient writers in Europe and America called "the law of nature."

This conclusion rests on the proposition that our positive law is predicated on the possibility of men's coexistence in society. When a situation arises in which the coexistence of men becomes impossible, then a condition that underlies all of our precedents and statutes has ceased to exist. When that condition disappears, then it is my opinion that the force of our positive law disappears with it. We are not accustomed to applying the maxim *cessante ratione legis, cessat et ipsa lex* to the whole of our enacted law, but I believe that this is a case where the maxim should be so applied.

The proposition that all positive law is based on the possibility of men's coexistence has a strange sound, not because the truth it contains is strange, but simply because it is a truth so obvious and pervasive that we seldom have occasion to give words to it. Like the air we breathe, it so pervades our environment that we forget that it exists until we are suddenly deprived of it. Whatever particular objects may be sought by the various branches of our law, it is apparent on reflection that all of them are directed toward facilitating and improving men's coexistence and regulating with fairness and equity the relations of their life in common. When the assumption that men may live together loses its truth, as it obviously did in this extraordinary situation where life only became possible by the taking of life, then the basic premises underlying our whole legal order have lost their meaning and force.

Had the tragic events of this case taken place a mile beyond the territorial limits of our Commonwealth, no one would pretend that our law was applicable to them. We recognize that jurisdiction rests on a territorial basis. The grounds of this principle are by no means obvious and are seldom examined. I take it that this principle is supported by an assumption that it is feasible to impose a single legal order upon a group of men only if they live together within the confines of a given area of the earth's surface. The premise that men shall coexist in a group underlies, then, the territorial principle, as it does all of law. Now I contend that a case may be removed morally from the force of a legal order, as well as geographically. If we look to the purposes of law and government, and to the premises underlying our positive law, these men when they made their fateful decision were as remote from our legal order as if they had been a thousand miles beyond our boundaries. Even in a physical sense, their underground prison was separated from our courts and writ-servers by a solid curtain of rock that could be removed only after the most extraordinary expenditures of time and effort.

I conclude, therefore, that at the time Roger Whetmore's life was ended by these defendants, they were, to use the quaint language of nineteenth-century writers, not in a "state of civil society" but in a "state of nature."

This has the consequence that the law applicable to them is not the enacted and established law of this Commonwealth, but the law derived from those principles that were appropriate to their condition. I have no hesitancy in saying that under those principles they were guiltless of any crime.

What these men did was done in pursuance of an agreement accepted by all of them and first proposed by Whetmore himself. Since it was apparent that their extraordinary predicament made inapplicable the usual principles that regulate men's relations with one another, it was necessary for them to draw, as it were, a new charter of government appropriate to the situation in which they found themselves.

It has from antiquity been recognized that the most basic principle of law or government is to be found in the notion of contract or agreement. Ancient thinkers, especially during the period from 1600 to 1900, used to base government itself on a supposed original social compact. Skeptics pointed out that this theory contradicted the known facts of history, and that there was no scientific evidence to support the notion that any government was ever founded in the manner supposed by the theory. Moralists replied that, if the compact was a fiction from a historical point of view, the notion of compact or agreement furnished the only ethical justification on which the powers of government, which include that of taking life, could be rested. The powers of government can only be justified morally on the ground that these are powers that reasonable men would agree upon and accept if they were faced with the necessity of constructing anew some order to make their life in common possible.

Fortunately, our Commonwealth is not bothered by the perplexities that beset the ancients. We know as a matter of historical truth that our government was founded upon a contract or free accord of men. The archeological proof is conclusive that in the first period following the Great Spiral the survivors of that holocaust voluntarily came together and drew up a charter of government. Sophistical writers have raised questions as to the power of those remote contractors to bind future generations, but the fact remains that our government traces itself back in an unbroken line to that original charter.

If, therefore, our hangmen have the power to end men's lives, if our sheriffs have the power to put delinquent tenants in the street, if our police have the power to incarcerate the inebriated reveler, these powers find their moral justification in that original compact of our forefathers. If we can find no higher source for our legal order, what higher source should we expect these starving unfortunates to find for the order they adopted for themselves?

I believe that the line of argument I have just expounded permits of no rational answer. I realize that it will probably be received with a certain discomfort by many who read this opinion, who will be inclined to suspect that some hidden sophistry must underlie a demonstration that leads to so many unfamiliar conclusions. The source of this discomfort is, however, easy to identify. The usual conditions of human existence incline us to think of human life as an absolute value, not to be sacrificed under any circumstances. There is much that is fictitious about this conception even when it is applied to the ordinary relations of society. We have an illustration of this truth in the very case before us. Ten workmen were killed in the process of removing the rocks from the opening to the cave. Did not the engineers and government officials who directed the rescue effort know that the operations they were undertaking were dangerous and involved a serious risk to the lives of the workmen executing them? If it was proper that these ten lives should be sacrificed to save the lives of five imprisoned explorers, why then are we told it was wrong for these explorers to carry out an arrangement which would save four lives at the cost of one?

Every highway, every tunnel, every building we project involves a risk to human life. Taking these projects in the aggregate, we can calculate with some precision how many deaths the construction of them will require; statisticians can tell you the average cost in human lives of a thousand miles of a four-lane concrete highway. Yet we deliberately and knowingly incur and pay this cost on the assumption that the values obtained for those who survive outweigh the loss. If these things can be said of a society functioning above ground in a normal and ordinary manner, what shall we say of the supposed absolute value of a human life in the desperate situation in which these defendants and their companion Whetmore found themselves?

This concludes the exposition of the first ground of my decision. My second ground proceeds by rejecting hypothetically all the premises on which I have so far proceeded. I concede for purposes of argument that I am wrong in saying that the situation of these men removed them from the effect of our positive law, and I assume that the Consolidated Statutes have the power to penetrate five hundred feet of rock and to impose themselves upon these starving men huddled in their underground prison.

Now it is, of course, perfectly clear that these men did an act that violates the literal wording of the statute which declares that he who "shall willfully take the life of another" is a murderer. But one of the most ancient bits of legal wisdom is the saying that a man may break the letter of the law without breaking the law itself. Every proposition of positive law, whether contained in a statute or a judicial precedent, is to be interpreted reasonably, in the light of its evident purpose. This is a truth so elementary that it is hardly necessary to expatiate on it. Illustrations of its application are numberless and are to be found in every branch of the law. In *Commonwealth* v. *Staymore* the defendant was convicted under a statute making it a crime to leave one's car parked in certain areas for a period longer than two hours. The defendant had attempted to remove his car, but was prevented from doing so because the streets were obstructed by a political demonstration in which he took no part and which he had no reason to anticipate. His conviction was set aside by this Court, although his case fell squarely within the wording of the statute. Again, in *Fehler* v. *Neegas* there was before this Court for construction a statute in which the word "not" had plainly been transposed from its intended position in the final and most crucial section of the act. This transposition was contained in all the successive drafts of the act, where it was apparently overlooked by the draftsmen and sponsors of the legislation. No one was able to prove how the error came about, yet it was apparent that, taking account of the contents of the statute as a whole, an error had been made, since a literal reading of the final clause rendered it inconsistent with everything that had gone before and with the object of the enactment as stated in its preamble. This Court refused to accept a literal interpretation of the statute, and in effect rectified its language by reading the word "not" into the place where it was evidently intended to go.

The statute before us for interpretation has never been applied literally. Centuries ago it was established that a killing in self-defense is excused. There is nothing in the wording of the statute that suggests this exception. Various attempts have been made to reconcile the legal treatment of self-defense with the words of the statute, but in my opinion these are all merely ingenious sophistries. The truth is that the exception in favor of self-defense cannot be reconciled with the *words* of the statute, but only with its *purpose*.

The true reconciliation of the excuse of self-defense with the statute making it a crime to kill another is to be found in the following line of reasoning. One of the principal objects underlying any criminal legislation is that of deterring men from crime. Now it is apparent that if it were declared to be the law that a killing in self-defense is murder such a rule could not operate in a deterrent manner. A man whose life is threatened will repel his aggressor, whatever the law may say. Looking therefore to the broad purposes of criminal legislation, we may safely declare that this statute was not intended to apply to cases of self-defense.

When the rationale of the excuse of self-defense is thus explained, it becomes apparent that precisely the same reasoning is applicable to the case at bar. If in the future any group of men ever find themselves in the tragic predicament of these defendants, we may be sure that their decision whether to live or die will not be controlled by the contents of our criminal code. Accordingly, if we read this statute intelligently it is apparent that it does not apply to this case. The withdrawal of this situation from the effect of the statute is justified by precisely the same considerations that were applied by our predecessors in office centuries ago to the case of self-defense.

There are those who raise the cry of judicial usurpation whenever a court, after analyzing the purpose of a statute, gives to its words a meaning that is not at once apparent to the casual reader who has not studied the statute closely or examined the objectives it seeks to attain. Let me say emphatically that I accept without reservation the proposition that this Court is bound by the statutes of our Commonwealth and that it exercises its powers in subservience to the duly expressed will of the Chamber of Representatives. The line of reasoning I have applied above raises no question of fidelity to enacted law, though it may possibly raise a question of the distinction between intelligent and unintelligent fidelity. No superior wants a servant who lacks the capacity to read between the lines. The stupidest housemaid knows that when she is told "to peel the soup and skim the potatoes" her mistress does not mean what she says. She also knows that when her master tells her to "drop everything and come running" he has overlooked the possibility that she is at the moment in the act of rescuing the baby from the rain barrel. Surely we have a right to expect the same modicum of intelligence from the judiciary. The correction of obvious legislative errors or oversights is not to supplant the legislative will, but to make that will effective.

I therefore conclude that on any aspect under which this case may be viewed these defendants are innocent of the crime of murdering Roger Whetmore, and that the conviction should be set aside.

Tatting, J. In the discharge of my duties as a justice of this Court, I am usually able to dissociate the emotional and intellectual sides of my reactions, and to decide the case before me entirely on the basis of the latter. In passing on this tragic case I find that my usual resources fail me. On the emotional side I find myself torn between sympathy for these men and a feeling of abhorrence and disgust at the monstrous act they committed. I had hoped that I would be able to put these contradictory emotions to one side as irrelevant, and to decide the case on the basis of a convincing and logical demonstration of the result demanded by our law. Unfortunately, this deliverance has not been vouchsafed me.

As I analyze the opinion just rendered by my brother Foster, I find that it is shot through with contradictions and fallacies. Let us begin with his first proposition: these men were not subject to our law because they were not in a "state of civil society" but in a "state of nature." I am not clear why this is so, whether it is because of the thickness of the rock that imprisoned them, or because they were hungry, or because they had set up a "new charter of government" by which the usual rules of law were to be supplanted by a throw of the dice. Other difficulties intrude themselves. If these men passed from the jurisdiction of our law to that of "the law of nature," at what moment did this occur? Was it when the entrance to the cave was blocked, or when the threat of starvation reached a certain undefined degree of intensity, or when the agreement for the throwing of the dice was made? These uncertainties in the doctrine proposed by my brother are capable of producing real difficulties. Suppose, for example, one of these men had had his twenty-first birthday while he was imprisoned within the mountain. On what date would we have to consider that he had attained his majority — when he reached the age of twenty-one, at which time he was, by hypothesis, removed from the effects of our law, or only when he was released from the cave and became again subject to what my brother calls our "positive law"? These difficulties may seem fanciful, yet they only serve to reveal the fanciful nature of the doctrine that is capable of giving rise to them.

But it is not necessary to explore these niceties further to demonstrate the absurdity of my brother's position. Mr. Justice Foster and I are the appointed judges of a court of the Commonwealth of Newgarth, sworn and empowered to administer the laws of that Commonwealth. By what authority do we resolve ourselves into a Court of Nature? If these men were indeed under the law of nature, whence comes our authority to expound and apply that law? Certainly *we* are not in a state of nature.

Let us look at the contents of this code of nature that my brother proposes we adopt as our own and apply to this case. What a topsy-turvy and odious code it is! It is a code in which the law of contracts is more fundamental than the law of murder. It is a code under which a man may make a valid agreement empowering his fellows to eat his own body. Under the provisions of this code, furthermore, such an agreement once made is irrevocable, and if one of the parties attempts to withdraw, the others may take the law into their own hands and enforce the contract by violence — for though my brother passes over in convenient silence the effect of Whetmore's withdrawal, this is the necessary implication of his argument.

The principles my brother expounds contain other implications that cannot be tolerated. He argues that when the defendants set upon Whetmore and killed him (we know not how, perhaps by pounding him with stones) they were only exercising the rights conferred upon them by their bargain. Suppose, however, that Whetmore had had concealed upon his person a revolver, and that when he saw the defendants about to slaughter him he had shot them to death in order to save his own life. My brother's reasoning applied to these facts would make Whetmore out to be a murderer, since the excuse of self-defense would have to be denied to him. If his assailants were acting rightfully in seeking to bring about his death, then of course he could no more plead the excuse that he was defending his own life than could a condemned prisoner who struck down the executioner lawfully attempting to place the noose about his neck.

All of these considerations make it impossible for me to accept the first part of my brother's argument. I can neither accept his notion that these men were under a code of nature which this Court was bound to apply to them, nor can I accept the odious and perverted rules that he would read into that code. I come now to the second part of my brother's opinion, in which he seeks to show that the defendants did not violate the provisions of N.C.S.A. (N.S.) § 12-A. Here the way, instead of being clear, becomes for me misty and ambiguous, though my brother seems unaware of the difficulties that inhere in his demonstrations.

The gist of my brother's argument may be stated in the following terms: No statute, whatever its language, should be applied in a way that contradicts its purpose. One of the purposes of any criminal statute is to deter. The application of the statute making it a crime to kill another to the peculiar facts of this case would contradict this purpose, for it is impossible to believe that the contents of the criminal code could operate in a deterrent manner on men faced with the alternative of life or death. The reasoning by which this exception is read into the statute is, my brother observes, the same as that which is applied in order to provide the excuse of self-defense.

On the face of things this demonstration seems very convincing indeed. My brother's interpretation of the rationale of the excuse of self-defense is in fact supported by a decision of this court, *Commonwealth* v. *Parry*, a precedent I happened to encounter in my research on this case. Though *Commonwealth* v. *Parry* seems generally to have been overlooked in the texts and subsequent decisions, it supports unambiguously the interpretation my brother has put upon the excuse of self-defense.

Now let me outline briefly, however, the perplexities that assail me when I examine my brother's demonstration more closely. It is true that a statute should be applied in the light of its purpose, and that *one* of the purposes of criminal legislation is recognized to be deterrence. The difficulty is that other purposes are also ascribed to the law of crimes. It has been said that one of its objects is to provide an orderly outlet for the instinctive human demand for retribution. *Commonwealth* v. *Scape*. It has also been said that its object is the rehabilitation of the wrongdoer. *Commonwealth* v. *Makeover*. Other theories have been propounded. Assuming that we must interpret a statute in the light of its purpose, what are we to do when it has many purposes or when its purposes are disputed?

A similar difficulty is presented by the fact that although there is authority for my brother's interpretation of the excuse of self-defense, there is other authority which assigns to that excuse a different rationale. Indeed, until I happened on *Commonwealth* v. *Parry* I had never heard of the explanation given by my brother. The taught doctrine of our law schools, memorized by generations of law students, runs in the following terms: The statute concerning murder requires a "willful" act. The man who acts to repel an aggressive threat to his own life does not act "willfully," but in response to an impulse deeply ingrained in human nature. I suspect that there is hardly a lawyer in this Commonwealth who is not familiar with this line of reasoning, especially since the point is a great favorite of the bar examiners.

Now the familiar explanation for the excuse of self-defense just expounded obviously cannot be applied by analogy to the facts of this case. These men acted not only "willfully" but with great deliberation and after hours of discussing what they should do. Again we encounter a forked path, with one line of reasoning leading us in one direction and another in a direction that is exactly the opposite. This perplexity is in this case compounded, as it were, for we have to set off one explanation, incorporated in a virtually unknown precedent of this Court, against another explanation, which forms a part of the taught legal tradition of our law schools, but which, so far as I know, has never been adopted in any judicial decision.

I recognize the relevance of the precedents cited by my brother concerning the displaced "not" and the defendant who parked overtime. But what are we to do with one of the landmarks of our jurisprudence, which again my brother passes over in silence? This is *Commonwealth* v. *Valjean.* Though the case is somewhat obscurely reported, it appears that the defendant was indicted for the larceny of a loaf of bread, and offered as a defense that he was in a condition approaching starvation. The court refused to accept this defense. If hunger cannot justify the theft of wholesome and natural food, how can it justify the killing and eating of a man? Again, if we look at the thing in terms of deterrence, is it likely that a man will starve to death to avoid a jail sentence for the theft of a loaf of bread? My brother's demonstrations would compel us to overrule *Commonwealth* v. *Valjean,* and many other precedents that have been built on that case.

Again, I have difficulty in saying that no deterrent effect whatever could be attributed to a decision that these men were guilty of murder. The stigma of the word "murderer" is such that it is quite likely, I believe, that if these men had known that their act was deemed by the law to be murder they would have waited for a few days at least before carrying out their plan. During that time some unexpected relief might have come. I realize that this observation only reduces the distinction to a matter of degree, and does not destroy it altogether. It is certainly true that the element of deterrence would be less in this case than is normally involved in the application of the criminal law.

There is still a further difficulty in my brother Foster's proposal to read an exception into the statute to favor this case, though again a difficulty not even intimated in his opinion. What shall be the scope of this exception? Here the men cast lots and the victim was himself originally a party to the agreement. What would we have to decide if Whetmore had refused from the beginning to participate in the plan? Would a majority be permitted to overrule him? Or, suppose that no plan were adopted at all and the others simply conspired to bring about Whetmore's death, justifying their act by saying that he was in the weakest condition. Or again, that a plan of selection was followed but one based on a different justification than the one adopted here, as if the others were atheists and insisted that Whetmore should die because he was the only one who believed in an afterlife. These illustrations could be multiplied, but enough have been suggested to reveal what a quagmire of hidden difficulties my brother's reasoning contains.

Of course I realize on reflection that I may be concerning myself with a problem that will never arise, since it is unlikely that any group of men will ever again be brought to commit the dread act that was involved here. Yet, on still further reflection, even if we are certain that no similar case will arise again, do not the illustrations I have given show the lack of any coherent and rational principle in the rule my brother proposes? Should not the soundness of a principle be tested by the conclusions it entails, without reference to the accidents of later litigational history? Still, if this is so, why is it that we of this Court so often discuss the question whether we are likely to have later occasion to apply a principle urged for the solution of the case before us? Is this a situation where a line of reasoning not originally proper has become sanctioned by precedent, so that we are permitted to apply it and may even be under an obligation to do so?

The more I examine this case and think about it, the more deeply I become involved. My mind becomes entangled in the meshes of the very nets I throw out for my own rescue. I find that almost every consideration that bears on the decision of the case is counterbalanced by an opposing consideration leading in the opposite direction. My brother Foster has not furnished to me, nor can I discover for myself, any formula capable of resolving the equivocations that beset me on all sides.

I have given this case the best thought of which I am capable. I have scarcely slept since it was argued before us. When I feel myself inclined to accept the view of my brother Foster, I am repelled by a feeling that his arguments are intellectually unsound and approach mere rationalization. On the other hand, when I incline toward upholding the conviction, I am struck by the absurdity of directing that these men be put to death when their lives have been saved at the cost of the lives of ten heroic workmen. It is to me a matter of regret that the Prosecutor saw fit to ask for an indictment for murder. If we had a provision in our statutes making it a crime to eat human flesh, that would have been a more appropriate charge. If no other charge suited to the facts of this case could be brought against the defendants, it would have been wiser, I think, not to have indicted them at all. Unfortunately, however, the men have been indicted and tried, and we have therefore been drawn into this unfortunate affair.

Since I have been wholly unable to resolve the doubts that beset me about the law of this case, I am with regret announcing a step that is, I believe, unprecedented in the history of this tribunal. I declare my withdrawal from the decision of this case.

KEEN, J. I should like to begin by setting to one side two questions which are not before this Court.

The first of these is whether executive clemency should be extended to these defendants if the conviction is affirmed. Under our system of government, that is a question for the Chief Executive, not for us. I therefore disapprove of that passage in the opinion of the Chief Justice in which he in effect gives instructions to the Chief Executive as to what he should do in this case and suggests that some impropriety will attach if these instructions are not heeded. This is a confusion of governmental functions — a confusion of which the judiciary should be the last to be guilty. I wish to state that if I were the Chief Executive I would go farther in the direction of clemency than the pleas addressed to him propose. I would pardon these men altogether, since I believe that they have already suffered enough to pay for any offense they may have committed. I want it to be understood that this remark is made in my capacity as a private citizen who by the accident of his office happens to have acquired an intimate acquaintance with the facts of this case. In the discharge of my duties as judge, it is neither my function to address directions to the Chief Executive, nor to take into account what he may or may not do, in reaching my own decision, which must be controlled entirely by the law of this Commonwealth.

The second question that I wish to put to one side is that of deciding whether what these men did was "right" or "wrong," "wicked" or "good." That is also a question that is irrelevant to the discharge of my office as a judge sworn to apply, not my conceptions of morality, but the law of the land. In putting this question to one side I think I can also safely dismiss without comment the first and more poetic portion of my brother Foster's opinion. The element of fantasy contained in the arguments developed there has been sufficiently revealed in my brother Tatting's somewhat solemn attempt to take those arguments seriously.

The sole question before us for decision is whether these defendants did, within the meaning of N.C.S.A. (N.S.) § 12-A, willfully take the life of Roger Whetmore. The exact language of the statute is as follows: "Whoever shall willfully take the life of another shall be punished by death." Now I should suppose that any candid observer, content to extract from these words their natural meaning, would concede at once that these defendants did "willfully take the life" of Roger Whetmore.

Whence arise all the difficulties of the case, then, and the necessity for so many pages of discussion about what ought to be so obvious? The difficulties, in whatever tortured form they may present themselves, all trace back to a single source, and that is a failure to distinguish the legal from the moral aspects of this case. To put it bluntly, my brothers do not like the fact that the written law requires the conviction of these defendants. Neither do I, but unlike my brothers I respect the obligations of an office that requires me to put my personal predilections out of my mind when I come to interpret and apply the law of this Commonwealth.

Now, of course, my brother Foster does not admit that he is actuated by a personal dislike of the written law. Instead he develops a familiar line of argument according to which the court may disregard the express language of a statute when something not contained in the statute itself, called its "purpose," can be employed to justify the result the court considers proper. Because this is an old issue between myself and my colleague, I should like, before discussing his particular application of the argument to the facts of this case, to say something about the historical background of this issue and its implications for law and government generally.

There was a time in this Commonwealth when judges did in fact legislate very freely, and all of us know that during that period some of our statutes were rather thoroughly made over by the judiciary. That was a time when the accepted principles of political science did not designate with any certainty the rank and function of the various arms of the state. We all know the tragic issue of that uncertainty in the brief civil war that arose out of the conflict between the judiciary, on the one hand, and the executive and the legislature, on the other. There is no need to recount here the factors that contributed to that unseemly struggle for power, though they included the unrepresentative character of the Chamber, resulting from a division of the country into election districts that no longer accorded with the actual distribution of the population, and the forceful personality and wide popular following of the then Chief Justice. It is enough to observe that those days are behind us, and that in place of the uncertainty that then reigned we now have a clear-cut principle, which is the supremacy of the legislative branch of our government. From that principle flows the obligation of the judiciary to enforce faithfully the written law, and to interpret that law in accordance with its plain meaning without reference to our personal desires or our individual conceptions of justice. I am not concerned with the question whether the principle that forbids the judicial revision of statutes is right or wrong, desirable or undesirable; I observe merely that this principle has become a tacit premise underlying the whole of the legal and governmental order I am sworn to administer.

Yet though the principle of the supremacy of the legislature has been accepted in theory for centuries, such is the tenacity of professional tradition and the force of fixed habits of thought that many of the judiciary have still not accommodated themselves to the restricted role which the new order imposes on them. My brother Foster is one of that group; his way of dealing with statutes is exactly that of a judge living in the 3900's.

We are all familiar with the process by which the judicial reform of disfavored legislative enactments is accomplished. Anyone who has followed the written opinions of Mr. Justice Foster will have had an opportunity to see it at work in every branch of the law. I am personally so familiar with the process that in the event of my brother's incapacity I am sure I could write a satisfactory opinion for him without any prompting whatever, beyond being informed whether he liked the effect of the terms of the statute as applied to the case before him.

The process of judicial reform requires three steps. The first of these is to divine some single "purpose" which the statute serves. This is done although not one statute in a hundred has any such single purpose, and although the objectives of nearly every statute are differently interpreted by the different classes of its sponsors. The second step is to discover that a mythical being called "the legislator," in the pursuit of this imagined "purpose," overlooked something or left some gap or imperfection in his work. Then comes the final and most refreshing part of the task, which is, of course, to fill in the blank thus created. *Quod erat faciendum.*

My brother Foster's penchant for finding holes in statutes reminds one of the story told by an ancient author about the man who ate a pair of shoes. Asked how he liked them, he replied that the part he liked best was the holes. That is the way my brother feels about statutes; the more holes they have in them the better he likes them. In short, he doesn't like statutes.

One could not wish for a better case to illustrate the specious nature of this gap-filling process than the one before us. My brother thinks he knows exactly what was sought when men made murder a crime, and that was something he calls "deterrence." My brother Tatting has already shown how much is passed over in that interpretation. But I think the trouble goes deeper. I doubt very much whether our statute making murder a crime really has a "purpose" in any ordinary sense of the term. Primarily, such a statute reflects a deeply-felt human conviction that murder is wrong and that something should be done to the man who commits it. If we were forced to be more articulate about the matter, we would probably take refuge in the more sophisticated theories of the criminologists, which, of course, were certainly not in the minds of those who drafted our statute. We might also observe that men will do their own work more effectively and live happier lives if they are protected against the threat of violent assault. Bearing in mind that the victims of murders are often unpleasant people, we might add some suggestion that the matter of disposing of undesirables is not a function suited to private enterprise, but should be a state monopoly. All of which reminds me of the attorney who once argued before us that a statute licensing physicians was a good thing because it would lead to lower life insurance rates by lifting the level of general health. There is such a thing as overexplaining the obvious.

If we do not know the purpose of § 12-A, how can we possibly say there is a "gap" in it? How can we know what its draftsmen thought about the question of killing men in order to eat them? My brother Tatting has revealed an understandable, though perhaps slightly exaggerated revulsion to cannibalism. How do we know that his remote ancestors did not feel the same revulsion to an even higher degree? Anthropologists say that the dread felt for a forbidden act may be increased by the fact that the conditions of a tribe's life create special temptations toward it, as incest is most severely condemned among those whose village relations make it most likely to occur. Certainly the period following the Great Spiral was one that had implicit in it temptations to anthropophagy. Perhaps it was for that very reason that our ancestors expressed their prohibition in so broad and unqualified a form. All of this is conjecture, of course, but it remains abundantly clear that neither I nor my brother Foster knows what the "purpose" of § 12-A is.

Considerations similar to those I have just outlined are also applicable to the exception in favor of self-defense, which plays so large a role in the reasoning of my brothers Foster and Tatting. It is of course true that in *Commonwealth* v. *Parry* an obiter dictum justified this exception on the assumption that the purpose of criminal legislation is to deter. It may well also be true that generations of law students have been taught that the true explanation of the exception lies in the fact that a man who acts in self-defense does not act "willfully," and that the same students have passed their bar examinations by repeating what their professors told them. These last observations I could dismiss, of course, as irrelevant for the simple reason that professors and bar examiners have not as yet any commission to make our laws for us. But again the real trouble lies deeper. As in dealing with the statute, so in dealing with the exception, the question is not the conjectural *purpose* of the rule, but its *scope*. Now the scope of the exception in favor of self-defense as it has been applied by this Court is plain: it applies to cases of resisting an aggressive threat to the party's own life. It is therefore too clear for argument that this case does not fall within the scope of the exception, since it is plain that Whetmore made no threat against the lives of these defendants.

The essential shabbiness of my brother Foster's attempt to cloak his remaking of the written law with an air of legitimacy comes tragically to the surface in my brother Tatting's opinion. In that opinion Justice Tatting struggles manfully to combine his colleague's loose moralisms with his own sense of fidelity to the written law. The issue of this struggle could only be that which occurred, a complete default in the discharge of the judicial function. You simply cannot apply a statute as it is written and remake it to meet your own wishes at the same time.

Now I know that the line of reasoning I have developed in this opinion will not be acceptable to those who look only to the immediate effects of a decision and ignore the long-run implications of an assumption by the judiciary of a power of dispensation. A hard decision is never a popular decision. Judges have been celebrated in literature for their sly prowess in devising some quibble by which a litigant could be deprived of his rights where the public thought it was wrong for him to assert those rights. But I believe that judicial dispensation does more harm in the long run than hard decisions. Hard cases may even have a certain moral value by bringing home to the people their own responsibilities toward the law that is ultimately their creation, and by reminding them that there is no principle of personal grace that can relieve the mistakes of their representatives.

Indeed, I will go farther and say that not only are the principles I have been expounding those which are soundest for our present conditions, but that we would have inherited a better legal system from our forefathers if those principles had been observed from the beginning. For example, with respect to the excuse of self-defense, if our courts had stood steadfast on the language of the statute the result would undoubtedly have been a legislative revision of it. Such a revision would have drawn on the assistance of natural philosophers and psychologists, and the resulting regulation of the matter would have had an understandable and rational basis, instead of the hodgepodge of verbalisms and metaphysical distinctions that have emerged from the judicial and professorial treatment.

These concluding remarks are, of course, beyond any duties that I have to discharge with relation to this case, but I include them here because I feel deeply that my colleagues are insufficiently aware of the dangers implicit in the conceptions of the judicial office advocated by my brother Foster.

I conclude that the conviction should be affirmed.

HANDY, J. I have listened with amazement to the tortured ratiocinations to which this simple case has given rise. I never cease to wonder at my colleagues' ability to throw an obscuring curtain of legalisms about every issue presented to them for decision. We have heard this afternoon learned disquisitions on the distinction between positive law and the law of nature, the language of the statute and the purpose of the statute, judicial functions and executive functions, judicial legislation and legislative legislation. My only disappointment was that someone did not raise the question of the legal nature of the bargain struck in the cave — whether it was unilateral or bilateral, and whether Whetmore could not be considered as having revoked an offer prior to action taken thereunder.

What have all these things to do with the case? The problem before us is what we, as officers of the government, ought to do with these defendants. That is a question of practical wisdom, to be exercised in a context, not of abstract theory, but of human realities. When the case is approached in this light, it becomes, I think, one of the easiest to decide that has ever been argued before this Court.

Before stating my own conclusions about the merits of the case, I should like to discuss briefly some of the more fundamental issues involved — issues on which my colleagues and I have been divided ever since I have been on the bench.

I have never been able to make my brothers see that government is a human affair, and that men are ruled, not by words on paper or by abstract theories, but by other men. They are ruled well when their rulers understand the feelings and conceptions of the masses. They are ruled badly when that understanding is lacking.

Of all branches of the government, the judiciary is the most likely to lose its contact with the common man. The reasons for this are, of course, fairly obvious. Where the masses react to a situation in terms of a few salient features, we pick into little pieces every situation presented to us. Lawyers are hired by both sides to analyze and dissect. Judges and attorneys vie with one another to see who can discover the greatest number of difficulties and distinctions in a single set of facts. Each side tries to find cases, real or imagined, that will embarrass the demonstrations of the other side. To escape this embarrassment, still further distinctions are invented and imported into the situation. When a set of facts has been subjected to this kind of treatment for a sufficient time, all the life and juice have gone out of it and we have left a handful of dust.

Now I realize that wherever you have rules and abstract principles lawyers are going to be able to make distinctions. To some extent the sort of thing I have been describing is a necessary evil attaching to any formal regulation of human affairs. But I think that the area which really stands in need of such regulation is greatly overestimated. There are, of course, a few fundamental rules of the game that must be accepted if the game is to go on at all. I would include among these the rules relating to the conduct of elections, the appointment of public officials, and the term during which an office is held. Here some restraint on discretion and dispensation, some adherence to form, some scruple for what does and what does not fall within the rule, is, I concede, essential. Perhaps the area of basic principle should be expanded to include certain other rules, such as those designed to preserve the free civilmoign system.

But outside of these fields I believe that all government officials, including judges, will do their jobs best if they treat forms and abstract concepts as instruments. We should take as our model, I think, the good administrator, who accommodates procedures and principles to the case at hand, selecting from among the available forms those most suited to reach the proper result.

The most obvious advantage of this method of government is that it permits us to go about our daily tasks with efficiency and common sense. My adherence to this philosophy has, however, deeper roots. I believe that it is only with the insight this philosophy gives that we can preserve the flexibility essential if we are to keep our actions in reasonable accord with the sentiments of those subject to our rule. More governments have been wrecked, and more human misery caused, by the lack of this accord between ruler and ruled than by any other factor that can be discerned in history. Once drive a sufficient wedge between the mass of people and those who direct their legal, political, and economic life, and our society is ruined. Then neither Foster's law of nature nor Keen's fidelity to written law will avail us anything.

Now when these conceptions are applied to the case before us, its decision becomes, as I have said, perfectly easy. In order to demonstrate this I shall have to introduce certain realities that my brothers in their coy decorum have seen fit to pass over in silence, although they are just as acutely aware of them as I am.

The first of these is that this case has aroused an enormous public interest, both here and abroad. Almost every newspaper and magazine has carried articles about it; columnists have shared with their readers confidential information as to the next governmental move; hundreds of letters-to-the-editor have been printed. One of the great newspaper chains made a poll of public opinion on the question, "What do you think the Supreme Court should do with the Speluncean explorers?" About ninety per cent expressed a belief that the defendants should be pardoned or let off with a kind of token punishment. It is perfectly clear, then, how the public feels about the case. We could have known this without the poll, of course, on the basis of common sense, or even by observing that on this Court there are apparently four-and-a-half men, or ninety per cent, who share the common opinion.

This makes it obvious, not only what we should do, but what we must do if we are to preserve between ourselves and public opinion a reasonable and decent accord. Declaring these men innocent need not involve us in any undignified quibble or trick. No principle of statutory construction is required that is not consistent with the past practices of this Court. Certainly no layman would think that in letting these men off we had stretched the statute any more than our ancestors did when they created the excuse of self-defense. If a more detailed demonstration of the method of reconciling our decision with the statute is required, I should be content to rest on the arguments developed in the second and less visionary part of my brother Foster's opinion.

Now I know that my brothers will be horrified by my suggestion that this Court should take account of public opinion. They will tell you that public opinion is emotional and capricious, that it is based on half-truths and listens to witnesses who are not subject to cross-examination. They will tell you that the law surrounds the trial of a case like this with elaborate safeguards, designed to insure that the truth will be known and that every rational consideration bearing on the issues of the case has been taken into account. They will warn you that all of these safeguards go for naught if a mass opinion formed outside this framework is allowed to have any influence on our decision.

But let us look candidly at some of the realities of the administration of our criminal law. When a man is accused of crime, there are, speaking generally, four ways in which he may escape punishment. One of these is a determination by a judge that under the applicable law he has committed no crime. This is, of course, a determination that takes place in a rather formal and abstract atmosphere. But look at the other three ways in which he may escape punishment. These are: (1) a decision by the Prosecutor not to ask for an indictment; (2) an acquittal by the jury; (3) a pardon or commutation of sentence by the executive. Can anyone pretend that these decisions are held within a rigid and formal framework of rules that prevents factual error, excludes emotional and personal factors, and guarantees that all the forms of the law will be observed?

In the case of the jury we do, to be sure, attempt to cabin their deliberations within the area of the legally relevant, but there is no need to deceive ourselves into believing that this attempt is really successful. In the normal course of events the case now before us would have gone on all of its issues directly to the jury. Had this occurred we can be confident that there would have been an acquittal or at least a division that would have prevented a conviction. If the jury had been instructed that the men's hunger and their agreement were no defense to the charge of murder, their verdict would in all likelihood have ignored this instruction and would have involved a good deal more twisting of the letter of the law than any that is likely to tempt us. Of course the only reason that didn't occur in this case was the fortuitous circumstance that the foreman of the jury happened to be a lawyer. His learning enabled him to devise a form of words that would allow the jury to dodge its usual responsibilities.

My brother Tatting expresses annoyance that the Prosecutor did not, in effect, decide the case for him by not asking for an indictment. Strict as he is himself in complying with the demands of legal theory, he is quite content to have the fate of these men decided out of court by the Prosecutor on the basis of common sense. The Chief Justice, on the other hand, wants the application of common sense postponed to the very end, though like Tatting, he wants no personal part in it.

This brings me to the concluding portion of my remarks, which has to do with executive clemency. Before discussing that topic directly, I want to make a related observation about the poll of public opinion. As I have said, ninety per cent of the people wanted the Supreme Court to let the men off entirely or with a more or less nominal punishment. The ten per cent constituted a very oddly assorted group, with the most curious and divergent opinions. One of our university experts has made a study of this group and has found that its members fall into certain patterns. A substantial portion of them are subscribers to "crank" newspapers of limited circulation that gave their readers a distorted version of the facts of the case. Some thought that "Speluncean" means "cannibal" and that anthropophagy is a tenet of the Society. But the point I want to make, however, is this: although almost every conceivable variety and shade of opinion was represented in this group, there was, so far as I know, not one of them, nor a single member of the majority of ninety per cent, who said "I think it would be a fine thing to have the courts sentence these men to be hanged, and then to have another branch of the government come along and pardon them." Yet this is a solution that has more or less dominated our discussions and which our Chief Justice proposes as a way by which we can avoid doing an injustice and at the same time preserve respect for law. He can be assured that if he is preserving anybody's morale, it is his own, and not the public's, which knows nothing of his distinctions. I mention this matter because I wish to emphasize once more the danger that we may get lost in the patterns of our own thought and forget that these patterns often cast not the slightest shadow on the outside world.

I come now to the most crucial fact in this case, a fact known to all of us on this Court, though one that my brothers have seen fit to keep under the cover of their judicial robes. This is the frightening likelihood that if the issue is left to him, the Chief Executive will refuse to pardon these men or commute their sentence. As we all know, our Chief Executive is a man now well advanced in years, of very stiff notions. Public clamor usually operates on him with the reverse of the effect intended. As I have told my brothers, it happens that my wife's niece is an intimate friend of his secretary. I have learned in this indirect, but, I think, wholly reliable way, that he is firmly determined not to commute the sentence if these men are found to have violated the law.

No one regrets more than I the necessity for relying in so important a matter on information that could be characterized as gossip. If I had my way this would not happen, for I would adopt the sensible course of sitting down with the Executive, going over the case with him, finding out what his views are, and perhaps working out with him a common program for handling the situation. But of course my brothers would never hear of such a thing.

Their scruple about acquiring accurate information directly does not prevent them from being very perturbed about what they have learned indirectly. Their acquaintance with the facts I have just related explains why the Chief Justice, ordinarily a model of decorum, saw fit in his opinion to flap his judicial robes in the face of the Executive and threaten him with excommunication if he failed to commute the sentence. It explains, I suspect, my brother Foster's feat of levitation by which a whole library of law books was lifted from the shoulders of these defendants. It explains also why even my legalistic brother Keen emulated Pooh-Bah in the ancient comedy by stepping to the other side of the stage to address a few remarks to the Executive "in my capacity as a private citizen." (I may remark, incidentally, that the advice of Private Citizen Keen will appear in the reports of this court printed at taxpayers' expense.)

I must confess that as I grow older I become more and more perplexed at men's refusal to apply their common sense to problems of law and government, and this truly tragic case has deepened my sense of discouragement and dismay. I only wish that I could convince my brothers of the wisdom of the principles I have applied to the judicial office since I first assumed it. As a matter of fact, by a kind of sad rounding of the circle, I encountered issues like those involved here in the very first case I tried as Judge of the Court of General Instances in Fanleigh County.

A religious sect had unfrocked a minister who, they said, had gone over to the views and practices of a rival sect. The minister circulated a handbill making charges against the authorities who had expelled him. Certain lay members of the church announced a public meeting at which they proposed to explain the position of the church. The minister attended this meeting. Some said he slipped in unobserved in a disguise; his own testimony was that he had walked in openly as a member of the public. At any rate, when the speeches began he interrupted with certain questions about the affairs of the church and made some statements in defense of his own views. He was set upon by members of the audience and given a pretty thorough pommeling, receiving among other injuries a broken jaw. He brought a suit for damages against the association that sponsored the meeting and against ten named individuals who he alleged were his assailants.

When we came to trial, the case at first seemed very complicated to me. The attorneys raised a host of legal issues. There were nice questions on the admissibility of evidence, and, in connection with the suit against the association, some difficult problems turning on the question whether the minister was a trespasser or a licensee. As a novice on the bench I was eager to apply my law school learning and I began studying these questions closely, reading all the authorities and preparing well-documented rulings. As I studied the case I became more and more involved in its legal intricacies and I began to get into a state approaching that of my brother Tatting in this case. Suddenly, however, it dawned on me that all these perplexing issues really had nothing to do with the case, and I began examining it in the light of common sense. The case at once gained a new perspective, and I saw that the only thing for me to do was to direct a verdict for the defendants for lack of evidence.

I was led to this conclusion by the following considerations. The melee in which the plaintiff was injured had been a very confused affair, with some people trying to get to the center of the disturbance, while others were trying to get away from it; some striking at the plaintiff, while others were apparently trying to protect him. It would have taken weeks to find out the truth of the matter. I decided that nobody's broken jaw was worth that much to the Commonwealth. (The minister's injuries, incidentally, had meanwhile healed without disfigurement and without any impairment of normal faculties.) Furthermore, I felt very strongly that the plaintiff had to a large extent brought the thing on himself. He knew how inflamed passions were about the affair, and could easily have found another forum for the expression of his views. My decision was widely approved by the press and public opinion, neither of which could tolerate the views and practices that the expelled minister was attempting to defend.

Now, thirty years later, thanks to an ambitious Prosecutor and a legalistic jury foreman, I am faced with a case that raises issues which are at bottom much like those involved in that case. The world does not seem to change much, except that this time it is not a question of a judgment for five or six hundred frelars, but of the life or death of four men who have already suffered more torment and humiliation than most of us would endure in a thousand years. I conclude that the defendants are innocent of the crime charged, and that the conviction and sentence should be set aside.

TATTING, J. I have been asked by the Chief Justice whether, after listening to the two opinions just rendered, I desire to re-examine the position previously taken by me. I wish to state that after hearing these opinions I am greatly strengthened in my conviction that I ought not to participate in the decision of this case.

The Supreme Court being evenly divided, the conviction and sentence of the Court of General Instances is *affirmed*. It is ordered that the execution of the sentence shall occur at 6 A.M., Friday, April 2, 4300, at which time the Public Executioner is directed to proceed with all convenient dispatch to hang each of the defendants by the neck until he is dead.

POSTSCRIPT

NOW *that the court has spoken its judgment, the reader puzzled by the choice of date may wish to be reminded that the centuries which separate us from the year 4300 are roughly equal to those that have passed since the Age of Pericles. There is probably no need to observe that the* Speluncean Case *itself is intended neither as a work of satire nor as a prediction in any ordinary sense of the term. As for the judges who make up Chief Justice Truepenny's court, they are, of course, as mythical as the facts and precedents with which they deal. The reader who refuses to accept this view, and who seeks to trace out contemporary resemblances where none is intended or contemplated, should be warned that he is engaged in a frolic of his own, which may possibly lead him to miss whatever modest truths are contained in the opinions delivered by the Supreme Court of Newgarth. The case was constructed for the sole purpose of bringing into a common focus certain divergent philosophies of law and government. These philosophies presented men with live questions of choice in the days of Plato and Aristotle. Perhaps they will continue to do so when our era has had its say about them. If there is any element of prediction in the case, it does not go beyond a suggestion that the questions involved are among the permanent problems of the human race.*

THE QUINN PAPERS

JOHN QUINN combined a successful career as a New York lawyer with a sympathetic and perceptive interest in artists and actors. When he died in 1922, he directed in his will that some dozen volumes of correspondence be deposited in the New York Public Library, there to be withheld from publication until 1988. The library accepted Quinn's correspondence on this condition and placed it in the Special Manuscripts Room, where it was open to perusal only by qualified scholars who agreed neither to copy nor to publish any part of it.

During the years following Quinn's death, many of the writers, actors, and artists with whom he had corresponded became important figures in the creative world, and his papers accordingly elicited considerable interest in artistic and literary circles. In 1959 Mr. Peter Kavanaugh, sometime poet, littérateur, and amateur printer, set about preparing a clandestine edition of excerpts from Quinn's correspondence. Kavanaugh reasoned that true justice to Quinn, to his correspondents, and to the public required that the letters be published while the writers were still widely known rather than after they had faded into obscurity. During a two-week period he alternately memorized portions of the correspondence in the Special Manuscripts Room and wrote out what he had memorized in nearby Bryant Park. Subsequently, he personally printed and bound 129 fifty-two-page volumes of excerpts from Quinn's letters. Later comparison showed that the passages in Kavanaugh's book were practically identical with corresponding parts of Quinn's papers.

In January, 1960, the New York Public Library sought a court order requiring Kavanaugh to destroy the books he had printed and to desist from further efforts to make Quinn's letters public. In court it developed that Kavanaugh had sent one copy to the British Museum, nine copies to a friend, Mr. Patrick Campbell, and had retained the remaining 119 copies. He had received no payment for the ten copies already distributed, had asked for none, and expected none. It was established that, at the court's request, Kavanaugh had asked Campbell to return the nine copies he possessed and that Campbell had refused.

This relatively minor incident gave rise to a number of questions having implications which are by no means minor and over which lawyers are still wrangling. Some of the more important questions are the following:

- Does the policy of the New York Public Library concerning access to Quinn's papers violate the terms of his will?
- Did Kavanaugh violate his agreement with the library? Specifically, did he "copy"? did he "publish"? If he did either, at precisely what moment was the act completed?
- Was Quinn justified in withholding his papers from publication as stipulated in his will?
- Were Kavanaugh's actions justified?
- Was the library justified in seeking legal enforcement of the restrictions it had placed upon use of the papers?
- How should a person dispose of private papers that are likely to be of interest to the general public?

WHAT CONSTITUTES "DELIVERY"?

SECTION 34 of Chapter 138 of the General Laws of Massachusetts reads as follows:

1. Whoever, being licensed under this chapter, employs any person under 21 years of age in the direct handling or selling of alcoholic beverages or alcohol, or

2. whoever makes a sale or delivery of any such beverages or alcohol to any person under 21 years of age, either for his own use or for the use of his parent or any other person, or

3. whoever, being a patron of an establishment licensed under sections 12 or 15, delivers or causes to be delivered in any public room or area of such establishment if licensed under section 12, or in any area of such establishment if licensed under section 15, any such beverages or alcohol for the use of a person whom he knows or has reason to believe is under 21 years of age

— shall be punished by a fine of not more than $200 or by imprisonment of not more than six months, or both.

Early in the summer of 1961, Massachusetts State Police officers arrested fourteen male college students, all twenty-one years of age or older, who were on a picnic at which they served drinks to their female companions, all of whom were under twenty-one years of age. The students were charged with violating the statute quoted above in that they had "delivered" alcoholic beverages to a minor (provision 2). In the Central District Court at Haverhill, Massachusetts, they were found guilty and fined twenty dollars each.

Throughout the prior history of provision 2 of Section 34, its scope had been confined to the *sale* of intoxicating beverages. The Supreme Court of Massachusetts considered this provision in three decisions antedating the Haverhill case, each of which dealt only with the illegal sale of liquor. The sole legal periodical to examine it took a similar view. The extra session of the Massachusetts legislature, which adopted Section 34 in 1933, did not record a single line of debate regarding the word "delivery" in provision 2 despite the far-reaching implications of the term as interpreted in the Haverhill decision. A father handing his twenty-year-old son a cocktail in their own home, for example, or giving his nineteen-year-old daughter a glass of champagne at her wedding would seem to be acting within the scope of provision 2 of Section 34, and even a clergyman administering communion with wine to a minor might be violating the law.

In the immediately adjacent provision 3, on the other hand, the terms "delivers or causes to be delivered" are used in a context that makes it clear they do not imply a sale or transaction of any kind.

> What constitutes "delivery" of an alcoholic beverage in the sense that the term is used in provision 2 of Section 34?

THE GREASY CARVING KNIFE

UNDER NEW YORK STATE law a host is responsible for protecting his guests from accidental injuries caused by traps and dangerous defects known to the host and unlikely to be discovered by the guests. Both parties, however, are expected to exercise reasonable caution. If a guest is injured exclusively by reason of his host's negligence, he may have valid grounds for suit; but if the guest is guilty of contributory negligence, no claim will stand.

Mrs. Patrick Manly thought she had valid grounds for claiming one hundred thousand dollars in damages when her close friend, Mrs. Ronald Packman, dropped a carving knife which cut Mrs. Manly's foot. The resulting painful injury required nearly a year to heal and left her subject to chronic swelling of the foot.

At a preliminary court hearing Mrs. Manly testified that she and her husband were dinner guests of Mr. and Mrs. Packman, whom they had known for ten years, and that she was seated next to Mrs. Packman while the latter carved a turkey prior to the meal. Mrs. Manly contended that her hostess was negligent in that she used the same hand to alternately cut and pick up slices of meat without pausing to remove grease from her hand and from the handle of the knife. In consequence of this negligence, Mrs. Manly argued, Mrs. Packman lost her grip on the knife, and it fell from her hand.

Mrs. Packman countered with the charge that her guest was also negligent because "she sat close to the table with her knees at the end of the table" where the hostess was carving the turkey. "This conclusively indicated contributory negligence on the part of Mrs. Manly and an assumption of the risks attendant upon sitting so close."

The presiding justice at the preliminary hearing refused either to present a summary judgment against Mr. and Mrs. Packman or to dismiss the suit, ordering instead that the issue be tried before a jury. The judge noted in his decision that since Mrs. Manly had observed the manner in which the carver's hand allegedly became greasy, her remaining nearby without bringing the "dangerous situation" to Mrs. Packman's attention raised the issue of contributory negligence. "But there might be considerations," he suggested, "which would inhibit a social guest from saying or doing anything which would reflect upon the actions of a hostess."

  § Was Mrs. Packman negligent?
  § Was Mrs. Manly negligent?

VINES V. MUTUAL INSURANCE COMPANY

AT ABOUT 4:30 P.M. on Tuesday, April 14, 1960, Robert Vines, age twelve, drowned in a swimming pool on the campus of Western University. Robert, a sixth-grade pupil in the demonstration grade school conducted by Western, had been dismissed from classes at the regular hour, 2 P.M., on the fourteenth, and had walked to his home. About 4 P.M. he returned to the university and was in and around the pool until the time of his death. Medical examination indicated that Robert had struck his head prior to drowning, presumably on the side or bottom of the pool. The pool was regularly available to students on Tuesdays from 4 to 5 P.M., and a lifeguard employed by the university was on duty.

Western University held a blanket student accident policy issued by the Mutual Insurance Company. One provision of the policy covered "all students of Western University who suffer accidental bodily injury during the period beginning one hour before school commences and ending one hour after the student is dismissed from school." Another provision of the policy covered a student "while participating in a school-sponsored activity, other than athletics, under the supervision of a proper school authority."

Kenneth and Sylvia Vine, Robert's parents, filed suit against the Mutual Insurance Company under terms of the accident policy issued to Western University for loss incurred by reason of their son's death.

- Was Robert a "student" of Western University within the meaning of the term as employed in the insurance policy?
- Was he participating in a "school-sponsored activity" at the time of his death?
- Was Robert participating in an activity "other than athletics"?
- Did a "proper school authority" supervise the swimming?
- Assuming for the moment that each of the above questions can be answered affirmatively, are the two provisions quoted from the policy necessarily ambiguous and contradictory?
- Assuming they are, should Kenneth and Sylvia Vine recover under terms of the policy?

THE SILVER DOLLAR FIRE

In November, 1955, Henry Gartland, an inspector with the New York City Fire Department, entered the Silver Dollar bar at Broadway and Forty-sixth Street in New York. Inspector Gartland had been assigned to make routine tests of the potential fire hazard of window displays and similar temporary decorations in public buildings. He lit a match and touched it to a Thanksgiving display furnished to the Silver Dollar by the Seagram Distilling Company and placed in one of the bar's street display windows by employees of the Silver Dollar. When a portion of the display ignited, Inspector Gartland snuffed out the flames and turned away to inform the proprietors.

Almost immediately the display exploded, and the bar was swept by flames. Six customers and a number of employees escaped uninjured, but Inspector Gartland and two additional firemen received minor injuries while fighting the blaze. The bar was severely damaged, and several other business establishments in and adjacent to the Silver Dollar building sustained relatively minor smoke and water damage.

Pietrofessa Brothers, Inc., owners of the Silver Dollar, filed a damage suit against the City of New York (which is responsible for the acts of its authorized agents, such as Gartland), and a number of smaller claims were entered by other injured parties.

Written law does not provide much guidance for fixing the blame in such a situation. An out-of-court settlement was eventually reached with the assistance of New York State Supreme Court Justice Abraham Geller.

> ◄§ Who do you think should pay the bills? the city? Seagram? Pietrofessa Brothers? some other party or combination of parties? Or should the fire be attributed to "an act of God"?

MILLER V.
B. & A. RAILROAD

THE FARMERS in and near Mackeys, South Carolina, specialize in growing green peas of a first-class variety. These farmers send their peas to Ben Miller, the general storekeeper of Mackeys, who, in turn, sends them to commission merchants in large eastern cities. On May 24 Mr. Miller turned over to the B. & A. Railroad one car of freshly picked peas to be shipped to Mr. Cornelius, a commission merchant in Washington, D.C. This car, according to the bill of lading, was to be "under refrigeration" and was to be delivered to its destination with "reasonable dispatch."

According to the usual schedule, this car should have reached Washington on Sunday, May 26. Owing to an unaccountable delay, it did not reach Washington until the afternoon of the twenty-eighth, and Mr. Cornelius received notification later that day that the car was on the track. His men unloaded several truckloads of the peas on the morning of May 29, and the peas were found to be in fairly good condition. Since the next day was Decoration Day, a national holiday, no peas were unloaded from the car. On the morning of May 31, when Mr. Cornelius' men returned to unload more of the peas, they found the interior of the car so hot that steam came out of the car doors. Upon examination of the refrigeration bunkers, the men found that there was no ice in them. When boxes of peas were opened, they were found to be spoiled, and the unloaded portion of the shipment was promptly condemned by a food inspector from the health department. Approximately two-thirds of the peas were condemned, one-third having been removed on May 29.

Mr. Miller, the legal owner of the peas, filed suit against the B. & A. Railroad, charging that he had lost perishable merchandise valued at twelve hundred dollars because of improper refrigeration and an unreasonable delay in transportation. Expert witnesses testified that under proper refrigeration freshly picked peas would remain in perfect condition for at least six days.

The railroad claimed that the peas were under refrigeration for a period long enough to have allowed for their unloading from the car, and that it was not responsible for a loss caused by the delay, since the car had reached Washington with "reasonable dispatch."

&§ Should Mr. Miller recover?

MAIL-SCHOOL INSTITUTE V. KOPPELL

MISS KOPPELL, a Chicago elementary-school teacher, answered an advertisement of the Mail-School Institute of New York, asking for information regarding instruction in typing, stenography, and bookkeeping. A few days later she was visited by a salesman from the institute who convinced her in an hour to pay three hundred and fifty dollars for the complete course, which she could study at her leisure. The institute guaranteed to find a position for every student who completed the course. Lessons were to be sent to the institute's building in New York for correction. Miss Koppell asked the agent to come back the next morning for her answer, thus giving her time to consider the offer thoroughly. The agent told her that if she delayed until the following day, the price for the course would be four hundred dollars. Miss Koppell thereupon signed the contract, agreeing to pay fifty dollars down and fifty dollars each month. She wrote the salesman a personal check for fifty dollars.

After giving the matter an hour's consideration, however, and consulting her physician, who told her she was physically unfit for the added work, she attempted to locate the agent. He had disappeared. At nine o'clock the next morning Miss Koppell went to her bank and withdrew all her money. At nine-thirty the agent appeared at the door and asked why she had closed her bank account. She told him her decision and asked to be released from the contract. He refused, threatened her good reputation as a teacher, and told her she would have to settle with his company.

Within a week Miss Koppell received a twenty-pound package through the mail from the institute; she returned it unopened. A series of collection letters followed which she did not answer. Finally, she received notification that suit was being filed against her by the company's representative in Chicago, and that legal steps had been started to collect the alleged debt.

&§ Should the institute collect from Miss Koppell?

WATSON V. ZELLER

ON JUNE 2, 1928, the plaintiff, Susanna Watson, was born out of lawful wedlock, and shortly thereafter she became the ward of Enid County, Oklahoma.

When Susanna was only a few months old, the defendants, Mr. and Mrs. Zeller, took her into their home and, for a valuable consideration paid to them by Enid County, agreed to keep and care for her until she reached the age of eighteen. Susanna entered the Zeller home under this arrangement in 1928 and lived there continuously until May 1, 1953, when she married Mr. Watson. During these twenty-five years she was known as Susanna Zeller. She was led to believe, and did believe, that she was the Zellers' real daughter. Between June 2, 1946, when Susanna became eighteen years old, and May 1, 1953, she performed a woman's work in the house and a man's work in the fields as directed by the Zellers. The Zellers never told her that she was not their daughter, but in 1953 other persons told her the true facts of her origin.

Alleging that her work for the Zellers, between June 2, 1946, and May 1, 1953, was of the value of seven thousand five hundred dollars and that the Zellers had practiced fraud upon her and cruelly deceived her by the concealment of the material facts of her real origin, to her damage in the sum of seven thousand five hundred dollars, Susanna sued Mr. and Mrs. Zeller for the total sum of fifteen thousand dollars.

⋘§ Should Susanna recover?

THE LOWENTHAL WILL

A St. Louis newspaper reported on September 10, 1960, that Surrogate William L. Bussman had upheld a provision of the will of Abraham S. Wagman which stipulated that "no descendant of the testator who marries a person not of the Jewish faith and not of Jewish blood can take any legacy. . . ."

Mr. Wagman, who died in 1930, provided in his will that descendants who married within the Jewish faith would receive ten thousand dollars on their twenty-first birthdays and become beneficiaries of a trust fund, now amounting to about three-quarters of a million dollars. When a grandson, Mr. Stephen R. Lowenthal, a member of the New York Stock Exchange, died in 1956, his daughter, Miss Anne C. Lowenthal, came in line to benefit from the will on her twenty-first birthday, September 25, 1960.

Miss Lowenthal, however, wished to marry her fiancé, John C. Murray, Jr., before the Army called him into service on October 1, 1960, and application was made to the Surrogate's Court for a legal interpretation of the will.

"The petitioner's situation," said Surrogate Bussman, "commands the court's sympathy. It is unfortunate that she cannot have both a marriage with the man of her choice and the inheritance. Present considerations which tug at her heart do not resolve the legal queries propounded, however. Miss Lowenthal has recently become affianced to John C. Murray, Jr., who is not a person born in the Jewish faith and not of Jewish blood. He has received orders to report to Fort Sill, Oklahoma, in October, 1960, for active service, and it is the intention of Miss Lowenthal to marry prior to that time. The prohibitive section of the will is discriminatory, but discrimination is the privilege of the testator. To discriminate in the disposition of property is frequently the motivation of the testator. He may exclude a child or other descendant from participation in his estate for sound reason or because of whim or prejudice which might seem unreasonable to others. The court is compelled to uphold the manifest of the testator's will. The determination here was written into the will and is binding on the petitioner."

    ❧ Was the girl right in trying to break the will?
    ❧ Was the testator right in making such a will?
    ❧ Is it against public policy to permit such a will to stand?

SHOULD SCHOOL RECORDS BE OPEN TO PARENTS?

IN SEPTEMBER, 1960, the New York State Department of Education — moving to conclude a conflict that had arisen in Levittown, Long Island — ruled that parents had the right to inspect their children's actual school records rather than settle, as they had in the past, for an "interpretation" of the records by a teacher or guidance counselor.

In November a New York State resident filed suit to secure access to school records concerning his son, a seventh-grade pupil. A school psychologist had recommended psychiatric treatment for the child, but the local school board insisted that the Department of Education's order was not binding on all school districts and, moreover, was "not sufficiently broad and interpretive."

A court thought otherwise. The school board was ordered to open its records to the parent, and the storm quickly subsided.

Or did it? Modern school records go far beyond mere course grades and

I.Q. ratings. They may include scores on aptitude tests, interest inventories, personality profiles; and observations, comments, and "evaluations" by teachers, remedial instructors, social workers, and psychologists. Even the school's interpretation of what parents have told teachers about the child's home and family life sometimes finds its way into a student's dossier.

Many administrators, teachers, and school psychologists believe it would be a serious mistake to permit parents to pore over accumulated reports in search of "the facts." Without explanation and interpretation the bald results of highly technical tests would be misunderstood or misinterpreted by many parents, and for some the data might be disturbing and even destructive. An association of psychologists has argued that "the content of test scores is not appropriate material for a layman without guidance and experience to understand."

On the other side of the question, it may be noted that much information in school records is readily supplied to prospective employers, that parents are continually urged to work with the schools as partners in the education of children, and that parents presumably need to understand the child as well as, if not better than, the school does. Protection from public scrutiny, moreover, inevitably encourages the recording of ill-considered judgments, the retention of material whose usefulness expires with the passage of time, and other abuses to which ingrown systems are subject.

Recognizing these difficulties, the State Commission of Education formed a committee to seek an equitable solution to the problem. Nearly a year after the initial dispute had apparently been laid to rest, the committee made public a series of recommendations endorsed by the Department of Education. The committee was of the opinion that the "official" school records of every child should be available to parents and guardians. Included within the committee's definition of "official" were the conclusions of psychiatrists or other guidance personnel which possess "long-term value." Such records should be discussed with parents, the committee believed.

Noting, however, that school reports could be incomplete and thus misleading, that some test scores were meaningless without professional interpretation, and that some psychological reports could harm a child if made public, the committee specified certain kinds of information which should not be made available to parents and guardians:

1. Working materials accumulated while a teacher or school staff member is studying a pupil and assessing his strengths and weaknesses; these are to be considered raw material for a final report.

2. Background data collected by psychologists, psychiatrists, therapists, and social workers; these should be kept from teachers and school administrators, as well as from parents.

3. Reports to school officials from outside agencies, such as social work groups, juvenile courts, hospitals, and correctional institutions; these are often confidential and should be available outside the school only if the agency that prepared them agrees.

Whether the committee's recommendations, which are now the official policy of the State of New York, represent a clarification or complication of the situation is open to question.

◄§ Do you agree with the committee's recommendations?

Part II

$\diamond$

ANALYZING THE CASE AND EVALUATING THE EVIDENCE

BEFORE ARGUMENT can begin, one must see clearly which points are at issue. Perhaps it is because this initial consideration is so obvious that it is so often overlooked. The spectacle of two opponents arguing at cross purposes on different issues is common, disheartening, and more likely to produce new confusion than clarity. Only when one perceives what must be proved is one in a position to set aside irrelevant evidence and to assess the strengths and weaknesses of that which remains. The ground is then prepared for intelligent, penetrating argument that will illuminate all facets of the question with the most revealing light available.

The cases in this section are intended to tax and increase the student's ability to analyze, evaluate, and reason. Proceed with caution. They are full of traps in the form of hidden issues and — especially — untrustworthy, irrelevant, and inconsistent evidence. The first case, *The People* v. *Lucas*, illustrates many problems that will be encountered under various guises in subsequent exercises. The easy way to prove anything, of course, is by direct evidence: a confession or the testimony of an eyewitness to a crime, for example. When relevant and reliable evidence exists, however, usually there is not much left to argue about. Most of the situations described in this section depend on circumstantial evidence. If, in the Lucas case, Morris' testimony were entirely credible, it would probably convict Lucas. Similarly, the recordings made by Lynott might secure conviction if they were not open to effective rebuttal. But Morris' background is questionable, doubts can be cast on Lynott's integrity, and the recordings are not clear enough to establish very much. Consequently, the prosecution supplements this evidence with a full circumstantial case: evidence tending to show that Lucas had the motive, the disposition, and the means to commit the crime with which he is charged.

The issues, then, are motive, disposition, means, and presence. How does one go about evaluating the evidence which bears on these issues? Full analyses of the evidence on both sides, as well as selected arguments marshaled for effective presentation to a particular audience and transcripts of oral arguments, are provided in the briefs, outlines, and speeches at the end of the Lucas case. Here we would point out the general principles on which the analysis of evidence is conducted. Evidence consists of facts — knowledge that can be determined objectively to the satisfaction of reasonable men; and testimony — knowledge that depends on the statement of an individual. In this exemplary case, for instance, it is a fact that Lucas placed a telephone call to Brockman on a given day. What he said to Brockman and even whether he actually spoke with Brockman are matters of testimony.

Concerning factual evidence, little need be said except that it is inherently more reliable than testimony and consequently is useful in destroying credence in testimony with which it conflicts. For example, given the distance from Mrs. Daley's back porch to the car in which she testified she saw Lucas, and the position of a street light with respect to the car, grave doubt can be thrown on her testimony.

Testimony may be offered by laymen, who are generally limited to stating what they did, saw, or said, but who are sometimes permitted to repeat what they heard and to give their opinion; it may also come from experts, who are generally asked to render an opinion on matters within their special field of knowledge. As in the Lucas case, expert testimony on one side is frequently offset by the conflicting testimony of an expert on the other side. The problem becomes one of weighing their qualifications and the inherent reasonableness of their opinions one against the other.

Lay testimony is subject to three main weaknesses, each of which is illustrated in the Lucas case: perjury, bias, and half-truths. To the extent that testimony in these cases can be attacked, the way is prepared by the witnesses' admissions during cross-examination. One's task is first to recognize and then to exploit the weak points. Perjury is sometimes revealed by trapping a witness in his own contradictory statements. The more pedestrian, but much more usual, way is to demonstrate that a witness's testimony is contradicted by known facts, other testimony, or strong probabilities. In the Lucas case much evidence has been introduced to provide the basis for attacking the testimony of Lynott and Morris in this manner.

"Bias" is used here to comprehend both motivations (such as friendship, antipathy, or indebtedness to one of the principals) which can persuade a witness that he saw or heard something that never transpired; and imagination, which can achieve the same result even more effectively. The witness who gives biased testimony does not want and would probably refuse to lie knowingly; beyond that demarcation line, however, his mental state may range all the way from absolute conviction that he is telling the truth to an unwillingness to consider his statements too closely. All such testimony can profitably be considered of one type because it is frequently impossible to divine a witness's true feelings. On the other hand, the wide range of factors which can lead to bias is worth noting because it suggests a variety of tactics for rebuttal. Good examples are provided in the Lucas case by the two lines of counter-argument prepared for rebuttal of the testimony of Mrs. Daley and Mr. Sentelle. By pointing out during cross-examination that neither eyewitness to the alleged planting of the bomb volunteered any information until questioned by the police, the defense opened the door for argument that their testimony was biased by police pressure. At the same time, the defense has sufficient information concerning distances and lighting conditions to urge that the witnesses could not possibly have seen what they claim.

The half-truth, finally, can be found in Miss Tilden's testimony. On direct examination she said that Lucas had twice followed a car in which she was riding. But alert cross-examination won the admissions that she really did not know whether or not she was being "followed," and that she was in no way alarmed when she saw Lucas behind her because he frequently delivered printing orders in that part of the city.

The arguments, that is, the interpretations of facts and opinions, which can be worked up from these points and many others appear in the exemplary briefs, outlines, and speeches, following the summary of evidence in the Lucas case. The instructor will indicate the extent to which he wants the student to follow these models in developing his own case. The briefs presented here are intended to be repositories of all the evidence and arguments available to the respective sides of the case. The outlines were drawn up as plans for speeches to be delivered to particular audiences on particular occasions. The speeches themselves are edited transcripts made from tape recordings of what the speakers actually said. The briefs, outlines, and speeches are the work of Harvard University undergraduates. Each speaker was limited to eight minutes, and the speeches were delivered extemporaneously.

Suggestions for Further Reading

BUSCH, FRANCIS X. *Law and Tactics in Jury Trials.* Indianapolis: The Bobbs-Merrill Company, Inc., 1949.

CORNELIUS, ASHER L. *The Cross Examination of Witnesses.* Indianapolis: The Bobbs-Merrill Company, Inc., 1929.

QUINE, WILLARD V. O. *Methods of Logic.* New York: Henry Holt & Company, Inc., revised edition, 1959.

STRYKER, LLOYD P. *The Art of Advocacy.* New York: Simon and Schuster, Inc., 1949.

TOULMIN, STEPHEN. *The Uses of Argument.* Cambridge: Cambridge University Press, 1958.

WAGNER, RUSSELL H. *Handbook of Argumentation.* New York: Thomas Nelson & Sons, 1936.

WELLMAN, FRANCIS L. *The Art of Cross-Examination.* New York: The Macmillan Company, fourth revised edition, 1936.

Additionally, a large number of argument and discussion textbooks are now in print which consider analysis of questions, evaluation of evidence, reasoning, and preparation of briefs and outlines.

THE PEOPLE V. LUCAS

QUESTION: *Did Lucas place explosives in Judge Kampson's house?*

FACTS

ON JUNE 25, 1935, at 11 P.M., the home of Judge Jared P. Kampson, of Allentown, Pennsylvania, was badly damaged by an explosion. Investigation showed that dynamite sticks, placed in the cellar under the rear of the house, had been used. No one was in the house at the time. The house is located at the corner of Main Street and Warren Avenue.

Judge Kampson is a county judge. He is under impeachment, charging him with exceeding statutory limitations in sentencing labor leaders to prison for alleged contempt of injunctions issued by him. The petition for impeachment was printed and circulated by James Lucas and is the third impeachment of Judge Kampson that Lucas has sponsored. The other two were dismissed.

A coal miners' strike, championed by Lucas, has been in progress for two years. One of the affected mines has closed permanently, one has announced its intention of doing the same, and one continues in operation with police protection.

Letters, unsigned, to Judge Kampson threatening his and his daughter's lives are placed in evidence. Six pamphlets, printed and signed by Lucas, protesting Judge Kampson's judicial decisions and actions are placed in evidence. The only important correspondences in language are these:

LETTERS:
 . . . your high-handed and illegal actions.
 Stop persecuting us or we'll take justice into our own hands.
 We're tired of knuckling to a gang of bosses and crooked lawyers.

PAMPHLETS:
 . . . actions that exceed legal powers and are dictatorial.
 Persecution has reared its ugly head; retaliation is sure to follow.
 The people of this community will not tolerate further abuse of legal powers.

The distance from Mrs. Daley's rear porch to the alley is forty feet. The Sentelle cottage faces the alley, twenty-five feet further down the alley than the Daley alley gate. The front porch is thirty feet from the alley.

Lucas' home is in the southern part of Allentown, fifteen blocks from his office in the center of town. Judge Kampson's house is ten blocks north of the center of town.

Five Dictograph records are admitted in evidence. Lucas concedes he is one of the two speakers on each record. On all the records Lucas' voice is faint and indistinct. On only one record is it articulate enough for his statements to be at all significant, and these are transcribed here:

LYNOTT. So, what did you do?

LUCAS. . . . Bill Morris, the damn fool kid, never could do a job right.

LYNOTT. Well, what about Kampson now?

LUCAS. Maybe he won't bother us any more. But what good will it do if he is . . . ?

LYNOTT. Listen, Jim, this is simply good business. I can help you and you can help me. We want a good reliable union man to print our mag . . .

LUCAS. Where's your money? Where's your union? You can't tell me . . .

TESTIMONY

WALTER LYNOTT, age forty-five, said he was a detective for the Delaware and Lackawanna Railroad for ten years. He has been out of work for about one year. He was hired by District Attorney Morno to investigate the bombing. He worked himself into the confidence of Lucas, whom he and others suspected of having done the bombing. Lucas told him he wanted Judge Kampson "out of the way" and had hired Morris to do it, but Morris had bungled the job. Lynott agreed to help Lucas and had Lucas come to his hotel room on August 4. Here he and Lucas discussed various methods of doing away with Kampson, and, since Dictographs had been concealed in the room, talked to him about the bombing. At 10 P.M. police entered the room and arrested both men. Lynott, of course, was later released.

HERMAN J. PIGOTT, age fifty, agent for the Dictograph Corporation in Philadelphia, said he had been called to Allentown by the district attorney and had placed five Dictographs in Lynott's room. After Lucas was arrested, he collected the records and listened to them. Lucas had pitched his voice so low that little was intelligible on the records. He did say, on two occasions, "I want Judge Kampson out of the way."

On cross-examination Pigott admitted he could not be absolutely certain he had heard more than "Judge Kampson" and "out of the way." Asked why Lucas' voice was so much fainter than Lynott's, he explained as follows: Lynott has a naturally clear, ringing voice, while Lucas' is "mushy" and indistinct; Lynott spoke especially plainly, while Lucas was secretive, almost whispering; Lynott tried to get Lucas to sit near the desk or telephone stand where microphones were concealed, but Lucas insisted on standing across the room near a window, which he opened, and through which street noises came. He admitted that his control board has a selective volume control but said the maximum volume was on for Lucas all the time.

WILLIAM MORRIS, age twenty-nine, said he is unemployed and has never had steady work. He did odd jobs for Lucas for several years — delivering, sweeping up, and the like. Lucas told him he would give him one hundred dollars to take a package into Judge Kampson's cellar, and that it contained evidence he wanted found there. He agreed to do it if Lucas would lend him his car since the package was too heavy to carry. Lucas refused, but agreed to drive him to the alley at the rear of the house. This was done, and Morris threw the package through the cellar window into the furnace room. When the explosion occurred, he became frightened and told the police about it.

On cross-examination, Morris admitted he had been a bootlegger for three years "off and on." He denied that he had been warned by the police and said he had not been arrested. Asked what Lucas said after the explosion, he answered: "I guess Kampson won't be in our way any longer." When he saw Lucas the next day, Lucas said: "Did you know the Judge wasn't at home?" He replied: "Sure, we passed them coming up Main Street." Lucas said: "You fool, why didn't you tell me?" He admitted not having worked for Lucas since May 12, but denied being fired. He admitted not reporting to the police until June 28. Morris said Lucas told him they shouldn't be seen together too much or they would be suspected.

H. O. QUICKMAN, age forty-eight, auditor of the Farmer's Feed and Supply Company, said he has known Lucas for many years, and has had printing done in Lucas' shop as late as April, 1935. He has employed Morris as day laborer on his farm at Lucas' suggestion, but found him untrustworthy. He saw Lucas and Morris talking together twice in an East Allentown tavern during June, 1935. On the evening of June 25 he saw Lucas and Morris driving south on Main Street about 9 P.M. He admitted he had been a friend of Morris' father before the latter's death, but denied that he has maintained any friendship whatever with the son.

JUDGE KAMPSON said that he had received threatening letters during the preceding two years, warning him not to issue injunctions against miners' unions nor to enforce laws against strikers. (The letters are placed in evidence.) He had left home, with his daughter, on the night of June 25, about 10:30 P.M., to get some papers at his office. On the way his daughter said, "There's the car that's been following me." He made note of the license number and was certain he recognized Lucas driving. (It is established that the license number Judge Kampson noted is the number issued for a car owned by Lucas.) He admitted that he did not say at the preliminary magistrate's hearing that he recognized Lucas. He said he was not asked. The car was on the other side of Main Street, going in the opposite direction. Another man was in the car with Lucas.

VERONICA KAMPSON, age twenty-four, said that early in June she had seen a car following her all the way home from the high school where she teaches. She noticed it because she had gone out of her way to take Helen

Tilden to her home in East Allentown, and the car was still behind her when she reached home. One other time it followed her when Miss Tilden was with her, and she pointed it out to Miss Tilden, who said, "Why, that's Jim Lucas, the labor agitator." On the night of June 25, when she was driving her father to his office, she saw the same car and pointed it out to her father. She had not at any time noted the license number. Two men were in the front seat.

HELEN TILDEN, age twenty-three, said she has known James Lucas for ten years. She lived in the same block as Lucas for two years, five years before, and has had dramatic club programs printed in his shop during the past two. She noticed Lucas' car following Miss Kampson in May and early June. She was sure she recognized Lucas in it both times. Asked how she knew it was "following" Miss Kampson, she said she supposed it was. Asked whether she told Miss Kampson, she said she didn't remember. Asked whether she was alarmed, she admitted she was not. Miss Tilden admitted that Lucas' car was often seen in East Allentown, delivering job printing.

M. T. BROWN, handwriting expert and chemist, said he had been a chemical engineer for twelve years and had studied handwriting as a hobby. Ten years ago he became a member of a firm of private detectives, specializing in handwriting. He has been engaged by both prosecution and defense in 109 cases, mostly in Philadelphia. He does not have a university degree, but attended the University of Pennsylvania for three years and spent one summer as an apprentice to handwriting experts in New York and one summer observing the methods of experts in this line in Europe. He said that all the letters received by Judge Kampson were written by Lucas. All show a novice's attempt to disguise his usual mode of writing, but all betray characteristics peculiar to Lucas.

MRS. MARY DALEY, age forty, said she lives on Warren Avenue, around the corner from Judge Kampson's house. She was awake on the night of June 25, and at 10:45 P.M. saw a car drive into the alley and stop near her alley gate. She tried to rouse her husband, but could not. She went down to her rear porch and saw a man leave the auto and return later. As the car backed out, she got a good look at both occupants. Mrs. Daley identified Lucas and Morris as the two men.

Asked on cross-examination whether she had ever seen Lucas or Morris before, Mrs. Daley admitted she had not. She admitted not reporting immediately after the bombing that she had seen the men. She said that a detective asked her if she had seen the men and that she then went with him to the county jail where she identified them. Asked why she did not volunteer her information after the bombing, she said her husband told her to stay out of it. Asked how she could see the men from her rear porch well enough to identify them, Mrs. Daley said the street light on Warren

Avenue at the alley entrance made it possible. She could not remember whether it was a clear, moonlit, or cloudy night; did not note the license number; could not describe the car. Both men had on hats, she said, and Lucas wore a light-gray overcoat and Morris wore a leather jacket.

JOHN SENTELLE, age sixty-eight, said he is employed by Judge Kampson as a gardener and handy man. He lives in a cottage in Kampson's yard, near the alley. He was awake on the night of June 25, about 10:50 P.M., and noticed a man coming out of the rear of Judge Kampson's house. He got out of bed and went to his porch. He saw the two men and watched the car back out of the alley. He identified them as Lucas and Morris. Sentelle admitted he did not report the matter until asked about it by Detective Sivich of the district attorney's office, and was then taken to the county jail to see the two men. He said he was afraid of being bombed, but had been assured of police protection if he told all he knew. He had never seen either man before; both of them had on hats. He could not describe the car. He said it was a clear, moonlit night. He said the car was parked in the alley opposite his front porch.

JAMES LUCAS, sixty-five, said he has lived in Allentown for forty years, following the trade of printer. For the past twenty years he has owned and operated his own job printing shop. He has been a member of the Typographical Union for thirty years and is secretary of the local union and chairman of the CIO for the Scranton district. From 1931 to 1934 he published a weekly called *Unemployment News*, distributed without charge to the unemployed. He financed this paper himself, securing contributions from unions with which he was in touch. A number of issues were confiscated by the police, and his shop was raided and searched five times. He had been asked by the local union of the United Mine Workers to help impeach Judge Kampson, and, together with the legal adviser of the union, had prepared the petition for impeachment. He denied all knowledge of any plot to bomb Judge Kampson's home, or having anything to do with it, or having sent anonymous letters to Judge Kampson.

Lucas said he was working in his printing shop until 10:30 P.M. and then went home, took a short walk, and was in bed by 11 P.M., on the night of June 25. He said Lynott came to him with a proposal to print a textile workers' magazine, to be financed by a union with headquarters in New York City. Lynott said he was authorized to give Lucas one thousand dollars for new equipment and additional help. Lucas said he had hesitated because he was not certain as to the financial standing of the union. Lynott had given him the name of the treasurer of the New York union, Samuel Jimerson, and he had telephoned a friend in New York, asking him to look up Jimerson and the union. The friend reported that Jimerson was an officer of a truck drivers' union and did not know Lynott, nor did he know anything about plans to have a magazine published in Scranton. Lynott asked him to come to his hotel room on the night of August 4. He went to tell Lynott that he would have nothing to do with the scheme. Lynott kept talking about the bombing of Judge Kampson's house and seemed annoyed because he, Lucas, didn't know anything about it and wouldn't talk about it. He admitted he had not fired Morris as his wife took care of the extra help and all financial matters in the shop. He did not remember talking with Morris since Morris stopped working there six weeks before the bombing.

CATHERINE LUCAS, fifty-five, said she works in her husband's printing shop. She was working there the night of June 25. She and her husband left about 10:30 P.M. and were home by 10:40. Her husband went out for a walk, came in at 11, and went to bed. The car was in the garage from 10:40 on. William Morris was not in the printing shop that day and hadn't been for six weeks. They had employed him as extra help because he was jobless, but he had been so unreliable that she told him about six weeks before the bombing not to come back.

MARTIN BROCKMAN, sixty, officer of a bakers' union in New York City, said he had known Lucas for about fifteen years as a casual business acquaintance through their mutual connection with union work. He corroborated Lucas' testimony regarding a telephone request for information. He said Lucas phoned him on July 15, and he replied by phone on July 28. Brockman fixed the date from memoranda kept in his office.

Certified excerpts from telephone company records were placed in evidence. They indicated: (1) that Lucas had placed a person-to-person call from Allentown to Brockman in New York on July 15, and that the call had lasted five minutes; (2) that Brockman had placed a person-to-person call from New York to Lucas in Allentown on July 28, and that the call had lasted eight and a half minutes.

GEORGE NEMOLAS, forty, said he operates a cigar store two blocks from the Lucas home. He remembered seeing Lucas walk past his window on the night of June 25, shortly before 11 P.M. He fixed the time then because he closes his shop at 11. He admitted that Lucas had lent him money from time to time and that he now owed him three hundred dollars. Nemolas admitted that he had been arrested and fined three times for illegal sale of liquor during prohibition.

EDWARD CHRISTY, thirty-five, unemployed miner, said he was in Lucas' shop on the night of June 25. Lucas was there at 10:20 P.M. He admitted not having a watch, but maintained that he was looking at the clock in Lucas' office because he had promised his wife not to stay late.

JOSEPH P. DELANEY, of Newark, New Jersey, said he has been a handwriting and typescript expert for thirty years — for ten years as an officer of the New York Life Insurance Company, in charge of identification, and for twenty years as an independent expert on authenticity of typing, printing, and handwriting for many banks, business firms, insurance companies, and litigants. He has never testified in a criminal case. He is not a college graduate. He has held a card in the International Typographical Union for many years because he began his career as a typesetter. He said the letters were not written by Lucas: the most distinguishing features of Lucas' handwriting, such as careful closing of the letters *a, o, s, g, p, b,* and *d,* are entirely lacking in the letters in evidence. He claimed that these and other equally important differences could not be achieved by any but the most expert forger. Asked to compare specimens of Lynott's and Morris' handwriting with letters in evidence, he was prevented from doing so by the judge's ruling such evidence inadmissible at this time.

WILLIAM McINTYRE, formerly detective in the Allentown police force, now retired on pension, said that he was asked by the Allentown chief of police in 1929 to warn William Morris not to sell liquor in Allentown anymore and that he did so warn him. On orders from the same chief of police he took Morris into custody in 1932. For reasons unknown to McIntyre, Morris was released without being charged.

GEORGE R. HERMAN, chief of police since 1925, said he never gave orders to warn or arrest Morris at any time. He admitted not remembering all persons warned, but said he kept records of all persons suspected, warned, or arrested for bootlegging, has those records, and is willing to submit them in evidence.

Additional facts admitted in the course of the testimony of McIntyre and the cross-examination of Herman (not admitted by Mrs. Daley or Sentelle, who were excused by the judge from testifying on these points for reasons satisfactory to both sides): Lynott and Lucas are the same height and build; both have dark complexions; Lynott is ten pounds heavier; their features are not dissimilar; there are no peculiarities of carriage or walk.

Brief for the Prosecution

INTRODUCTION

I. The case arises from charges made before a jury by the district attorney of Allentown, Pennsylvania, that James A. Lucas planned and supervised the placing and exploding of a bomb in the house of Judge Jared P. Kampson.

II. The history of the case is as follows:

A. Relations between the CIO, and the UMW, and the coal mine operators in Allentown are strained, for

1. There has been a strike in progress for two years in the coal mines, and

2. The strike has had serious consequences, for
   a. One mine has shut down, and
   b. Another mine has announced that it will shut down, and
   c. The third mine is open only under police protection.
B. It is evident that ill-will exists between the labor unions and certain judicial and police authorities in the city, for
   1. The CIO believes that there has been improper infringement of their freedom of the press, for
      a. Lucas' printing shop was raided by the police five times between 1931 and 1934, and
      b. A number of issues of *Unemployment News* were confiscated.
   2. There is evidence that the UMW and the CIO feel that Judge Kampson has been unjust, for
      a. They declare that sentences imposed by him on labor leaders for contempt of injunctions have exceeded statutory limitations, and
      b. They have circulated three petitions for the impeachment of Kampson on these charges.
C. James Lucas has championed Labor's side in this struggle, for
   1. He is the Allentown chairman of the CIO, and
   2. He has published six signed pamphlets, protesting judicial decisions and actions, and
   3. He initiated the three petitions for Kampson's impeachment.
III. The facts on which all parties to the case agree are as follows:
A. Kampson's house was badly damaged at 11 P.M. on June 25, 1935, by the explosion of dynamite placed in the basement of the house; no one was in the house at the time of the explosion, and
B. Certain features of geography of Kampson's neighborhood, to wit:
   1. Kampson's house is at the corner of Main Street and Warren Avenue, facing Main; an alley runs off Warren behind the house, and
   2. The Daleys live in a house on Warren Avenue, next to the alley, its back porch is forty feet from the alley, and
   3. On the Kampson property is a second house in which the handy man, Mr. Sentelle, lives; it faces the alley, and its front porch is thirty feet from the alley; the house is twenty-five feet further from Warren than is the gate to the Daley house.
   4. There is a street light on Warren at the entrance to the alley.
C. Kampson's house is ten blocks north of the center of town; Lucas' is fifteen blocks south, and
D. A comparison of anonymous letters sent to Kampson and six pamphlets published by Lucas reveal that three sentences in each one

are somewhat similar in language and ideas; the sentences are quoted in the case, and

    E. A conversation between Lucas and Walter Lynott in Lynott's hotel room on August 4 was recorded, but only fragments, quoted in the case, are audible, and

    F. Lucas and Lynott are similar in appearance, for
        1. They are of the same height and build, and
        2. They both have dark complexions and similar features, and
        3. They have similar walks and carriages.

IV. The essential matters of testimony in dispute are:

    A. Lucas says that he did not write the anonymous, threatening letters to Kampson; Brown, a handwriting expert, identified the handwriting as Lucas', crudely disguised; another expert, Delaney, said that the writing is not Lucas', and

    B. Lucas says he was in his office all evening on June 25 until 10:30 P.M., when he went home, took a walk, and went to bed; Mrs. Lucas corroborates this; Christy says Lucas was in his shop at 10:20; Nemolas says Lucas walked past his shop just before 11; Morris says Lucas drove him to Kampson's house where he planted the bomb at about 10:45; Kampson and his daughter say they saw Lucas and Morris driving north on Main at 10:30; Daley and Sentelle say they saw Lucas and Morris in the alley at 10:45; and

    C. Lucas says he had not seen Morris for six weeks prior to the bombing; Morris says he accompanied Lucas on June 25; Quickman says he saw the two together twice earlier in June; Quickman, Kampson, his daughter, Daley, and Sentelle all say they saw the two together on the night of June 25.

V. The issues are:

    A. Did Lucas have sufficient motive to bomb Kampson's house?
    B. Did Lucas intend to harm Kampson?
    C. Did Lucas cause Morris to plant a bomb in Kampson's house?

PROOF

James Lucas caused the bombing of Judge Kampson's house, for

I. Lucas had strong motives for wanting to kill Judge Kampson, for

    A. Kampson had sentenced several of Lucas' friends to prison for contempt, and

    B. Lucas had failed in two previous attempts to remove Kampson through impeachment proceedings, and

    C. Lucas felt that Kampson was acting illegally, for
        1. Lucas' pamphlets referred to "actions that exceed legal powers," and
        2. These same pamphlets spoke of "persecution."

II. Lucas intended to harm Kampson, for

   A. The testimony of H. J. Pigott, agent for the Dictograph Corporation, reveals that Lucas said twice in Lynott's room, "I want Judge Kampson out of the way," and

   B. The threatening letters were written by Lucas, for

      1. M. T. Brown, handwriting expert, so testified, and

      2. His testimony is sound, for

         a. He has had much experience with criminal cases, and

         b. He was able to detect Lucas' writing despite efforts to disguise it.

      3. The testimony of Joseph P. Delaney that the handwriting is not Lucas' is unreliable, for

         a. He is a member of the same union as Lucas, and

         b. He has had no experience in criminal cases.

   C. Lucas was seen following Veronica Kampson's car on several occasions, for

      1. Veronica Kampson so states, and

      2. Helen Tilden noticed Lucas following Miss Kampson on two occasions.

   C^1. This may be deemed an effort to intimidate, for

      1. The anonymous letters mentioned that the life of Kampson's daughter, Veronica, was in danger, and

      1^1. These letters have been proved to have been written by Lucas (II-B).

III. Lucas caused Morris to bomb Kampson's house, for

   A. Morris' testimony relates this fact, and

   A^1. Morris' testimony is convincing, for

      1. It accords with the testimony of Judge Kampson, Veronica Kampson, Mary Daley, and John Sentelle, for

         a. All speak of seeing Morris in the car with Lucas, and

         b. Mrs. Daley and Sentelle saw one man get out of the car after it had stopped in the alley.

      2. Morris had reason to tell the truth, for

         a. Lucas had lied to him about the bomb, saying it was only "evidence," and

         b. Morris had reason to believe Lucas would try to get rid of him, for

            (1) Lucas warned him they should not be seen together, and

            (2) He knew that Lucas considered him to be untrustworthy.

   B. Both Kampson and his daughter testified that they saw Morris and Lucas driving toward their house shortly before the bomb exploded, and

C. Both Mrs. Daley and Mr. Sentelle said that they saw Morris and Lucas in the alley, and

C¹. The testimony of each gains credibility from its consistency with the other, for

    1. Both said one man left the car, and

    2. Both said the two men wore hats, and

    3. Both placed the car in about the same position in the alley, for

        a. Sentelle said the car was in front of his porch, and

        b. Mrs. Daley said the car stopped *near* her alley gate, and

        c. These two specific positions are a maximum of only twenty-five feet apart.

D. The testimony by Lucas that he did not cause the bombing is unreliable, for

    1. His testimony is contradicted by that of several other witnesses, for

        a. His statement that he had not seen Morris for six weeks is contradicted by Quickman's testimony, and

        b. His statement that he stayed in his shop until 10:30 P.M. is contradicted by Quickman who saw him at 9:30, in a car with Morris, and

        c. His statement that he drove from his shop to his home at 10:30 P.M. is contradicted by Kampson and his daughter, and

        d. His statement that he took a walk from 10:40 to 11 P.M. is contradicted by the testimony of Mrs. Daley and Mr. Sentelle.

E. The testimony of Catherine Lucas in support of her husband is unreliable because biased, and

F. The testimony of Catherine Lucas in support of her husband is irrelevant because she admitted that she did not see him between 10:40 and 11 P.M.

G. The testimony of Edward Christy that Lucas was in his shop at 10:20 P.M. is unreliable, for

    1. He is an unemployed miner, and

    2. He is sympathetic to Lucas.

H. The testimony of Edward Christy that Lucas was in his shop at 10:20 P.M. is irrelevant, for there was ample time to plant the bomb after 10:20.

I. The testimony of George Nemolas that he saw Lucas walking near his house shortly before 11 P.M. is unreliable, for

    1. He is in debt to Lucas, and

    2. He has a record of disrespect for the law.

J. Lynott could not have driven Morris to the Kampson house, for

    1. Both Mrs. Daley and Sentelle declared without doubt that the man with Morris was Lucas, and

2. Mr. Quickman had seen Lucas with Morris earlier in the evening, and
3. There is no evidence that Lynott even knew Morris, and
4. Lynott's character cannot be impugned on the grounds that he gave false information to Lucas, for such conduct was consistent with his assigned duty to become a confidant of Lucas.

CONCLUSION

Since

1. Lucas had strong motives for wanting to kill Kampson, and
2. Lucas intended to harm Kampson, and
3. Lucas caused Morris to bomb Kampson's house.

Therefore,

James A. Lucas is guilty of having caused the bombing of Kampson's house.

Brief for the Defendant

INTRODUCTION

(Substantially the same as in the Brief for the Prosecution.)

PROOF

James A. Lucas did not cause the bombing of Kampson's house, for
I. Lucas did not write the threatening letters, for
   A. His past history of dealing with the labor matter shows that he is unlikely to employ illegal means, for
      1. He issued pamphlets which were legalistic in tone, for
         a. They emphasized the illegality of the actions of Kampson, and
         b. They emphasized that the "people of the community," acting collectively, should rectify the wrong, and
         c. They are carefully reasoned and not inflammatory or bitter.
      2. He undertook to stop Kampson through the legal instrument of impeachment.
   B. The testimony as to the identity of the writer is inconclusive, for
      1. The two experts conflict in their testimony, for
         a. Delaney says that Lucas did not write the letters, and
         b. Brown says that Lucas did write them.
      2. The experts were not allowed to examine the handwriting of other suspects.

C. The excerpts from the letters and the pamphlets do not prove a common writer, for
  1. They are different in tone, for
     a. The pamphlets are legalistic, whereas
     a^1. The letters threaten illegal action, and
     b. The pamphlets are reasoned and calm, whereas
     b^1. The letters are bitter and emotional.
  2. They are but three sentences out of context from six pamphlets and several letters, and
  3. We can be confident that they were chosen carefully by the prosecution for their similarities, not because they are typical.
D. The letters do not prove the identity of the bomber, for
  1. They do not prove genuine intention by the writer to kill Kampson, and
  2. Assuming that the writer did indeed wish to kill Kampson, there is no direct proof of connection between this wish and the attempt.

II. The bombing attempt and the two occasions when Miss Kampson thought that Lucas was following her are not connected, for
A. Lucas was not following Miss Kampson, for
  1. He often delivered materials in East Allentown, and
  2. He had no motive, for
     a. On neither occasion did Kampson accompany his daughter, and
     b. The episodes could not help him plan Kampson's murder, and
     c. He did not attempt to frighten Miss Kampson to alarm her father.
B. The two instances did not alarm Miss Tilden, for she was accustomed to seeing Lucas in East Allentown, and
C. The two instances did not alarm Miss Kampson, for
  1. She did not make note of the license number, and
  2. She did not report the incidents to the police, and
  3. Her father did not report the incidents to the police.

III. Lucas was not present at the scene of the bombing on June 25, for
A. The testimony of Daley and Sentelle is unreliable, for
  1. Positive identification of the driver of the car seen by Daley and Sentelle was impossible, for
     a. The driver never stepped out of the car, and
     b. The distances were too great, for
        (1) Sentelle was at least thirty feet from the car, and
        (2) Daley was at least forty feet from the car, and
        (3) Both were considerably further from the car when it was beneath the street light.

      c. The lighting of the driver's face was poor, for
        (1) He wore a hat, and
        (2) The street light was behind the car when it was in the alley, and
        (3) No other artificial lighting was nearby, and
        (4) Light could not shine on the driver's face because of the shadows cast by the brim of his hat and the roof of his car.
      d. The driver could not be seen clearly by Daley as the car backed onto the street, for
        (1) The distance was very great, and
        (2) The car would have paused beneath the light for only a second at most, and
        (3) The same factors still shaded the driver's face from overhead lighting.
      e. Neither Sentelle nor Daley had ever seen Lucas before, and
      f. Lucas and Lynott have similar appearances.
    2. The circumstances of the identification were odd, for
      a. Both witnesses testified only when urged to do so by the police, and
      b. Lucas was identified under irregular procedures, for
        (1) He was identified in his cell, rather than being chosen from a line-up of people of similar appearance, and
        (2) He was identified together with Morris who had been clearly seen by the witnesses, but who was not necessarily associated with Lucas in the bombing, and
        (3) Under these circumstances it was natural to assume that the man in the cell with Morris was the man who had been with him in the car.
    3. The car seen in the alley has not been identified, and
    4. Lucas was not the man seen driving the car in the alley, for
      a. His wife testified that he was at home at 10:40 and 11 P.M., and
      b. He was not in his car at 10:50 P.M., for
        (1) His wife testified that the car was in the garage, and
        (2) Nemolas saw Lucas out walking at about 10:50 P.M.
B. Morris' testimony is not reliable, for
    1. He has shown himself untrustworthy in the past, for
      a. He admits bootlegging, and
      b. Quickman fired him as untruthworthy, and
      c. Mrs. Lucas fired him as unreliable.
    2. He has a motive for lying, for
      a. He has a grudge against Lucas, for

(1) The Lucases fired him, and

(2) It was very difficult to get a new job at the time, and this increased his bitterness.

   b. He is susceptible to bribes, for

     (1) He needs money, and

     (2) He has a criminal past.

   c. He may get special treatment for lying, for

     (1) He will have turned state's evidence, and

     (2) He will have helped to convict a man whom the police and judicial departments clearly consider a nuisance.

C. Lynott's testimony is unreliable, for

  1. He was anti-union, for

   a. He was associated with management in his former job, and

   b. He was hired to induce a union leader, Lucas, to incriminate himself, and

   c. He was a labor spy, for

     (1) He was a railroad detective, and

     (2) Railroad detectives are commonly used to control union activities (1935).

  2. He has much to gain from testifying against Lucas, for

   a. He desperately needs a job, and

   b. This will secure his employment with the police force, for

     (1) His testimony is a valuable link in the prosecution, and

     (2) The police force is much interested in the success of the prosecution, and

     (3) It will have demonstrated his ability.

  3. His testimony is contradicted by facts, for

   a. He alleges that he won Lucas' confidence, for

     (1) He says Lucas told him about the bombing, and

     (2) He says Lucas enlisted his aid in planning a second attempt on Kampson's life.

   a^1. At the same time, evidence shows that Lucas did not trust Lynott, for

     (1) Lucas called Brockman on July 15 and asked him to check on Lynott's story about the union magazine, and

     (2) On July 28 Brockman called Lucas, telling him that Lynott was lying, and

     (3) The dictograph recordings clearly show that Lucas was being very cautious.

   b. Lynott states that on August 4 Lucas declared that he wanted Kampson "out of the way," but

   b^1. The Dictograph recordings show that Lucas did not believe it would solve his problems to stop Kampson from harassing him, for

(1) Lynott said, "Well, what about Kampson now?" and
(1¹) Lucas replied, "Maybe he won't bother us any more. But what good will it do if he is . . .?"

CONCLUSION

Since

1. Lucas did not write the threatening letters, and
2. There is no connection between the bombing and the two occasions on which Veronica Kampson thought Lucas was following her, and
3. Lucas was not at the scene of the bombing.

Therefore,

James A. Lucas did not cause the bombing of Kampson's house.

Outline of a Speech for the Prosecution

PROPOSITION: *Lucas caused the bombing of Judge Kampson's house.*

Strategy	Ideas

INTRODUCTION

Make introduction as interesting as possible to gain attention.

I. Allentown, Pennsylvania, was in a severe economic condition in June, 1935. (Sketch circumstances briefly.)

DISCUSSION

Start with motives; they are interesting and easily understood. They may develop a suspicion of Lucas that will carry over into the more decisive part of the case.

I. The evidence shows that Lucas had strong motives to kill Judge Kampson.
   A. Many of Lucas' labor colleagues had been sent to jail by Kampson.
   B. Lucas had failed in two previous attempts to oust Kampson through impeachment.
   C. Lucas believed that Kampson was acting illegally.
      1. Pamphlets mention that Kampson exceeded legal powers.
      2. They mention "persecution."

II. Lucas manifested intentions of harming Kampson.

   A. Pigott's testimony reveals that Lucas said, "I want Judge Kampson out of the way."

   B. M. T. Brown testified that the threatening letters were written by Lucas.

Attack Delaney here, knowing that defense will probably attack Brown. I can't lose over-all and may gain some support for Brown.

      1. This testimony is to be believed in preference to that of Joseph P. Delaney.

        a. Delaney belongs to the same union as Lucas.

        b. Delaney has never dealt with criminal cases before.

   C. Lucas followed Veronica Kampson.

Play on the inherent distaste for a sinister man following an innocent young lady. Briefly summarize the argument to this point before launching into the heart of the case. Hit hard on the consistency of and the motivation behind Morris' testimony.

      1. Miss Kampson testified to this.

      2. So did Helen Tilden.

III. Lucas caused Morris to bomb Kampson's house.

   A. Morris testified to this.

   A¹. His testimony is convincing.

      1. It coincides with the statements of Judge Kampson, his daughter, Mary Daley, and John Sentelle.

      2. Morris had reasons for reporting Lucas' crime.

        a. Lucas had lied to him about the dynamite.

        b. Lucas had implied that he didn't want Morris around.

        c. Morris knew that Lucas considered him untrustworthy.

   B. The testimony of Judge Kampson and his daughter supports this view.

   C. The testimony of Daley and Sentelle supports this view.

Press consistency here also.

   C¹. The testimony of Daley and Sentelle is believable because consistent.

      1. Both saw one man return to the car.

      2. Both said the two men wore hats.

Emphasize that all defense witnesses have motives for giving false testimony.

   D. Lucas' testimony concerning his whereabouts is unreliable.

Strategy

Ideas

1. Quickman contradicts his statement that he had not seen Morris.
2. Quickman contradicts his statement that he was in his shop until 10:30 P.M.
3. Daley and Sentelle contradict his statement that he was out walking from 10:40 to 11 P.M.

E. Catherine Lucas' testimony is unreliable because biased.
F. Nemolas' testimony is unreliable.
   1. He is in debt to Lucas.
   2. He has a record of fines and arrests.
G. Edward Christy's testimony is unreliable.
   1. He is an unemployed miner.
   2. Unemployed miners inevitably see in Lucas a champion.

This should be strong support for Lynott. To override it, the defense will have to spend a considerable amount of time to the detriment of the rest of its case.

H. Walter Lynott could not have taken Morris to Kampson's house.
   1. Daley and Sentelle say that the man with Morris was Lucas.
   2. Quickman had seen Lucas with Morris earlier.
   3. There is no testimony that Lynott even knew Morris.
   4. Lynott's character cannot be impugned by his false statements to Lucas because this was part of his plan to secure justice.

CONCLUSION

Summary for emphasis and for appearance of certitude.

I. We have shown that in every area the finger of guilt points to Lucas.
   A. Sufficient motives were present.
   B. There were definite attempts at intimidation.
   C. Lucas was the actual force behind the bombing.
II. This act is deplorable.

Attempt here to divert any support for Lucas based on sympathy with organized labor.

   A. It violates law.
   B. It discredits the labor movement.
   C. It intimidates law-abiding citizens.

Outline of a Speech for the Defendant

PROPOSITION: *Lucas did not cause the bombing of Judge Kampson's house.*

Strategy	*Ideas*

INTRODUCTION

Brave assertion; attempt to gain attention and cause the jury to hesitate before deciding case.

I. The prosecution has proved only that it has great ability to gloss over the facts of the case in an attempt to stampede the jury to its point of view.

   A. Its case depends on choosing only the testimony which supports its case.

Dismiss troublesome evidence quickly.
Hint of a main argument which will be discussed later.

   B. It relies in large part on circumstantial evidence.

   C. It does not critically examine the source of the evidence it cites as showing directly James Lucas' role in the bombing

More emphasis on hesitation before decision.

   D. Let us consider carefully the value of the evidence which the prosecution has presented.

Again, we must slow down. Hint of issue of reasonable doubt.

II. We must deliberate carefully to determine whether or not Lucas is guilty beyond all reasonable doubt.

   A. We must not let an innocent man be unjustly punished.

Warning; cast doubt on reliability of witnesses.

   B. We must not allow the pro-union or anti-union sentiments of any witnesses, or any other prejudices, pass unnoticed.

Repeat issue of reasonable doubt to make impression.

   C. If there is a reasonable doubt as to Lucas' guilt, he must be freed.

DISCUSSION

Skim over to emphasize unimportance of the issue; circumstantial evidence does not benefit the case.

I. There is much circumstantial evidence in the case which we should not value too greatly.

   A. The identity of the writer of the anonymous letters is unknown.

      1. Testimony by experts conflicts as to his identity.

Note of sarcasm; belittle prosecution here.

      2. The experts even disagree on the degree of expertise of the unknown forger's work.

Strategy	Ideas

Hint of irregularity in the proceeding; vague.

    3. We have been denied the right to see if Lynott or Morris wrote the letters.

B. The letters are not necessarily connected with the bombing.

Show irrelevance briefly.

    1. They may have been written by a crank who did not intend to carry out the threat.

    2. Even if the writer intended to kill Kampson, he is not necessarily the one who made the attempt on June 25.

C. The alleged following of Miss Kampson is unimportant.

    1. Lucas may have been delivering printing orders.

    2. The incidents alarmed no one at the time.

    3. The incidents showed no malice or motive.

Begin main assault on four key prosecution witnesses; press vigorously and in detail; repeat and elaborate.

II. Identification of the driver was impossible under the circumstances.

A. The lighting was insufficient.

    1. The driver was inside the car at all times, thus out of the direct moonlight.

    2. The driver's hat further shielded his face from the light.

    3. When the car was in the alley, the street light was behind it.

    4. Therefore, the street light was behind the driver who was facing forward.

B. Only the head and shoulders of the driver would be at all visible.

Emphasize.

C. Neither Daley nor Sentelle had ever seen Lucas before they identified him in jail.

D. The distances were great.

    1. Mrs. Daley was at least forty feet away.

    2. Sentelle was at least thirty feet away.

Emphasize if prosecution raises question of street light; otherwise not necessary.

    3. When the driver was under the street light, he was a great distance from both, and his face was again sheltered by the car roof and his hat.

Throughout point II concentrate on raising doubts.

E. The circumstances of the identification in jail were suspicious.

    1. There was no line-up.

    2. Lucas was identified when with Morris, not separately.

Do not dwell on Morris because attack on him is weakest of the four. Cannot prove he is lying, but can raise doubts.

III. Morris' testimony is unreliable.

  A. He has shown himself to be untrustworthy.

    1. Quickman fired him as untrustworthy.

    2. Mrs. Lucas fired him as unreliable.

    3. He has a record of bootlegging.

  B. He could be bribed.

    1. He needs money.

    2. He has a grudge against Lucas.

      a. The Lucases fired him.

      b. He may have been embittered because it is so hard to find a job (1935).

Step up attack on fourth witness, the only one who seems to have been lying deliberately; emphasize strongly in such a way as to strengthen attack on Morris.

IV. Lynott's testimony is unreliable.

  A. He is prejudiced in this case.

    1. He had been hired by a railroad to keep unions down.

    2. He needed money and a job.

    3. He wanted to secure a guilty verdict to prove his usefulness to the police.

    4. He wanted to secure a guilty verdict to win the gratitude of the police, who consider Lucas a nuisance.

  B. His testimony is contradicted by the facts.

    1. He says that Lucas wanted Kampson out of the way.

    2. Dictograph shows that Lucas did not believe this would solve his problems.

Clinching argument. Difficult for prosecution to slide around telephone company records.

  C. His testimony is contradicted by the facts in another instance.

    1. He stated that Lucas trusted him.

    2. Dictograph shows that Lucas felt Lynott had lied to him.

    3. Telephone records show that Lucas' suspicions were confirmed.

CONCLUSION

Repeat main argument.

I. The four witnesses who directly implicate Lucas in the crime are all unreliable.

Repeat unimportance of circumstantial evidence.

II. We cannot convict Lucas on this weak, circumstantial evidence, for we cannot say he is guilty beyond reasonable doubt.

Ridicule idea of charge by showing absurd bungling. Helps to raise doubts.

III. It is absurd to think that Lucas would take so many risks in committing a crime.

Seek snowball effect; speed up as I go down the list to increase effect.

A. Hiring an accomplice he knows to be unreliable.

B. Appearing at the scene of the crime in person and in his own car.

C. Driving the car into the alley frontwards, thereby being unable to escape quickly.

D. Not checking to see if the intended victim was at home.

E. Exploding the bomb at time when the intended victim might conceivably be out.

F. Carrying out the crime in such a way and at such a time as to arouse people in two neighboring houses.

G. Not having a good alibi when he would have known he would be the first suspect.

H. Talking to a stranger whom he distrusts about a crime he has committed and another he is planning.

Pause; then ask final rhetorical question soberly.

IV. Has the prosecution produced conclusive evidence to prove Lucas' guilt beyond a reasonable doubt?

Speech for the Prosecution

THE CITY of Allentown, Pennsylvania, in June, 1935, was in a dire economic condition. A coal strike had been in progress for two years, and Judge Jared P. Kampson had sentenced some of the leaders to prison for contempt of injunctions he had issued against the strike. On the night of June 25, 1935, at 11 P.M., Judge Kampson's house was blown up by sticks of dynamite placed in the basement.

The task of the prosecution in this case is to prove that one James Lucas, a prominent labor leader in Allentown, was responsible for the bombing. In attempting to prove this, the prosecution will first show that Lucas had sufficient motive for the crime. Second, we will show that Lucas had definite intentions of harming Judge Kampson. And third, we will approach the more decisive part of the testimony which you have heard and show that Lucas was, in fact, responsible for this bombing.

First, in regard to the motive of this case: Judge Kampson, as we have noted, had sentenced Allentown labor leaders to prison for violating injunctions he had issued against them. This quite obviously had angered Lucas, who is a prominent labor leader and leader of the CIO in this district. Also, not only had Kampson sentenced labor leaders to prison, but he had been acquitted in impeachment proceedings twice brought against him by Lucas. It was becoming apparent to Lucas that he would have to resort to more forceful measures if he were to rid himself of this obnoxious judge. Finally, Mr. Lucas had printed pamphlets directed against Judge Kampson. In those pamphlets he used words such as "persecution" and "dictatorial means" — words which show that Lucas considered Judge Kampson an unfair and evil man against whom he would, in turn, have to employ evil means. So Mr. Lucas had a motive for this bombing, a motive born of hatred and of frustration.

Lucas had more than a motive, however. He had manifested direct intention of committing violence against Judge Kampson, both before and after the bombing. Evidence of this intention to commit violence occurs in a conversation recorded in the room of an investigator, a man named Lynott. Lynott worked his way into Lucas' confidence by posing as a labor leader from New York. He invited Lucas to his hotel room, in which he had concealed five dictographs in various positions. He recorded the conversation between himself and Lucas in that room. Unfortunately, the conversation is blurred. Lucas' voice is soft, and much of what he said is indistinct. But a representative of the Dictograph Corporation, Mr. Pigott, testified, as you have heard, that Lucas, in the conversation, was twice heard to say, "I want to get rid of Judge Kampson." So testimony regarding what took place in Lynott's room is one evidence of Lucas' intentions.

The second piece of evidence comprises some threatening letters sent to Judge Kampson. Testimony conflicts as to the authorship of these letters. One handwriting expert, M. T. Brown, said these letters were the work of Lucas. He noted attempts in them to disguise the writing style, but he said certain characteristic forms emerge in the letters, showing they were written by James Lucas, the accused. The prosecution must contend with an opposing witness, Delaney, another handwriting expert, who said in contradiction of Mr. Brown that these letters were not written by Lucas. The prosecution feels that Mr. Delaney's testimony is not worthy of our belief because he is a member of the same union, the Typographical Union, in which Lucas is a prominent member; also, because Mr. Delaney has never worked in criminal cases before, as Mr. Brown has. Brown's carefully reasoned opinion that Lucas did write the letters deserves your thoughtful consideration.

Certain interesting patterns emerge in these letters — in these threatening letters — which we believe show who their author was, quite independently of Mr. Brown's testimony. Take a look at the letters, and compare them to the pamphlets Lucas admitted writing. One phrase in the letters runs as follows, "Your high-handed and illegal actions." Compare this with a phrase in the pamphlets which says, "Actions that exceed legal powers and are dictatorial." There is an even more striking likeness. In the letters we find, "Stop persecuting us or we'll take justice into our own hands." And in the pamphlets, Lucas wrote, "Persecution has reared its ugly head. Retaliation is sure to follow." The phrasing in the pamphlets and the letters is remarkably similar. It argues that Lucas did, in fact, write the letters as well as the pamphlets.

The third source of evidence regarding Lucas' intent to harm Judge Kampson, in addition to the conversation in Lynott's room and the letters, can be seen in Lucas' following of Judge Kampson's daughter, Veronica. Veronica Kampson testified that on several occasions she detected James Lucas' car following her home from the school where she was employed. And on two of those occasions she was accompanied by one of her fellow schoolteachers, Miss Helen Tilden, who testified that she recognized Lucas in the car. Since Miss Tilden had, at one time, been Lucas' neighbor, there can be no question regarding her competence to make the identification. And Miss Kampson testified that after she had dropped Miss Tilden off, Lucas continued to follow her across Allentown to her home. This action, perhaps harmless enough on the surface, takes on an ominous appearance when we remember that in the letters Lucas wrote, the lives of both Judge Kampson and his daughter were threatened.

From this evidence we can see that Lucas had a motive, and that Lucas had indicated his resolve to resort to force to intimidate Judge Kampson, even to kill him if necessary. That he did, in fact, resort to violent measures is proved by the testimony of William Morris and others. Morris testified that Lucas offered to pay him one hundred dollars to deliver the package which contained the dynamite and to put it in Kampson's basement; also, that Lucas explained to him that this was just evidence he wanted found around the house. Morris objected because the package was too heavy. He wanted to use Lucas' car; Lucas refused; and finally Lucas said, "O.K., I'll drive you over to the house." They drove to the house; Morris dumped the dynamite into the basement; the house blew up.

The defense, I am sure, will attempt to discredit this very damaging testimony from Morris, and they will undoubtedly use the fact that his character was not the finest. He is accused of having been a bootlegger. He is reputed to be untrustworthy. The one point in Morris' testimony which stands out, however, is its consistency with the testimony of other witnesses — with the testimony of Judge Kampson, his daughter, Mary Daley, and John Sentelle. Judge Kampson and his daughter report that they saw Morris and Lucas driving toward the Kampson home minutes before the dynamite was planted there. Mrs. Daley and Mr. Sentelle report that they saw Morris and Lucas arriving at the house at approximately 10:45 P.M., and that Morris got out of the car, walked to Kampson's house, and returned to the car in a few minutes. All of this is very damaging to Lucas, the more so because the testimony of each witness is entirely consistent with that of every other witness. The testimony leads us to the conclusion that Lucas is indeed guilty of this bombing.

He should be made to suffer the consequences of his unlawful act. The bombing is deplorable not only because it violates the law of this land, but also because it reflects unfavorably upon all organized labor. Such an action, moreover, intimidates fair and high-minded citizens who are willing to stand up to criminal elements. A verdict of guilty is needed here to satisfy the law, to rid the union movement of an unworthy leader, and to reaffirm the integrity of our courts and our law-enforcement agencies.

Speech for the Defendant

GENTLEMEN OF THE JURY: Let us carefully consider the exact case which the prosecution has presented. And in doing so let us remember one thing, one very basic thing in any criminal case — if we are to condemn a man to spend most of the remainder of his life in jail, we must be certain of his guilt beyond all reasonable doubt. In this light let us examine exactly what evidence the prosecution has put forth, and let us consider how reliable it is.

The prosecution, first of all, picks only those facts, those bits of circumstantial evidence — which the prosecution itself admits are circumstantial — only those bits of evidence which point toward the conclusion that the prosecution supports. It is most uncritical in examining the evidence provided by the four key witnesses. As a matter of fact, one of the key witnesses in this case has been ignored completely. I speak of Mr. Lynott. It is very curious that Lynott is so important to the prosecution and yet so thoroughly ignored.

Before we discuss the merits of the case, let me say one word of caution. A great deal of prejudice has been shown here today. Let us not assume that a union leader is necessarily a violent man. James Lucas is a respected man in his community. He is a leader of the CIO, he is a pamphleteer, he is a printer. He has been a member of this community for forty years.

No sign exists that he has ever engaged in a violent act over his entire life. His pamphlets are not violent or bitter. They are, indeed, very legalistic. They emphasize that Judge Kampson has violated the law. They ask the people of the community to seek retribution, not illegally, but through established legal channels.

Who are the four key witnesses in this trial? They are Mrs. Daley and Mr. Sentelle, who say that they identified Lucas at the scene of the crime. They are Morris, who says he was an accomplice, and Lynott, who says Lucas confessed to him.

Is it possible that Sentelle and Mrs. Daley could tell who Lucas was, that they could tell who the man inside the car was? Let us re-create the conditions at the scene of the crime at 10:45 P.M. on June 25. It was very dark. Everyone admits this. There was only one light available. It was a street light. And where was this street light? It was behind the car. The car went into the alley forwards, and the light was at the corner of the street and the alley — therefore, behind the car and behind the driver of the car. He never got out of the car. He wore a hat which shaded his face, making it still darker. The roof of the car — a 1935 model with a roof that extended well beyond and down over his head — the roof also darkened his face. Any moonlight would have come from above his head, and the brim of his hat and the roof of the car would have kept it off his face. There is no evidence of any other artificial lighting. Indeed, both the alleged witnesses say they were in bed. It is quite unlikely that they would have turned on lights if they were going to investigate suspicious activities in the alley and did not want to alarm the people there.

And let us also look at the circumstances of the identification when they went to the police station. Neither Mrs. Daley nor Mr. Sentelle volunteered the information. Both were very reluctant. Both testified on the initiative of the police, and both identified Morris and Lucas while they sat together in adjacent cells, without the benefit of a line-up. In other words, Morris, who could have been seen clearly, who I do not deny for a minute was involved in the bombing, was in the jail with another man. It was no more than natural for Mrs. Daley and Mr. Sentelle to assume that this was the same man they had seen at the scene of the crime. Lucas was not picked out of a line-up of men who looked somewhat similar. Instead, he was there alone with this man who was indeed guilty. This is a very odd, a very strange way to secure an identification, especially when Mrs. Daley and Mr. Sentelle had never seen Lucas before. How could they identify him?

Now, let's look at the other two witnesses. There is Mr. Morris. How reliable a witness is he? He admits that he has been a bootlegger on and off. There is some suspicion that the police had warned him; that he had been released by the police under mysterious circumstances. He was fired as untrustworthy by Mr. Quickman and as unreliable by Mrs. Lucas. This is hardly the kind of man on whom we can rely. And he has an excellent motive for lying now. He needed money and could easily have been bribed. He has a criminal record. He was dishonest. If he turned state's evidence, if he helped convict a man whom the police wanted to convict very badly because he has been a nuisance to them for years, then Morris could expect to receive easy treatment.

And who is the final witness, the witness the prosecution so conveniently forgets because he is so troublesome? Mr. Lynott, the man hired by the police, whose testimony is necessary to prove that Lucas is guilty, if, indeed, he is guilty. Lynott's testimony is completely contradicted by the facts. Lynott says, first of all, that Lucas trusted him, trusted him enough to talk to him about the bombing attempt, trusted him enough to come and plan another murder attempt. And yet, we see from the Dictograph records that Lucas did not trust Lynott; that he did not trust him on the basic issue for which the two men met, that is, the union magazine. I quote from the Dictograph transcription:

> LYNOTT. Listen, Jim, this is simply good business. I can help you and you can help me. We want a good reliable union man to print our mag . . .
> LUCAS. Where's your money? Where's your union? You can't tell me . . .

Is it likely that Lucas would confide in a man whom he did not trust on such a simple and basic thing as this? A perfect stranger to him? I submit that it is not.

Not one of these four main witnesses is solid. All the evidence which they present is unreliable for different reasons. And not only is their evidence unreliable, but the charge made against Mr. Lucas is absurd. Can you imagine that an intelligent man, a man capable of writing these quite intellectual pamphlets, of leading the CIO — can you imagine that a man such as this, a man sixty-five years old with almost a lifetime of experience behind him, would commit a crime in partnership with a man whom he felt was untrustworthy and disloyal? That he would go to the scene of the crime in his own car, in person? That he would go at such a time and in such a way as to arouse the suspicions of people in two different houses so they would come to their porches and look to see who was there? Can you imagine a man being so stupid as not to check to be sure that the people he wanted to harm or kill were inside the house, and to explode a bomb when they conceivably might not be at home? Can you imagine a criminal — who did not want to be seen — driving into an alley forward at 10:45 at night, forward so that he could not get out and escape quickly? Can you imagine an intelligent man confiding in another man who is a stranger to him, and whom he does not trust? There is unrefuted evidence, remember, that Lucas was in touch with Brockman in New York City and knew Lynott was lying to him.

This charge is absurd. How could a man make all these mistakes, these very basic mistakes? Why didn't he provide himself with a good alibi for the whole evening? With a time bomb, you have to have an alibi for the whole evening, because no one knows when the bomb was set. Lucas doesn't have an alibi for the early part of the evening. He would have known that he would be the first suspect.

Is it likely that Lucas would commit a crime under these absurd circumstances? Is the testimony that the prosecution has brought forward reliable? Their whole case is based on circumstantial evidence with great, gaping holes in it.

Gentlemen of the Jury: Please bear one thing in mind as you ponder the decision you must make. Lucas must be proved guilty beyond a reasonable doubt. There is a doubt, a reasonable doubt — much more than a reasonable doubt in this case.

THE HARVEY CASE

QUESTION: *Are Adams, Brown, and Clark guilty of the murder of Matthew Harvey in the first degree?*

FACTS

MATTHEW HARVEY, Negro, was a skilled mechanic employed by the Tennessee Coal, Iron, and Railroad Company, of Westfield, Alabama. On the night of February 9, 1933, the sheriff was called to the Harvey home by Mrs. Harvey, and found Harvey dead outside his house, with four bullet wounds.

At the coroner's inquest no witnesses could be found, and an open verdict was rendered. Mrs. Harvey had disappeared the night of the murder, and her whereabouts could not be determined at the inquest.

The case was reopened three weeks later at the insistence of several civil rights organizations. Mrs. Harvey, who had returned to Westfield by this time, was taken to the company plant where she identified four men as the ones who had shot her husband. These men, guards at the plant, admitted shooting Harvey. During the trial the fourth, Davis, dissociated himself from the others and was temporarily released from the charge but was held as a material witness. The other three were charged with first-degree murder and pleaded not guilty by reason of self-defense.

The Coal, Iron, and Railroad Company guards, under Alabama law, have the status of peace officers, with power to preserve order in the company plant and in the village of Westfield.

TESTIMONY

Evans, superintendent of that section of the Coal, Iron, and Railroad Company plant in which Harvey was employed, said that Harvey came to work drunk at 1 P.M. on February 9; that he continued to drink while at work; that he was quarrelsome and argued with and struck a white assistant; that he was ordered home, but refused to go until Evans forcibly ejected him about 3 P.M. Evans described Harvey as "a good mechanic, but a loud talker, insolent to white men, a bully to Negroes, hated by all because of his unusual size, strength, and mean disposition." Evans said that he had sent three guards, Adams, Brown, and Clark, to Harvey's house that evening to tell him not to come to work the next day; that he had cautioned the guards to avoid trouble with Harvey; that he wished to avoid a possible race riot. Asked why he had not given this information at the coroner's inquest, he said that he thought no good could come of it, and that it would lead to trouble among his workers and between Negroes and whites in Westfield.

The three guards, Adams, Brown, and Clark, testified that they had gone to Harvey's home about 10 P.M. to advise him not to come back to work; that they were met at the door by Harvey, who had a flashlight and a revolver in his hands; that they urged him to put away his revolver and come into the yard where they could talk without disturbing Mrs. Harvey; that Harvey finally agreed to accompany them into the yard, but refused to put away his revolver; that when they advised Harvey not to come to work anymore, he became very angry and leveled his revolver at them; that they then shot Harvey, each man firing once; that Davis had been with them and had also shot Harvey; that they were on duty at the time of the shooting because they were assigned to the 4 P.M. to midnight shift.

The guards insisted their job was to preserve order at the mill; they said they were simply acting as peace officers attempting to prevent an incipient race riot. They admitted that Harvey was a highly skilled mechanic. They could not recall ever having seen him drunk before. Adams, a native of Ohio, who had come from the North two years before, admitted that Harvey had repaired his car on one occasion, and said, "Harvey was one of the best machinists in Westfield." The guards denied that they had been drinking before going to the Harvey home, and denied having been in a speak-easy during the day. They said that Davis, who was on duty in another part of the plant, happened to meet them as they were going to Harvey's. He had offered to accompany them; he was told, "come along if you want to."

FINCH, a guard on the midnight to 8 A.M. shift, and a native of Illinois, testified that he roomed in the same building as Adams. He said that Adams returned to the house on February 9 about 11 P.M. Earlier in the evening Finch had heard that Adams and others were going to visit Harvey; and when he later asked Adams what had happened, Adams said, "He pulled a gun on us, and we had to shoot him."

THE CORONER testified that there were two bullet wounds in Harvey's chest and two in his abdomen.

THE SHERIFF testified that he had found a revolver near Harvey's body. It was loaded but had not been fired recently. He said the body was found about one hundred yards from the house.

MRS. HARVEY testified that on February 9 she and Harvey had gone to bed about 9:30 P.M. and were awakened by loud knocks and curses; that she got up and was going to the door, when it was forcibly opened and four men rushed in; that they brushed her aside, seized her husband, made him dress, forced him outside, and shot him; that she called the sheriff and immediately left with her three children for Montgomery, where she stayed with her mother to escape "the horrors of the situation." She admitted that Harvey had been drinking most of the morning of the ninth, but said he was ill with neuralgia. She denied that he drank frequently. She admitted that he continued to drink after coming home from work in the afternoon, and that she had had difficulty in getting him to go to bed that evening. Mrs. Harvey denied that he had had a flashlight or revolver in his hand at any time that evening. She admitted that he owned a revolver, but said it was kept in a bookcase. She admitted that she did not see Harvey killed. She admitted that the revolver found near Harvey's body was his.

DAVIS, the fourth guard, testified that he had met Adams, Brown, and Clark in a speak-easy in Birmingham (only a few miles from Westfield). The three were drinking and telling how they were going to "bump off that Harvey nigger." Davis said he decided to go along and try to protect Harvey, but that he had no opportunity. He claimed that he had left the employ of the Coal, Iron, and Railroad Company because he "disapproved of these killings." He denied being approached by representatives of the civil rights organizations which were aiding the prosecution. He admitted that he had not had a job since leaving the Coal, Iron, and Railroad Company. He denied shooting Harvey and said that he had admitted it at first because the company lawyer had told him he would get into more trouble by denying it.

Attempts to locate the speak-easy proprietor and his employees were unsuccessful. The address given by Davis proved to be an empty building, formerly occupied by a restaurant which had gone out of business about February 15, 1933.

THE INGRAM CASE

QUESTION: *Should the Baker Hero Fund Silver Medal be awarded posthumously to Rex Ingram?*

FACTS

ON AUGUST 10, 1929, a newspaper dispatch from Elizabeth, Tennessee, reported, "Nine boy scouts were saved from drowning in Masses Creek yesterday by Rex Ingram, local scoutmaster, when a cloudburst inundated the scout camp near here. Ingram and four boys were drowned."

Masses Creek is really a small river which drains a wide area and is full of falls and rapids. In one section it is normally two hundred feet wide and two to four feet deep for about a quarter-mile. The boy scout camp is located in this section of the creek, about seventy-five feet from the north bank on a low, sparsely wooded island. The cabin is fifteen feet high from sill to ridgepole and is still standing. Within fifty feet of the front door three large trees, the lowest branches of which are about twelve feet from the ground, are still standing.

The Elizabeth meteorologist stated that on August 9, nine and a half inches of rain fell between 5:30 and 7:30 P.M. Three and a half inches of rain had fallen in the preceding twenty-four hours. The water level of Masses Creek rose sixteen feet between 9 A.M. and 10 P.M. on August 9 and thereafter began to fall. This was the highest it had risen in the history of the local weather bureau; also, the rainfall was by far the heaviest on record. Local records going back over a thirty-year period showed that during June, July, and August the creek had risen only twice to within six feet of the level reached on August 9, 1929, and had never exceeded a ten-foot rise from its normal height.

Rex Ingram was twenty-five years of age, a native of Elizabeth, and a graduate of the local high school and of the University of Tennessee, where he had played varsity football for three years. He had served as scoutmaster for four years, 1925–29. He was also secretary of the Southern Textile and Rayon Products Company of Elizabeth, of which his father was president and principal stockholder. His scout duties occupied about half his time.

The Baker Hero Fund Commission sent Mr. C. V. O'Connor, a paid investigator, to Elizabeth to interview witnesses.

TESTIMONY

GEORGE YOUNG, fourteen years of age and the oldest boy in the party, said that there was a plank bridge between the island and the north bank of the creek; the stream was normally less than knee-deep at this point. When it began to rain heavily, the boys and Ingram went into the cabin and tried to stop leaks and keep themselves and their possessions dry. Later, one of the boys reported that the creek was over the bridge. This was about 6:30 P.M. They then made a fire, ate supper, and prepared to spend the night in the cabin. About 7 P.M. water began to come into the cabin. Mr. Ingram put on his coat and went out. He got the skiff and tied it to a nearby tree. As the water continued to rise rapidly, some of the smaller boys became afraid. Ingram put the four smallest in the boat, rowed across, and landed them on the bank. He rowed both ways himself. It took about forty-five minutes because the current tended to carry him downstream into the main channel. When he got back, the water was up to the boys' shoulders, and they were all frightened. Ingram had them get up on the roof. It was still drizzling, and Ingram feared the boys would catch cold or slip off the roof. He took George and four boys into the skiff. George was taken along to row. Ingram fended off the logs and debris with a long pole. They almost capsized once because of a sunken log. It was nearly dark by this time and still raining. Mr. Lincoln met them when they landed. George was sent to Lincoln's home to telephone for help.

H. B. LINCOLN, owner of the farm across from the camp, is sixty-five years old, afflicted with diabetes and heart trouble. He supplied the camp with eggs, milk, and similar foods. When the rain was nearly over, he went down to the creek and found the first four boys starting toward his house and Ingram about to start back. Ingram seemed tired but self-possessed. Ingram said the rest would be all right in the cabin; Lincoln agreed. He said he had never seen the water so high but expected it to go down soon. Later, Ingram came back with the second boatload, landing nearly a quarter-mile below the cabin. Ingram was definitely exhausted, but anxious to get back to the other boys. A short time later neighbors and city people came with cars and turned their headlights on the cabin. The water was within a few feet of the ridgepole on which Ingram and the boys were resting. Then two expert boatmen arrived with ropes and equipment and were about to set out for the cabin when the scout skiff, with Ingram and the boys in it, was observed in the water. The current seemed swifter than ever, and the boat turned around several times. It struck a log and sank. Ingram could be seen swimming and holding up two boys for a moment, but he soon submerged and was not seen again.

J. H. SLOAN, banker, president of the local boy scout organization, said that Ingram was the regularly elected scoutmaster, and received no pay on his own request; that Ingram had asked for the position; that the board had recommended abandoning the camp because of its dangerous and unhealthy location, but that Ingram said he would resign if it were abandoned. Sloan said that he had warned Ingram of his responsibility in all situations; that in his opinion Ingram had not shown good judgment in remaining at camp so long after the creek rose; that his act in taking the boys across showed bravery, but poor judgment under the circumstances; Sloan admitted he had been beaten in a lawsuit with Ingram's father.

The local scout regulations as found in the secretary's minutes were typewritten. Under the duties of scoutmaster this sentence was found, "It shall be the duty of the scoutmaster to safeguard the boys under all ordinary circumstances." The last two words had apparently been written over an erasure. The secretary was Arnold Thies, chief accountant of the Southern Textile and Rayon Products Company. He denied having tampered with this statement and produced the penciled minutes, as of June 1, 1925, showing the sentence as originally typed. Both the penciled and the typed pages were borrowed by the investigator. A documentary expert employed by the Baker Hero Fund Commission later testified that the original words on the typed copy before erasure were "circumstances whatever."

L. A. WHITE, athletic director of the local high school, expert canoeist, swimmer, and life-saving expert, said he had known Ingram since he started in high school. He said Ingram was of powerful physique, rugged, heavy, and fearless; that he was idolized by the boys because of his athletic prowess; that he was not a good swimmer and knew little of boats or rowing; that he was vain, proud, and headstrong. White said that Ingram had not been in training since he had been scoutmaster; that he was impatient and not resourceful and, in his opinion, ought never to have been scoutmaster; that he had not taught the boys to swim; that in his opinion, Ingram, if exhausted as reported, should have known better than to try to take the last load across and should have tied the boys to tree limbs, or put them in the skiff and tied it to a tree. White felt, however, that under the circumstances, Ingram had shown considerable bravery, though the situation could have been avoided by a scoutmaster possessing ordinary foresight and good judgment.

BART KYLE, the elder of the Kyle brothers, who appeared with ropes and equipment, was questioned next. (The Kyle brothers are fishermen, expert swimmers and boatmen, and owners of a grappling outfit. They are often employed throughout the state to recover bodies lost by drowning.) Bart Kyle said that he and his brother were starting out in a boat to get the boys when Ingram's boat capsized; that they were unable to reach the boys before they were carried away; that they went over to the cabin and found the current very swift all over the island and many trees and limbs floating in the water; that the island was composed of sand and gravel. He said that in his opinion the creek was so high that it might have changed its main course and flowed right through the island at any time; staying on the island under these circumstances would have seemed as risky as trying to get to the bank. His younger brother corroborated this testimony.

NOTES

Regulations of the Baker Hero Fund Commission limit the scope of awards in this manner:

1. To acts in which conclusive evidence may be obtained showing that the person performing the act voluntarily risked his own life in saving or attempting to save the life of a fellow human being, or who voluntarily sacrificed himself in a heroic manner for the benefit of others.

2. Such acts must have been performed by persons whose duties in following their regular vocations do not necessarily require them to perform such acts.

3. Three classes of awards — bronze, silver, and gold medals — are established. A silver medal is awarded only to those who can be shown to have realized the risk involved before taking action.

4. In initiating the Baker Hero Fund Commission, Mr. Baker expressed a desire that in all cases the commission consider the character of the person nominated for an award.

GUSTAVSON V. SVEDBERG RESTAURANTS, INC.

QUESTION: *Is Svedberg Restaurants, Inc., guilty of the false imprisonment of Miss Jessie Gustavson?*

FACTS

SVEDBERG RESTAURANTS, INC., operates a chain in Minneapolis and St. Paul. As a result of incidents which Miss Jessie Gustavson alleges occurred in one of these restaurants, she sued Svedberg for damages on the ground of false imprisonment.

The restaurant in question has a seating capacity of 150. The distance from the cashier's desk to the street door is twenty-four feet. A mezzanine or balcony surrounds the lower or main dining room. Meals are not served on the balcony except by special arrangement. The entrance to the balcony is forty feet from the street door.

TESTIMONY

MISS JESSIE GUSTAVSON testified that she is twenty-two years of age and resides with her parents and her aunt; that on September 2, at about 6 P.M., she entered the restaurant in question with her aunt; that her aunt complained of feeling ill, and that she found her a seat on the mezzanine. Miss Gustavson said that she then returned to the main dining room and ate alone; that when she had finished her meal, about 6:45, she motioned to her aunt to come down; that she then went to the cashier and paid her bill; that as she and her aunt were about to leave by the main door, a bell rang over their heads; that they looked around and saw the cashier beckoning to them to return. Miss Gustavson testified that they returned to his desk and he sharply asked, "Where is the other check? There is only one for the two of you, and each person must have a check." She said that she told him her aunt had not eaten and had not even been in the dining room; that by this time the headwaiter had come up to the desk; and that he called the waiter who had served her; that the second waiter confirmed her statement concerning her aunt; that when she and her aunt turned to leave, the headwaiter asked her aunt if she had not had wafers and tea on the mezzanine. She said that much discussion ensued, most of it in Swedish, which she did not understand, and that they were finally told they could leave, at exactly 7:18 P.M.

Asked how she fixed the time so precisely, she said she was watching the clock above the cashier's desk as she was worried about keeping a 7:45 engagement and was twenty-five blocks from home. Asked how she fixed the time of completing her meal, she said she could only approximate it, but thought it was, if anything, earlier than 6:45 since she remembered glancing at the clock before ordering dessert and noticed it was 6:30. Asked whether the colloquy between her aunt and herself and the cashier and waiters was continuous or was interrupted by other persons paying their checks, she said one or two did so, but very few were in the restaurant at the time. Asked whether she had expressed a desire to leave before finally being permitted to do so, she said she had started to leave several times and the cashier had said each time, "Just a moment now," or something to that effect. Asked if she could speak Swedish, she said she could not and maintained that she could not understand it unless it was spoken slowly. She admitted having studied Swedish for two years at Concordia College and receiving A grades in it. She denied joking with the waiters either in Swedish or English.

Miss THORA ULF, age forty-five, said she began to feel ill on first entering the restaurant and retired to the balcony. She took a seat next to the railing and tried to recover, but the odor of the food kept her from doing so. After a while a waitress asked her if she wanted something to eat. She replied that she didn't think so. She was not feeling well at the moment but might go down to the dining room later and have coffee. The waitress urged her to have a cup of tea, brought her one, and insisted that she drink it. Not wanting to seem impolite, she drank about half a cup. If there were any wafers, she didn't remember eating them. It did not occur to her to pay for the tea. She had not ordered it and was given no check for it. When asked by the headwaiter if she had had tea, she had been surprised into answering in Swedish, her native language, "Great heavens, are you going to make me pay for that? I didn't want it anyway." The headwaiter replied in Swedish that it had been ordered for her and she should expect to pay for it. She replied that she certainly wouldn't, and though she had eaten at Svedberg Restaurants for many years, she never would again. She said the headwaiter then changed his tone and begged her at great length to forget the matter. She interrupted him to ask if they might leave and he said they could, but the cashier would not let them go until their conversation had been repeated to him in English. Otherwise, she corroborated in every detail Miss Gustavson's testimony relating to the controversy at the cashier's desk. Asked if she had been joking with the headwaiter she said, "Positively not. I never joke with such persons, and I was in no mood for joking then. I was both ill and angry." Asked if her niece could speak Swedish, she said she could not, but admitted Swedish was frequently spoken in the house by the elder Gustavsons and herself.

JOHN O'HARA, the restaurant cashier, said a fixed rule in all Svedberg Restaurants requires the cashier to secure a check from each person who leaves. Because he is not allowed to leave his cash register, a bell system is used to attract the attention of persons who do not deposit checks. It is very rarely necessary to ring the bell. Miss Gustavson and her aunt had almost reached the door when he noticed there was only one check. It was a busy hour, and he was trying to accommodate a number of hurrying patrons. He rang the bell, and Miss Gustavson explained that her aunt had not eaten. He summoned the headwaiter and then their waiter and found this was true. He thanked the women and said, "That's all." Then the headwaiter asked about the special order.

A lengthy conversation in Swedish followed between the two women and the two waiters, which he did not understand. All four were laughing and seemed to be enjoying themselves. Other patrons had difficulty in getting to his desk, and he finally asked the two women to step out of the passageway. The aunt asked if he wanted her to pay for the tea. He impatiently said, "No," and the two women smiled and left. Asked if he had told the women either to stay or to go, he said he first asked if they would mind waiting until the matter was cleared up because he was tired of the waiters' careless mistakes. The women did not object. He was annoyed at their staying so long after the matter was cleared up. Asked how long he kept them waiting, he said not over five minutes, only long enough to find out that the aunt had not eaten in the dining room. Asked how long the women remained after that, he said about ten or fifteen minutes. He could not fix the exact time for it had not seemed significant then.

ANDERS JOHNSON, headwaiter, said he heard the bell ring, and later went to the desk when O'Hara beckoned. Finding what the trouble was, he summoned Ole Svenson, Miss Gustavson's waiter. Johnson then recognized Miss Ulf as the woman in the blacony to whom an order of tea and cinnamon toast had been served. He had checked the order taken by the waitress who regularly served special orders. He was surprised that Miss Ulf spoke Swedish as he did not think she was Swedish, and spoke to her in that language to test her knowledge. Miss Ulf spoke Swedish much better than he, and Miss Gustavson did not speak the language fluently but she understood everything. The two women laughed and joked about the tea, offering to pay for it, but he told them to forget it. Nothing was said about whether it was ordered or not. He said they talked for ten minutes, not longer. He knew this because he went off duty at 7:15 and had been watching the clock when the bell rang. It was then almost 7 P.M. After the women left he had time to clean up before 7:15.

GLADYS BURNS, waitress, said she serves tea and sandwiches and the like on the mezzanine in the afternoon and clears tables in the dining room evenings. She saw Miss Ulf seat herself at a balcony table and went up to her to take her order. Miss Ulf said she felt faint and might eat later but would like a cup of tea and cinnamon toast. She secured this for her and had the order checked by the headwaiter, as was necessary for all orders served in the mezzanine after 5:30 P.M. She had received no check from the headwaiter and had made none out because she had turned her checks in at 5:30 as was the custom.

MISS JOSEPHINE JOHNSON, a high school English teacher for thirty years, said she was eating in the Svedberg Restaurant on September 2, and heard the bell ringing and the discussion between the two women and the restaurant staff. She came up to pay her check about 7 P.M., waited several minutes before she could be attended to, and could not help hearing the conversation. She understands Swedish very well and speaks it to some extent, being of Swedish extraction. She heard the aunt say to the headwaiter, "Is this monkey of a cashier going to let us out of here? I'm not going to pay for what I didn't order if he keeps us here all night." The headwaiter said, "Madame, are you sure you didn't order toast and tea? I checked the order myself." All this was in Swedish. She denied knowing or ever having seen the women before. Confronted with the fact that Jessie Gustavson was in a class she taught eight years before, she said she has more than a hundred students each term and does not remember her at all. She admitted not speaking Swedish in her home and said she has had little opportunity to hear or speak it for twenty-five years, except for one month spent touring in Sweden seven years earlier. She learned to speak Swedish when a child, and it was spoken in her home until she went to normal school.

O. L. STROM, Professor of Scandinavian Languages and Literature at Concordia College, said that the only two courses in Swedish taken by Miss Jessie Gustavson at Concordia were Old Swedish and Swedish Literature; Proficiency in modern Swedish was not required. Miss Gustavson could not converse in modern Swedish at the end of her college course two years ago. He admitted that she was a member of the Swedish Club, which was conducted in Swedish, but maintained she was practically a "silent member."

NOTES

The following statements of law are to be accepted in this case:

Any general restraint, even though effected without actual contact of the person, is imprisonment. Any demonstration of physical power, which to all appearances can be avoided only by submission, operates as effectually to constitute an imprisonment, if submitted to, as if any amount of force had been exercised. If a person is restrained of his personal liberty for an appreciable length of time by fear of a personal difficulty, it amounts to imprisonment.

"False" imprisonment is defined in law as improper, unwarranted, unjustified, without cause. Any citizen may imprison another to prevent a felony or other crime, and hotel and restaurant keepers, merchants, and others may imprison to prevent a fraud, but all these do so at the risk of civil suit for alleged false imprisonment.

THE GIORDANO CASE

QUESTION: *Is Giulo Giordano guilty of fraud?*

FACTS

JOHN MALDEN, an English instructor, noticed on Assistant Professor Bruska's desk a theme entitled "Immigration Restriction: A Challenge to Democracy," by Giulo Giordano, '48. He called Professor Bruska's attention to certain alleged similarities between this theme and the one submitted in his own section by Bernard Hilsen, '48, "South European Immigration: Fact and Fiction." The important similarities are:

I. The central idea of Giordano's paper is that the United States' discrimination against South-European immigrants is unjustified.
   A. The ethnic inferiority of South Europeans has not been and cannot be proved.
   B. The apparent tendency of Southern Europeans in America to enter

lawless activities and to retain low standards of living can be explained.

    1. They have had less time to adapt themselves than have the Northern Europeans with whom they are compared.

    2. They have been forced to remain in unwholesome sections of large cities, having found all the desirable urban and rural sections already occupied by previous immigrants.

C. Such unjustified discrimination makes American democracy a sham.

I^1. The central idea of Hilsen's paper is that the United States' discrimination against South-European immigrants is unjustified.

A. The supposed inferiority of Southern Europeans in the United States as judged by their failure to become good citizens is unsound reasoning since this group found the country saturated with immigrants and was forced to accept a lower economic and social status.

B. Southern Europeans are a desirable addition to America, for they bring a needed emotionalism and love of the arts into American culture and civilization.

C. Unjust discrimination against these peoples is a blow to good relations with the South-European countries, especially Italy.

II. Six sentences, not consecutive in either case, from each of the themes read as follows:

A. FROM GIORDANO'S THEME:

    1. "Of the millions of persons of foreign birth now in the country, we must admit that nearly half are of South-European stock. . . ."

    2. "What is the basis for the legislation of 1924 and subsequent immigration laws which give to the South-European nations such absurdly low quotas? Is it based on sound scientific or sociological grounds?"

    3. "It is assumed that the newer immigration is poor and ignorant and of debased living and moral standards because it seems to prefer the tenement and the mining camp to American standards of living and culture."

    4. "It is an open question whether this new immigration, if given a virgin soil, and the opportunities of the Scandinavians and Irish and Germans, would not develop the same qualities of mind and character which we assume to belong to the Anglo-Saxon overlords. . . ."

    5. "Former Commissioner of Immigration Howe has said that the alleged prevalence of crime among recent aliens is caused by the economic environment in which they must remain in a country filled with immigrants, and is not the result of inherent ethnic inferiority."

6. "Can America look with pride and satisfaction upon a discrimination against one class of immigration, when it rests on a basis as unscientific and false as it is undemocratic and insulting?"

B. FROM HILSEN'S THEME:
1. "Of the 15 million persons of foreign birth now in the United States, undoubtedly a large number are of South-European stock."
2. "The question is whether or not the legislation of 1924 which reduced to absurdly low figures the quotas for South-European nations is justified on any scientific or sociological grounds."
3. "This assumed that the new immigration is poor and ignorant because it is ethnically unfitted for American life and prefers the tenement and mining camp to American standards of living and culture."
4. "It is an open question whether this new immigration, if given a virgin continent, and the opportunities so made available, would not develop the same qualities of mind and of character that we assume to be the exclusive characteristics of the Anglo-Saxons."
5. "Former Commissioner of Immigration, Frederick C. Howe, has said that: 'The prevalence of crime and vice among the alien population is traceable to poverty and bad conditions of living rather than to ethnic causes, and insofar as it exists it tends to disappear as the conditions which breed it pass away.'"
6. "It is not strange, then, that Italy and other of the South-European countries have considered such a policy a gratuitous insult, when it rests on a basis as false, unscientific, and undemocratic as it does."

Other similarities occurred, but none as close as those given above. The introductions and conclusions were quite different. Professor Bruska remembered mentioning to Giordano an article by Howe entitled "The Alien," in *Civilization in the United States* by Harold E. Stearns. On pages 340, 341, and 346 of the 1922 edition of that book there are sentences similar to sentences 3, 4, and 5, above. The theme in question was a term theme and counts as part of the final examination. Hilsen's grade in the course without considering the theme or final examination is B—, and Giordano's is C.

Professor Bruska asked the Student Honor Tribunal to determine whether or not Giordano was guilty of fraud. The tribunal defines fraud as "willfully and intentionally giving or receiving improper aid in examinations or reports." A theme is construed by the tribunal to be a report.

TESTIMONY

PROFESSOR BRUSKA said that he had called Giordano into conference. Giordano at first appeared sullen and disinclined to talk, but later became more communicative, even frank. Giordano told him he first met Hilsen at a restaurant where he, Giordano, waited on tables; that he had asked Professor Bruska, after the theme was assigned, for a good topic to write on; and that Professor Bruska had suggested this subject and recommended the Howe article; that a week or two later he tried to get the book at the library and found that it was out. Giordano said that he walked home with Hilsen the next day and discovered that he had the book; that he asked to borrow it; and that Hilsen asked him to come up to his room and read it there, which he did that night. He said that he discussed the topic with Hilsen then and the following evening; that he wrote the theme the day after his first visit to Hilsen's room; that Giordano read his own theme aloud to Hilsen on the second night; that he could not account for the similarities between his and Hilsen's theme except that they had used the same language in discussion and the same reference.

Professor Bruska could not remember when Giordano had asked him for material on the subject, but felt it unlikely that he would have suggested this particular topic to Giordano. Yet he did remember mentioning Howe's essay to Giordano.

MALDEN said that he had called Hilsen into his office and confronted him with the two themes and the article by Howe. He said Hilsen told him in a frank, straightforward manner that he had conceived the idea of the theme as a result of a class discussion on immigration. The article by Howe was only one of several he had read; among others he had read Franz Boas' articles; that he took the book containing Howe's article from the library for home use; that he had known Giordano only slightly, having walked home from the campus with him several times; that he told Giordano he was writing on this topic; that Giordano showed much interest in it and suggested they discuss it together; that Giordano came up to his room on two different nights; there he read the article by Howe and took notes on it; and that they discussed the topic. Hilsen said that Giordano asked to see his theme and read it. Giordano did not take notes from it or copy it as far as he knew, although he, Hilsen, was working at another desk on another subject at the time. Malden said that Hilsen cheerfully admitted the close similarities in language between the two papers, but maintained he had never seen Giordano's essay.

GIORDANO reiterated his previous statements to Professor Bruska; he denied telling Hilsen that he did not know what topic to write on; he denied suggesting that they discuss the subject; he denied asking to read or actually reading Hilsen's theme.

HILSEN repeated everything he had said to Malden; he remembered speaking to Giordano in the restaurant; he seemed genuinely surprised at Giordano's conflicting testimony.

R. A. BRAUN, Hilsen's roommate, appeared before the tribunal at his own request. He said he was present both nights when Giordano was there; that on the second evening he heard Giordano ask to see Hilsen's theme, saw him read it, and saw him take notes on it. Asked where Hilsen and Giordano sat, he said Hilsen was at his own desk and Giordano at the other desk, usually occupied by Braun. Asked if he too was studying, he said he was. Asked where he was studying, he said in the same room. Asked if he was writing, he said he was, but had later retired to the bedroom. Asked if he usually studied there, he said no, but that he had retired to the bedroom because Hilsen and Giordano disturbed him with their talk. Asked if he could see Giordano from the bed, he said he could see the back of his head. Asked how he could be studying and watching Giordano's head at the same time, he said he was unable to concentrate on his book because of the conversation.

GIORDANO was recalled. He denied that Braun was in the study room when he entered the second night, and said that if Braun was in the bedroom, he did not see him.

HILSEN was recalled. He said that he did not remember whether Braun had retired to the bedroom, and that he did not remember where Braun was studying on the second night.

SUGGESTIONS

The direct and substantial contradictions between the testimony of Giordano and Hilsen provide a strong temptation to leap immediately to the conclusion that one, or both, is lying. Avoid this assumption until you have satisfied yourself that misunderstanding and faulty memories cannot account for the contradictions. If they can, possibilties for interpretation will emerge which the perjury hypothesis effectively obscures.

Something is to be learned by comparing the bent and flavor of Howe's and Boas' writings with corresponding qualities in Giordano's and Hilsen's themes.

THE McCOLLUM CASE

QUESTION: *Should McCollum's will be set aside on the ground of mental incapacity?*

FACTS

WILLIAM McCOLLUM, sixty-five, of Chaffee, North Dakota, widower, died and left six children, three sons and three daughters, all unmarried. He also left three small grandchildren by a deceased married daughter, Mrs. George Davis. McCollum left an estate valued at about $175,000. His will provides for the division of the estate into seven equal parts, one part to each of his surviving children and another to the orphan grandchildren. By the terms of the will, the lands and property are to be sold and a trust fund established. The children are to receive interest on their shares for life, and the grandchildren are to receive interest on their shares until all children are deceased. When McCollum's last child has died, the principal of the trust fund is to be divided among the surviving grandchildren.

The six children are anxious to secure outright control of their share of the estate and ask that the will be set aside due to the mental incapacity of McCollum. Each of the six will then inherit, outright, one-seventh of the estate. The children of Mrs. Davis, jointly, will receive the remaining seventh and no more.

The six children, Lincoln, Henry, Ada, Mary, June, and Edward, are between twenty-two and thirty-five years of age. All had become estranged from McCollum; the boys have been working away from home, and Lincoln, the oldest, rents a farm not far from McCollum's.

TESTIMONY

THE REV. EMERSON DeWITT, seventy-one, retired minister, said that he had known McCollum all his life; that McCollum was a grasping and miserly man, very profane and irreligious; that when Mrs. Davis was married, he, DeWitt, had conducted the ceremony in the parsonage; and that McCollum did not attend. Mrs. Davis told him her father was bitterly opposed to the marriage. He said that the next day when he had met McCollum in the street, the latter had cursed him; that when Mrs. Davis died, McCollum would not visit her home; that he did attend the church funeral, but sat in the back row; that when he, DeWitt, spoke to McCollum afterward and tried to comfort him, McCollum had replied, "Yes, she's in hell now."

LINCOLN McCOLLUM testified that his father had never cared for anything but making money; that he, Lincoln, had been taken from school at fourteen and had been made to work on the farm until he was nineteen, at which age he went to work for the neighboring farmer; that while at home, he had no wages at all, had to wear his father's made-over clothes, and was never allowed to drive a horse or car except on business for his father; that his father had never given his mother any money, except for bare necessities; that she had bought her clothes and provided food items not raised on the farm, by selling produce from a truck patch, by churning butter, and the like. He said his mother had not been allowed to have proper medical attention, and he attributed her death to his father's miserliness and lack of natural affection.

JUNE McCOLLUM, twenty-two, said she alone of all the children had remained on the farm. She said that when Henry McCollum lost a job in Fargo, North Dakota, because of illness, he had come home, but that her father had forbidden him to come into the house; that she had fixed a place for him in a dilapidated cottage on the farm, which had been occupied by Negro tenants; that she had had to slip coal and wood into the cottage to keep it warm, even though her father had given express orders to the contrary. She admitted that during the last few years her father had given her an allowance of fifteen dollars a month to clothe herself. She said that she was not permitted callers and could only occasionally attend movies and fairs with her father.

DR. A. L. MARTIN of Fargo said he was a physician and surgeon. He said that he had been called to Mrs. Davis' home to consult with the local physician in the case of her oldest son; that he had diagnosed the case as mastoiditic, urged an operation, and insisted that the boy be sent to the hospital at once; that Mrs. Davis told him they had no money; that when Mrs. Davis said her father had plenty of money but was not on speaking terms with her, Martin had gone to see McCollum; that the latter had refused to pay for anything for the boy, saying that Mrs. Davis had married a "wastrel" against his wishes, and that he had long since washed his hands of them; that McCollum appeared sound of body and sane in every respect, except for an obsessive hatred for his daughter and her husband. In Martin's opinion if a person hated all his children for no more reason than McCollum was said to have had, he was the victim of an insane delusion.

J. L. HAINES, Ford agent and garage owner in Chaffee, sixty-eight, testified that he had known McCollum for twenty-five years. He said that he had sold McCollum wagons and buggies and, in the last ten years, two Ford trucks; that McCollum was stingy and unprincipled in business dealings — he was a "sharp trader"; that McCollum had told him his oldest son, Lincoln, was a thief and was stealing his wheat; that McCollum had said that he "didn't want to leave his children a cent," and that he would like to leave his farm in such heavy debt that it would take years to pay it off; that McCollum had said he "wanted to leave it in such a way that the children would have to work like dogs to get a living out of it." Haines admitted that he could not remember exactly when this conversation took place; that he had heard part of it at one time and part at another. He was certain that he had heard all of it not more than two years prior to McCollum's death. He admitted that he had often tried to sell McCollum a pleasure car, and that they had quarreled frequently over repairs to McCollum's trucks.

JOHN GAULT, president of the Chaffee State Bank and chief executor of the will, testified that he had known McCollum for forty years. Gault said that McCollum had started in life as a hired man on a farm and through industry and business ability had become one of the wealthiest farmers in the community. Gault thought him honest and fair in all his dealings, prompt to pay his bills, and prominent and tireless in cooperative enterprises, such as the Cass County Fair Association, the Dairymen's League, and the Grange, to which he had given much of his time without pay. He said that McCollum had often spoken to him of his disappointment that his sons would not stay on the farm; that McCollum had said that if the boys would stay with him until they were twenty-one, he would buy them farms; that all of them had left voluntarily before they were twenty-one; that McCollum objected to Davis as a son-in-law because he thought him a ne'er-do-well who had inherited a farm and lost it through laziness and poor management; that McCollum had spoken well of his other daughters and was especially proud of June's good school record and of her general popularity.

DR. E. L. HOLT testified that he had been a physician in Chaffee for twenty-three years. During this time he was often called to McCollum's home. He said that he had attended both husband and wife in their last illnesses; that Mrs. McCollum had died of influenza in 1918 when there was a general epidemic of that disease; that she might possibly have recovered if she had had special nurses or hospital care, but that the local hospital had been full during her illness and that he had been unable to secure special nurses for any of his patients at that particular time. He said that in his opinion McCollum was sane in every way up to the moment of his death; that he was fully aware of the natural claims of his children; that his failure to leave his estate outright to them was not caused by a delusion but by a settled idea. Holt stated that no autopsy of McCollum had been performed; he said that none was required since McCollum had died of paralysis caused by high blood pressure and overexertion.

MISS HELEN DEVORE, a retired schoolteacher, testified that she had taught in the district school attended by the McCollum children; that all of them had studied under her; that all, except Lincoln, had completed the eighth grade; that none, except June, had any interest in study; and that all were very hard to manage. She said that McCollum had told her he wanted the children to go through high school if she thought they were fitted for it, and that she had advised it only for June. She admitted that McCollum was the principal director of the school, and that he had been influential in her having retained her position.

GEORGE OLDS, forty-five, owner of the farm next to McCollum's, testified that he knew McCollum and his sons very well for fifteen years or more. He said that McCollum was a good farmer, both competent and shrewd in managing his farm — one of the largest and best stocked in the county when he died; that he had had several differences of opinion with McCollum, the most severe being a dispute over who should pay for a tile drain necessary to prevent the erosion of Olds' fields caused by extensive drainage from McCollum's neighboring fields. Olds said a threatened lawsuit was settled amicably out of court because McCollum did not want to pay excessive legal fees; that he had employed all of McCollum's sons at some time, especially Lincoln; that they were all good workers, except that they could not be trusted with horses or machinery; that they were impatient, lost their tempers, and were cruel to animals; that they had all been given a chance to share in the proceeds from the fruit and dairy enterprises on the McCollum farm, which were extensive and always profitable, but that each time they quarreled with their father and left in anger because he insisted on his methods of husbandry as opposed to theirs; that Henry had told Olds he had left his father because McCollum would not buy a new milking machine, but insisted on having the old one repaired. McCollum was a very active promoter of agricultural organizations, had given financial support to the declining Cass County Fair, and was a stockholder in the Dairymen's League and a wheat marketing association.

NOTES

The following statements of law are to be accepted in this case:

To invalidate a will it is not necessary to show the testator incapable of understanding that he was making a disposition of his property, but only that he was incapable of comprehending the nature and extent of his property or of understanding the claims of persons who were or might be naturally the objects of his bounty. Capacity for the transaction of ordinary business has been adopted generally as the trial for testamentary capacity, but with it are combined the requirement of capacity to understand the business of making a will, capacity to comprehend the disposition and effects of disposing of his property, and the capacity to appreciate his relation to the natural objects of his bounty.

The capacity to understand claims to bounty comprises the knowledge, memory, and capacity to comprehend his relation to the persons who were or might be naturally the objects of his bounty, and the relative merits of their claims, and the capacity of making a rational selection among them, according to his settled purposes.

Delusion has been held to be the true and only test of the presence or absence of insanity or mental incapacity. Within the delusion rule, strong, violent, and unjust prejudice, not founded on any delusion, does not show mental incapacity which will invalidate a will. Whenever a person believes something extravagant exists, against all evidence — which thing has not any existence in fact, but in his imagination alone — and he is incapable of being reasoned out of such a conception, he will be held to have an insane delusion which will invalidate a will affected by such extravagant belief.

The question as to whether a testator's prejudice against the natural object of his bounty amounted to an insane delusion is one of fact, depending on whether or not, under all circumstances, it is deemed such as might not have resided in a sound mind.

SUGGESTIONS

The first requirement here is to puzzle out the meaning, in terms of this particular situation, of the rather complicated law which is relevant.

The facts and opinions must be mastered, but the more general pictures which can be inferred reasonably from them may provide the strongest arguments. Detailed examination of testimony which conflicts on minutiae must not obscure these larger considerations.

The task, it must be remembered, is to interpret the will, not to give vent to personal feelings concerning McCollum or his children.

THE PEOPLE V. DEMPSEY

QUESTION: *Should Patrolman Dempsey be indicted on a charge of manslaughter for killing Herbert Hausman?*

FACTS

ON AUGUST 22, 1936, at 3:35 P.M., two men, John Brechtl and Martin Bachorik, both nineteen, waylaid the manager of the Mendoza Fur and Dyeing Works, 712 East 133rd Street, the Bronx; robbed him of the payroll of $4,913.87; and killed the police guard, Webb, who attempted to fire on them. They then fled in the manager's car to St. Anne's Avenue and turned up 149th Street. In that vicinity they changed to a Yellow Taxi, driven by Hausman. They drove on to Third Avenue and then to the Boston Post Road. At 169th Street they killed Motorcycle Policeman Churchill. They followed 169th Street to Webster Avenue, drove a short way on Park Avenue, and turned onto 161st Street. At Jerome and 161st Street, Fireman Lopes, his wife, and daughter, in a Ford car, were injured by the bandits' shots. The three-year-old daughter, Gloria, later died from her injury. From this point they were pursued by Patrolmen Walker and Dempsey and Detective Kiley in a commandeered taxi driven by William Nugent. Moving over to 155th Street, the bandits crossed McCombs Dam Bridge over the Harlem River, turned into St. Nicholas Avenue, and crossed on 160th

Street to Riverside Drive. They went up Riverside Drive. At 181st Street, Fireman Hyde, who had been following from 169th Street, was seriously injured. A little later two pursuing drivers were wounded by the bandits' gunfire. The bandits turned east, went down Dyckman Street to Sherman Avenue, and circled around the area bounded by Broadway, Sherman, Dyckman, and Nagle Streets. On the second round, a truck blocked Dyckman Street, and the car came to a halt. Pursuing cars barricaded the streets, and Patrolman Dempsey shot Hausman at 4:05 P.M. On examination of the car the other two occupants were also found to be dead.

The bandits had covered about twelve miles in all. In addition to the bandits, two policemen, a taxi driver, and a child had been killed, and at least seven persons injured by their shots. Five pistols and thirty-two unused cartridges in boxes were found on the floor of the cab, as was the satchel containing the payroll. Two pairs of white canvas gloves were in the back seat of the car.

The two bandits were identified from fingerprints as having attempted to hold up a roadhouse proprietor at Kingston, New York, on October 19, 1935. They had been arrested at that time and served thirty days in jail for carrying concealed weapons. Hausman had no police record.

A grand jury was asked to consider whether or not Patrolman Dempsey should be indicted on a manslaughter charge for killing Hausman.

TESTIMONY

WILLIAM NUGENT said he was formerly a private chauffeur, had been out of work for six months and secured a job as a taxi driver on August 19, 1936. He joined the chase at 167th Street and Webster Avenue, and his car was commandeered by two policemen and Detective Kiley at 161st Street and Jerome Avenue. "Kiley was riding the running board all the time, shooting at them. But when he had emptied his gun, he had to come inside on the baggage seat, and I had to slow up a little so he could reload. We shot into Riverside Drive, and I almost skidded into a wall. They raced down Riverside Drive and opened fire something terrible. Two shots hit the dashboard, one right after the other. One shot went into the seat on one side of me; the other shot went in the other side, right between my arm and my side. Then we got to Broadway, and two of their bullets ripped both my front tires. They rounded the corner on two wheels, east of Broadway and Dyckman Street, and Kiley fired into their gas tank. The tank exploded, and there was a big flash and a lot of smoke. A vegetable truck blocked them there, and we pulled along their left side.

"Two other cabs full of cops and detectives came tearing alongside of us. Kiley, the cops, and I piled out. The man who was driving jumped out of the front seat with a red-hot gun in his hand. He was right out beside us. I ran over and grabbed a hammer that was lying on the tailboard of the truck. As he was trying to escape, I hit him on the side of the head with all I had behind it. Dempsey then let him have it — four shots. While this was going on, the other cops pulled the doors open and let the gangsters have it — ten or fifteen shots each. And that settled them. And it settled me, too. I'm through with hacking. This sort of thing never happened to me before, and I hope it never happens again."

MRS. MARGARET HAUSMAN, twenty-three, wife of Herbert Hausman, said she had been his wife since 1930. They have two small children. She said her husband had been in the marine hardware business until a year ago, when, acting on a policeman's suggestion that there was more money in hacking, he had secured a license and started taxi driving. For the last three months he had been out of work, but on August 18, 1936, he was employed by the Monarch Taxi Company. He was not assigned to a particular station, but cruised about for fares. She said that Hausman did not have a gun, stayed at home when not working, and was always looking in the want ads for a better job. "If Herbert had been a gangster, surely it stands to reason that we would not be so poor. Why, I haven't a cent in the house this minute. I haven't even enough money to buy food for the children, let alone bury him. You can't tell me a wife wouldn't know whether her husband is a gangster or not. If all the cops in Christendom told me that Herbert was working with those thieves, I wouldn't believe them."

PATROLMAN DEMPSEY said he had shot Hausman after he reached toward his pocket as if to draw a pistol. Dempsey said he had been on duty at the 161st Street Police Station when a message from Police Headquarters was received by the sergeant in charge, ordering them to look for a Yellow Taxi with the number later found to be Hausman's and believed to be transporting men wanted for robbery and murder. He had left at once.

DETECTIVE KILEY and PATROLMAN WALKER said they were also at the 161st Street Station and left with Dempsey. They corroborated Dempsey's statement and said that at the finish of the chase Dempsey jumped out of the cab first. They all had revolvers in their hands. Hausman jumped out, reached in his pocket, and Dempsey fired.

INSPECTOR JOHN J. SULLIVAN, in charge of detectives of all boroughs, said that a 32-caliber revolver was found in Hausman's coat pocket after the shooting. He said it was empty and had recently been fired. Asked if Hausman's fingerprints were on the pistol, he admitted they were not, but that other, unidentifiable fingerprints were on the gun. The inspector admitted that he had not tried to trace ownership of the pistol and claimed this was impossible. He admitted Hausman had no permit to carry a revolver, and said that he was at Police Headquarters when informed of the Mendoza affair. He was told that shortly before the report of the robbery and murder had been sent in, a message was received from James Peters. Nothing had been done about this message until the Mendoza information was received. At once, about 3:45 P.M., he ordered all available detectives and patrolmen in all Bronx and Manhattan stations to stop the Yellow Taxi described in Peters' message. A few minutes later a phone call was received from William Miller, and this information was relayed to all stations. He fixed the time at which this final word was sent out as 3:50 P.M.

PETER GARVIN, desk sergeant at the 161st Street Station, said that the first word received about the Yellow Taxi came at 3:45 P.M. from James Peters. The only other message came at 3:53, saying that Churchill had been killed while trying to arrest the occupants of the taxi and warning that they were probably coming across town.

JAMES PETERS, thirty-five, unemployed, said he was walking down 149th Street sometime after 3:30 P.M. on the afternoon in question, when a car went down the middle of the street and through a red light at a high rate of speed. About the middle of the next block the car turned toward the curb and stopped suddenly. Two men in white gloves jumped out and got into a Yellow Taxi that had stopped at this point, a little to the right of the middle of the street. The taxi then proceeded up 149th Street at "tremendous speed" and disappeared in the traffic. He telephoned the license numbers of the car to the the nearest police station, describing the car, the occupants, and the incident. Asked why he did this, he said he was tired of seeing people go through red lights and exceed the speed limits. He wasn't working and thought there might be "something in it" for him if the occupants of the car were wanted by the police. He waited half an hour beside the abandoned car, but when no police came he went to a movie. He had received no reward and was still unemployed.

WILLIAM MILLER, owner and manager of a retail cigar store next door to a subway station, on Westchester Avenue, said he had reported to the police that a taxi had driven up to the Jackson Avenue elevated subway station on Westchester Avenue at about 3:40 P.M. on August 22. Two men wearing white gloves had run into the subway station, leaving the taxi motor running, and had returned in about three minutes and driven off. Miller identified the dead bandits as the two men he had seen. He had been curious about the affair because the men wore white gloves. He had been on the sidewalk when they drove off. He had noted the license number, which was the same as that of the taxi in which the bandits were killed, and reported it to the police together with an account of the incident. The taxi drove away very swiftly and recklessly, swerved to the left, almost colliding with a truck, and disappeared in a great burst of speed. He phoned the nearest police station immediately. He could not identify Hausman as the driver because he had not paid any attention to him. He remembered that the driver had remained in the taxi when the others went into the subway station. He did not notice whether the two men carried anything into or out of the subway station.

FRANCIS X. SHEEHY, mechanic at this station, also testified that two men, wearing white gloves, had entered the station and then seemed to change their minds suddenly. They rushed back out of the turnstiles; they had neither satchels nor boxes. He identified the bandits as the two men he had seen.

GEORGE KARMANIAN, who has a shoe repair shop on Dyckman Street, said he saw one of the bandits in the back seat point a revolver at Hausman's head when the bandit car passed his shop the first time.

NICK ROMANO, restaurant proprietor on 161st Street, testified that one bandit was menacing Hausman with a revolver and one was firing at pursuing cars when the Yellow Taxi passed his place.

HARLEY HIGGINS, forty-nine, a New York police reporter for twenty years, now employed by the New York *World*, said he and news photographer Dennis Riordan had been in a taxi on an assignment and joined the chase at 160th Street, where Patrolmen Ankeny and Schwartz stopped them and directed them up Riverside Drive. Their taxi was driven by Sisson. They passed a number of pursuing cars and narrowly escaped crashing at 181st Street when the driver of the car ahead (Hyde) was shot. They pulled ahead of this car and saw one taxi between them and the bandits' cab. The bandits kept firing from the back window, and at a curve two blocks beyond 181st Street a bullet struck Sisson in the shoulder. Higgins grabbed the wheel, and Riordan and the policemen got Sisson into the back seat. Higgins then drove. One car had passed them, but its driver was shot and forced to pull to the curb shortly thereafter. By this time they had reached Dyckman Street. Here the Yellow Taxi swerved up Dyckman, turning left at several corners, apparently because of traffic jams. The bandits were firing continually until they had made a circuit and entered Dyckman for the second time. When they stopped, Higgins' car was right behind Nugent's. Higgins jumped out in time to see Nugent and the policeman in his taxi get out and run forward. Hausman opened the left front door of the bandits' taxi and stepped out. As he did so, Dempsey, who had run around from behind Nugent's taxi, shot him. Higgins said he did not see whether Hausman had a gun in his hand or not when he got out. He did not remember whether Hausman raised his hands in surrender.

On cross-examination, Higgins admitted that Hausman was shot just as he got out. His left hand was on the car, his left foot on the running board, and his right foot on the pavement as Dempsey opened fire. He also admitted that when he ran up to look at Hausman, there was no gun in Hausman's hands. No search was made of Hausman's pockets then; Kiley had Hausman placed in a police ambulance, along with the two other dead men, and they were taken away at once.

DENNIS RIORDAN, twenty-seven, a Fordham University graduate and photographer for the New York *World* for five years, confirmed Higgins' story,
except that he said he got out on the right side and did not see Hausman
until he was shot. He had seen both bandits moving about in the back
seat immediately before the taxi stopped; then he could no longer see
them, though his view was unobstructed. No shooting occurred after the
cars turned into Dyckman Street the second time. He was not permitted
to take pictures of the Yellow Taxi, or of anything else. His camera was
not confiscated or broken by the police. He could not swear positively that
any shooting was done by the bandits after they turned off Riverside Drive,
but was sure that the police in Nugent's car were firing until the car stopped.
He said a large crowd collected when the shooting was over.

SUGGESTIONS

Begin by plotting out all available information concerning the events
that transpired on August 22 between 3:35 and 4:05 P.M. By working out
the interrelationships between the characters and events, find out insofar
as possible where each person was, what he was doing, and especially,
what he knew, at each critical point. Then proceed to the second step in
the analysis — deciding as precisely as possible what the situation was, both
physically and psychologically, when Dempsey squeezed off the shot that
killed Hausman. Whether or not Dempsey should have fired hinges on
what he could reasonably have believed at that instant. Then evaluate the
testimony, both as to its relevancy and its reliability. Much of the testimony
is relevant only when used as the basis for a very special kind of inference.

THE PEOPLE V. TOWER

QUESTION: *Is Joshua Tower guilty of murder in the first degree?*

FACTS

JULIAN R. WATERS, principal of the Martin Private School for boys, near
Westham, Massachusetts, was killed by a rifle bullet on December 14, 1938.
Waters was twenty-eight years of age, unmarried, a Harvard and Oxford
graduate, a Rhodes scholar, and a teacher for five years at Mercersburg
Academy before coming to Martin in September, 1938. He showed promise
as a scholar and educator. He was the youngest person ever to have been
a member of the American Rhodes Scholar Board which chooses Rhodes
scholars. His father was John R. Waters, an internationally famous clergy-

man, publicist, and diplomat, who was then serving as a member of the League of Nations' Commission for the Control of Narcotics. Waters was near his desk in his study when the bullet was fired. The study is in the northwest corner of his one-story cottage. The window through which the shot was fired is on the north side.

TESTIMONY

Dr. R. T. Harris said he was called to Waters' cottage at 9:30 P.M., December 14, by Giorgio Cupola, Waters' servant. He found Waters seated and slumped over his desk, dead. Waters could not have been dead more than half an hour. He extracted the bullet the next day, turning it over to Sheriff White. The bullet had penetrated the skull behind the left ear and lodged against the right skull wall a little above and opposite to its entrance. Death was instantaneous. Dr. Harris lives three blocks from Waters' cottage.

Giorgio Cupola, thirty-five, unmarried, said he had been trained as a chef in Italy. He has been cook and house servant to the principal since September, 1936. He has had no misunderstandings of any kind and liked his two employers very much. His wages have been raised yearly. He was in his room listening to the radio when he heard the shot and breaking of glass. He ran into Waters' room, found him unconscious, ran to the telephone, and called Dr. Harris. It was about 9:25 P.M., as he noticed by the clock in Waters' room. Cupola does not know of anyone who disliked Waters; everyone seemed fond of him. He did not see anyone around that evening. He was afraid to go outside after the shooting.

Horace White, sheriff of Westmoreland County, said he was summoned by Waters' servant, Cupola, on the night of December 14. He found Harris in the room. Harris had already moved the body to a cot in the office. There were no signs of any kind of struggle and no evidence beyond broken glass on the window ledge and floor. The lower two-foot-square pane was about one-third broken in. He fitted the glass together, except for an area about one inch in diameter where the glass had been pulverized. (The reconstructed pane is offered in evidence.) The point at which the bullet pierced the glass was five feet above the level of the yard immediately surrounding the cottage. With Dr. Harris' help he seated Waters in his study chair and found that even if his head rested on the desk, the bullet-hole in his head was four inches above the point where the bullet entered the window. The chair and desk were nine feet from the window. A desk light was on the left corner of the desk, and a ceiling light was eight and a half feet from the floor, just above the desk. The yard is level, north of the house, for six yards. Then it rises steeply for thirty yards, at about a 25 per cent grade. No trees or fences are to the north, only a low hedge eight yards from the window. A light snow was falling that night. No snow had been on the ground before 8 P.M. About ten o'clock he went out to look for footprints and found three or four. They were in sheltered spots (small depressions in the ground) on the north slope about fifty feet from the house and were barely visible due to the continuous snowfall. Because of the wind and the very cold temperature, the snow did not pack well. He measured the footprints, and they were all the same size, about twelve inches long and four and five-eighths inches at their widest point. By the time he had finished measuring them, they were practically obliterated. He did not ask Tower what size shoe he wore.

Sheriff White further stated that the next day Dr. Harris gave him the bullet, which was a .30-.30 long. He inquired at the general store in Westham, the only local shop selling rifle cartridges, and found they had never sold anything but .22 cartridges. In Springfield, the nearest city, he found five hardware and two sporting goods stores that stocked .30-.30 longs. None of the clerks could remember selling any of them to anyone living in or near Westham. Together with three deputy sheriffs Sheriff White investigated all Westham residents who might have known Mr. Waters, and they did not find a .30-.30 rifle, nor did they hear of anyone owning one. He asked Tower, who answered that he had never owned a rifle.

JOHN SELLMAN, vice-principal, forty-five, married, said he has been a teacher at Martin's for twenty years. Waters was very well liked by all the students and teachers, except for Tower. Tower disliked the change Waters had made in chapel exercises. They had been compulsory every day until this fall when Waters made it optional, retaining compulsory church service on Sunday. Attendance, being optional, was very small. Waters thought religious instruction in the Bible course, which is compulsory for all, should be continued and improved. He visited the Bible classes frequently, offering many suggestions for improvement. Tower teaches all the Bible classes and ancient history as well. Tower was very displeased with these criticisms. He spoke against changing the course and for compulsory chapel in each of the monthly faculty meetings. Waters told Sellman that Tower would have to be asked to resign if he did not improve the Bible course. Tower's complaint was that Waters wanted religion taught as a social study in Christian Ethics, whereas he wanted to teach evangelical Christianity. He said Tower had told him that Waters was an atheist. Waters impressed Sellman as deeply religious, but opposed to traditional, outworn formalism and anxious to revive true Christian values. The Martin School is nonsectarian, but a majority of its directors have always been Methodists. Waters, like his predecessors, was a Methodist.

JAMES DOYLE, inspector in the Homicide Bureau of the attorney general's office, said he was sent by his office on January 3 to investigate the Waters case. He talked with the sheriff, teachers, townspeople, and two directors of the school. After three days he went to Tower's home and, having a search warrant, searched the premises. He found a .30-.30 rifle in the garage (offered in evidence) and two boxes of unused cartridges, .30-.30 long. Tower had maintained he had never possessed any of that type. Doyle wired the chief of the Homicide Bureau at Philadelphia, who sent him the following deposition by the chief of the shipping department at Sears Roebuck and Company: "One box of .30-.30 long cartridges, catalog #35T1493, sent to Joshua Tower, Westham, Massachusetts, on November 15, 1932" (offered in evidence).

Doyle testified that he is a ballistics expert, holding a certificate from the School of Ballistics, Police College, Montreal, Canada. He examined the rifle barrel by means of micro-photographs and offered in evidence photographs of the rifling, of the bullet which killed Waters, and of six other .30-.30 long bullets which were fired from the same rifle. There were nineteen idiosyncrasies in markings, which convinced him that the bullet that killed Waters could have been fired from no other rifle than that of Tower. Fifteen of the characteristics are identical in all bullets fired from the rifle. Of the other four, all less well marked than the fifteen, two characteristics may be faintly seen in two other bullets, under a microscope of higher power than the one used in the photograph. The remaining two, the faintest of all, are not visible under any microscopic examination. But such discrepancies are easily explained by the effect of discharging a high-powered cartridge in a rifle barrel. Usually the correlation of markings in successive bullets fired from the same barrel is much lower than fifteen out of nineteen in seven shots because of the abrasive effects on the rifling.

He admitted that there are no especially telltale marks visible to the eye and no distinctive rifling defects, but said there are idiosyncrasies which could not be duplicated under any conditions; that is, there is less chance of duplication than in the case of fingerprints. The rifle is a Winchester Master Marksman, one of the two best rifles of this caliber made for general sale in the United States. Its sale is small, mainly to expert marksmen. It is completely handmade. No cobwebs and very little dust were on the rifle when it was found. The barrel had been cleaned and oiled recently.

MARTIN JAMIESON, Ph.D., principal emeritus, seventy-eight years old, said he lives in Westham, near the Martin School of which he was principal for forty years, succeeding his grandfather, John Martin. He continued to take a deep interest in the school this past year, being especially anxious to help Waters get a good start. He strongly approved Waters' appointment; he never heard of Waters having enemies or of anyone feeling unfriendly toward him, except Tower. The students were all very favorably impressed with Waters. Waters consulted him about the change in chapel, and while he did not entirely agree with his reasons for the change, he was not averse to making chapel optional. He was forced to admit to Waters that the chapel services had become perfunctory and sometimes distasteful to him; two of the directors — Mr. Roberts and Mr. Wilson, who are graduates of the school and have boys there now — had been urging him to change. Waters told him twice that the change greatly disturbed Tower. Jamieson attended a faculty meeting in December, listened to Tower's complaints, and spoke in favor of the change.

Jamieson further stated that Waters spoke to him once about the need for improving the Bible course. He told Waters that he had never liked Tower, but regarded him as an excellent teacher and would be sorry if he left the school. Tower had been in difficulties twice to his knowledge. Mrs. Johnson, the matron of Townsend Hall, complained to him four years ago that Tower had tried to force his attentions on her. She is married, has a home in the country near Tower's farm, and walks home on nice evenings or week ends. He called Tower in; Tower denied any misconduct, but the principal warned him to desist. She then complained again, giving him details and names of witnesses who would swear that Tower had made improper proposals to her and forced her to call for aid. He confronted Tower with the charges — which he vehemently denied. Jamieson called a meeting of the board of directors and had Mrs. Johnson, her witnesses, and Tower appear. Mr. Roberts, who is a lawyer and the school's eldest director, took charge of the examination. Tower was forced to admit to some of the charges, and the board was convinced that he was thoroughly ashamed. Tower promised to have nothing further to do with Mrs. Johnson, and, by a close vote, the directors sustained Jamieson's motion that Tower be retained.

The other incident involved a complaint he received from Mr. Dorn, the father of a girl who was helping in the school kitchen. Dorn said Tower was annoying his daughter. Dorn threatened to bring charges against Tower if there was any more trouble. Jamieson called Tower in immediately, and he at first denied knowing the girl. When Jamieson offered to call the girl in, however, Tower conceded that he knew her but said he had only given her a ride home at her request. Tower promised to have nothing further to do with her. No other instances of this kind occurred insofar as he knew.

MRS. ESTHER JOHNSON, OLIN DORN, and his daughter EVA DORN corroborated Dr. Jamieson's testimony insofar as it related to them.

JOSHUA TOWER, fifty-five married, said he resides with his wife and two grandchildren on his poultry farm three miles from the Martin School. Tower is a graduate of Connecticut State College where he specialized in poultry husbandry, and of Drew Theological Seminary where he obtained B.S., B.D., and S.T.M. degrees. He settled on his farm thirty years ago and, in ten years, after building it up into a very profitable poultry farm, he entered the theological seminary. He was in ministerial work for several years and rented out the farm. Eight years ago he was elected Bible instructor in the Martin School and returned to his farm. He has two married daughters and had an unmarried son who died. He did not shoot at or kill Waters. He was not near his cottage on the evening of December 14. From 4 P.M. on he was at his farm; at 8:30 he was reading in his study. He had disagreed with Waters on the change in chapel and on the changes in the Bible course that Waters proposed.

When Inspector Doyle asked Tower if he had a rifle, he answered that he did but had not used it since summer and did not know where it was, unless it was in the barn. He went to look for it there, but Doyle went to the garage where he found it. He called Doyle's attention to the dust and cobwebs on it. Tower told Doyle he had never used .30-.30 long cartridges in it and did not believe he had any. He purchased the rifle in 1932 while in Boston and ran out of cartridges about a year later, ordering some from Sears Roebuck and Company. He did not at any time realize that they were .30-.30 longs. He needed a rifle to kill the rats that were molesting his chickens.

He did speak to three directors about the change in chapel. Only one, the Rev. Mr. Thompson, agreed with him. He did not threaten to resign or to injure Waters in any way. Waters never suggested that he resign nor did he threaten to leave him off next year's budget. Mrs. Johnson and Mr. Dorn, who complained to Dr. Jamieson, are his neighbors. He never molested or insulted them or their children. Both are extremely jealous of his success in chicken-raising. Both have allowed their turkeys and hogs to trespass on his farm and were angry when, after repeated requests, he served written notice requiring them to repair fences and keep their livestock on their own property. He offered in evidence statements signed by Justice of the Peace Andrew Knowles corroborating the sending of written notices prior to the alleged incidents of molestation. He never had any instruction in shooting and never handled a gun of any kind until he first took up poultry-raising. His only experience was shooting at rats. He can hit one at any distance if the rat doesn't move. He has never needed spectacles, though he cannot see distant objects as well as he once could. He suffers from sinusitis a good deal. He knows Sheriff White, but has never talked with him. White did not ask him if he had a rifle. White never talked with him at any time. Tower wears size 9B shoes.

Mrs. Joshua Tower said her husband was home all evening on December 14. She admitted not seeing him after 8 P.M. because, as was his custom, he went to his study. She would have heard him if he had left the house. She never heard him say he was angry with Waters. She admitted she had been separated from Mr. Tower for six years and had returned to care for her deceased son's two children. She admitted having told friends in Westham that Tower ran after other women and struck her when she remonstrated with him.

DOUGLAS WIGGINTON, a ballistics expert listed in the Directory of the Department of Jurisprudence of the State of Connecticut, said he has been supervisor of rifling at the Remington Arms Company for ten years and has spent the last fifteen years as rifle repairman, acting as ballistics expert in criminal cases from time to time. He has appeared in over thirty trials, twice previously in this court, both times for the defendants. Wigginton has not appeared for the state at any time. He examined the bullets and micro-photographs and found no more similarities between the markings on these bullets than between seven others from different .30-.30 rifles, fired in the presence of Mr. Doyle and officers of this court. (These seven micro-photographs are submitted in evidence.) Three of the seven bullets show twenty-three idiosyncrasies in common. He found only ten correlations between the seven bullets fired from the Tower rifle, and five of these are identical with markings on four bullets fired from each of four other rifles. Wigginton sees no relation between the photographs of rifling in the Tower rifle barrel and the bullets fired from it. He has abandoned the theory that such comparisons prove anything, except where noticeable defects occur.

He offered in evidence a statement by Dr. Rambaud of the French School of Ballistics at Marseilles, formerly professor of microscopy at the Sorbonne and leading European authority on ballistics, which said, in part: "Generally speaking, there is rarely any significance to be attached to micro-photographic comparisons of rifle barrels and the bullets fired. In machine-bored, cheaply made barrels there may be some value in these comparisons. Otherwise, none at all." He admitted that this rifle had been fired more than two hundred times, but pointed out that the barrel had been carefully cleaned and oiled. He had never testified before in a court case involving .30-.30 longs. He agreed that characteristic markings should, theoretically, be more evident in longs than shorts, but said that longs also abrade barrels more. He agreed that no two rifle barrels, even the best made, impart exactly the same bullet markings. He agreed that, except for gross defects in cheaply made products, hand-made barrels should, theoretically, yield more idiosyncrasies than machine-made ones.

MR. HARMON T. ROBERTS of Springfield, Massachusetts, a director of the Martin School, corroborated that part of Dr. Jamieson's testimony that involved himself. He also testified that Waters told him about December 5 that he had asked Tower to change the Bible course, give up the course, or resign before February 1; that Tower had refused all of these suggestions; and that the matter was to be brought up at the directors' meeting during the Christmas vacation.

MR. JARED N. DORMUND, chairman of the board of directors, said Waters had told him early in December that Tower was the only uncooperative faculty member. He expected trouble with him because of his ideas on

Bible teaching and might have to bring the matter up in the board meeting. Dormund told Waters he would back up any recommendation concerning Tower that Waters cared to make because he was tired of the complaints about his course and his personal conduct. He said the complaints about the course did not come from Dr. Jamieson or the teachers but from students and parents.

REV. THOMPSON of Ware, Massachusetts, director of the school, said Tower is the best teacher of the Bible he has ever known; his *Syllabus of Biblical Instruction,* published by Revell and Company, is a standard secondary-school textbook; all the boys he has talked to were very favorably impressed with his instruction. Tower was pastor of the church which Thompson had attended as a youth and was responsible for his attending the Martin School and entering the ministry. He had always found Tower to be a dynamic, positive Christian character. Tower had spoken to him in November about the change in chapel, and he had strongly agreed that it should be compulsory. He said Tower did not seem angry at Waters, but was deeply concerned about the change in chapel and had made the hundred-mile trip to Ware specifically to talk to him about it. He admitted that Tower once spoke to him about the principalship in 1937, but when Thompson asked if he would want to live at the school and give up his poultry farm, he said, "No, if I have to do that to be principal, I'll let the matter drop." Tower's name was not considered when candidates were discussed by the directors.

SPART V. HALPERN

THIS IS AN action in negligence to recover damages for the death of Mary Judith Spart, a child about nine years and four months of age, who died as a result of injuries sustained by her when she was struck by an automobile owned and driven by the defendant, Harold E. Halpern. The action was brought by Cyril F. Spart, father of the decedent.

The question here is not "What happened?" but rather "What does it mean?" The judge's charge explains how the terms "negligence" and "burden of proof" are to be interpreted. The question is, "Do the facts show Halpern to have been solely responsible for the child's death through negligence?"

FACTS

Shortly after 2 P.M. on Sunday, May 25, 1947 — a clear, dry day — Halpern left his home, about five miles from Mecklenburg, New York, in a

1941 Chevrolet four-door sedan. He drove through the city of Ithaca, about seventeen miles from his home, stopped near the city on Triphammer Road, and then proceeded toward Syracuse, his ultimate destination, where he wished to see a young lady he knew but with whom he had no appointment. About 4 P.M., as he was proceeding east on the Ithaca-Dryden State Highway in Willow Glen Corners — about eight miles from Ithaca — he came upon a straight, slightly uphill stretch of road which was 22 feet and 10 inches wide. He saw two little girls standing about 2 or 3 feet back from the edge of the paved portion of the roadway and about 750 feet in front of him. Nothing obstructed his view as he approached the children. Cars on the north side of the road were proceeding west, but none were proceeding east on the south side, either in front of or behind Halpern.

Halpern was traveling at about forty-five miles per hour and did not appreciably change speed, nor did he blow his horn as he approached the children.

Halpern stated that when he was about 375 feet from the girls, they looked toward him and, thereafter, looked straight across the road. Just a short distance west of where the girls were standing, a car traveling west on the north side of the highway passed Halpern. He claimed that as soon as the car traveling west passed him, the girls darted out into the road. He was then about 10 feet from them. Halpern further stated, "I was right up awful close to them, and they started going across the road, and I hit the horn with my arm, and the smallest girl [a younger sister of the decedent] stopped. The bigger girl, well, when I hit the horn, she had made a jump and I don't know whether she made two steps or one."

The instant he blew his horn, Halpern turned his car sharply to his left — toward the north — and struck the decedent when she was just north of the center line of the road. He did not apply his brakes until after the impact. The left front wheel of his car went off the north edge of the road; he then veered back to the south into his proper lane, stopping more than 300 feet from the point of impact. The decedent, who weighed about fifty-eight pounds, was struck by the left front of the car, thrown onto the hood, and then against the left corner post of the windshield, and finally thrown from the car as it veered back to the south side of the road. She landed in a creek bed about 99 feet from the point of impact. Her younger sister apparently remained within 3 or 4 feet of the south edge of the pavement and was brushed lightly and knocked down by the right rear fender of Halpern's car. She was uninjured.

There were two automobiles on the north side of the road, proceeding west from Dryden toward Ithaca and about four hundred and five hundred feet, respectively, east of the scene of the accident at the time of impact. The drivers of both these cars stated that they were traveling at about forty-five miles per hour and that, in their estimation, Halpern was travel-ing at about the same speed as he approached the girls. Both these drivers were accompanied by their wives. All four persons testified that the two girls stood about two to three feet away from the south edge of the paved portion of the road, and when Halpern's car was very close to them, they started to cross the road from south to north. None of the witnesses noticed the girls look toward Halpern at any time, but the witnesses stated that they had not watched the girls continuously from the time they first saw them until the accident. They further testified that when the children were three or four feet onto the road, the smaller child seemed to hesitate, but the older child started to run diagonally across the road and away from Halpern's car (toward the northeast). They agreed that Halpern veered sharply to his left immediately before striking the decedent, struck her just north of the center of the road, went off the north side of the road with his left front wheel, and then veered sharply back to his right, the body of the girl being thrown from his car when he made this last turn.

There was no evidence to indicate any mechanical deficiencies with re-spect to Halpern's car or physical deficiencies with respect to the defendant or the decedent. It was established that, at the time of the accident, Judy and her sister were on their way from their home to visit a neighbor who lived north of the highway. Judy had crossed the road daily when she got off the school bus opposite from her home. The decedent's scholastic records revealed that she had scored at the fifth-grade level on achievement tests although she was only in the third grade.

The defendant conceded that Judy's death resulted from injuries sus-tained in the accident. These injuries included a fractured dislocation of the neck, compound fracture of the right tibia and fibula, and fracture of the left tibia and fibula.

EXCERPTS FROM THE JUDGE'S CHARGE TO THE JURY

IN THIS case the plaintiff seeks to recover damages for the wrongful death of Mary Judith Spart which the plaintiff alleges was occasioned by the negligence of the defendant in the action. . . . At the outset, the mere fact that an accident occurred here, the mere fact that this little girl was killed, in and of itself does not render anyone liable in damages nor does it entitle anyone to recover damages. The case is based upon negligence or care-lessness and, in order for the plaintiff to recover, you must be satisfied that the little girl's death resulted from the negligence of the driver of the Hal-pern car, Harold E. Halpern, and without any negligence on the part of Judy which contributed thereto. This gives you, in a nutshell, the issue that will finally be submitted to you. I will elaborate, of course, upon what con-stitutes negligence as I go along. . . .

Let me first define negligence generally. Perhaps some of you are as familiar with that definition as I am. Negligence in the eyes of the law means simply this: the failure to use that degree of care which an ordinarily prudent person would have used under the same circumstances. To put it another way, negligence is doing something that an ordinarily prudent person would not have done under the same circumstances. That is the general rule. Here are more specific rules that may be helpful in determining whether or not that degree of care was used by either the driver of this vehicle or by Judy. I can't tell you with any degree of exactness whether either one or both of these parties were negligent. That is, negligence is not capable of an exact definition. I can't say to you that such an act is negligence and such an act is not. It is a question for jurors to determine using their experience and common sense applied to a set of facts to determine whether it is reasonable care or not and, when they apply the general rules to the facts in a particular case, their answer in each case determines whether or not it is negligence. Some things, as I have said, may be of assistance in determining whether or not any of the parties charged with negligence here were guilty of negligence, that is, whether or not they used the degree of care that a reasonably prudent person would use under the same circumstances.

I will read to you a portion of the Vehicle and Traffic Law of this state, which is the law and was at the time of this occurrence, and which may have some bearing on the issues which you will determine in this case. So much of Section 67 of the Vehicle and Traffic Law which applies or might apply here reads as follows:

Upon approaching a pedestrian who is upon the traveled part of any highway and not upon a sidewalk and upon approaching an intersecting highway or a curve, a hill or a corner in the highway where the operator's view is obstructed, every person operating a motor vehicle or motorcycle shall slow down and give a timely signal with his bell, horn, or other device for signaling.

The statute uses the word *timely* signal. If you find that this section is applicable to the facts here, timely again does not have an exact definition. It means simply a warning or signal given at a time which will enable others to act upon it and will give warning to others; again it is a question of reasonableness, and it is for you to say what would be timely. Was it a reasonable warning or not?

Section 85 of the Vehicle and Traffic Law, Subdivision 4, reads as follows:

Every pedestrian crossing a roadway at any point other than within a marked or unmarked crossing shall yield the right of way to vehicles and street surface cars upon the roadway provided that this provision shall not relieve the driver of a vehicle or street surface car from the duty of exercising due care for the safety of pedestrians.

This means exactly what it says: a pedestrian or person walking upon the highway other than at a crosswalk or regularly marked crossing shall give vehicles the right of way, but that does not relieve the driver of the vehicle from using due care to prevent injury or striking the pedestrian

Let's look for a moment at the duties of the parties involved in this unfortunate occurrence. It is the duty of a driver of a vehicle on the highway to obey the laws of the state, to obey the statutes and rules of the road. It is the duty of a driver to be alert and watchful, to look and to see what is there to be seen. It is the duty of a driver to give due regard to the conditions prevalent and the circumstances under which he is operating the vehicle. That is, to mention a few of them, the weather, visibility, highway conditions, whether or not the highway is being used by others and in what manner, and all of the surrounding circumstances that have a bearing on the manner in which he operates his vehicle. Having those things in mind, it is his duty to have his vehicle under reasonable control at all times. It is his duty to operate it at a careful and prudent speed that does not endanger the lives or limbs of others using the highway.

In this state, at the time of this occurrence, the maximum speed permitted by law was fifty miles an hour, but speed again has to do with reasonableness. Different speeds may be reasonable under different circumstances. It is for a jury to say what was reasonable and what was not, but every person operating a vehicle on the highway is obligated to operate at a speed which is reasonable, careful, and prudent under the circumstances. Generally, it is the duty of a driver of a vehicle to use reasonable care at all times to prevent accidents and injury to others.

A similar duty is imposed upon a pedestrian using the highway. Any person not in a vehicle but using the highway to cross or travel on must be vigilant and watchful and see what is there to be seen and use reasonable care for his or her own safety and to prevent accident. The law does not impose any specific time or specific point in a person's progress when they must look, but it does require that a person look before crossing a highway traveled by vehicles to ascertain that he may safely cross. Having that in mind, it is the duty of such a person to do whatever a reasonably prudent person would do under the same circumstances to prevent accident and injury either to someone else or to themselves.

It appears here that the deceased Judy Spart was a child and, I believe, between nine and ten years of age. This is a factor which you may give such consideration as you feel it deserves in resolving the question of negligence of either one of these parties. That is, if you find as a fact that the defendant, Harold Halpern, saw Judy near the highway, if he saw that she was a child, and there was something to indicate that she might cross the highway, then he is bound to consider, at least insofar as a reasonably prudent person would consider, the likelihood of a child of that age crossing the road when perhaps an adult would not do so. He is bound to know to the extent that a reasonably prudent person would know that children do things that adults do not do; that they sometimes act upon impulse; that they don't have the foresight of adults or they don't have the judgment of adults. So you may consider that factor in determining whether or not Harold Halpern used reasonable care under the circumstances in this case.

You may also give such consideration as you feel it warrants to the child's age in determining the question of her negligence contributing to the accident. In determining whether or not she was negligent, you should consider that the same laws that apply to adults applied to her. The same duties in general applied to her but you may consider, in determining whether or not she used the care that a reasonable person would, her age, her intelligence, the degree of maturity she had reached, her ability to understand and to exercise care. Again you will use your experience and judgment and determine whether or not Judy used that degree of care which a reasonably prudent person of the same age, intelligence, and understanding would have used under those same circumstances. If she did, then she is not negligent because the law does not require more of her than of a reasonably prudent child of the same age and intelligence.

There is a rule of law which you may find applicable to one or both of the parties in this accident and it is that when an emergency suddenly confronts a person, if they did not create that emergency by their own carelessness, the law does not demand the same calm, cool judgment as it would if there were no emergency, but only requires them to exercise that judgment which a reasonably prudent person would have exercised when confronted with the same emergency. . . .

That is about all I can say to you on the subject of negligence generally as it applies to either one of these parties, either Harold Halpern in the operation of the vehicle, or Judy Spart in the way she conducted herself on this occasion.

The burden is upon the plaintiff in this case to establish to your satisfaction by a fair preponderance of the evidence that the defendant Harold E. Halpern was negligent in a manner which caused or brought about this death and the damages which the plaintiffs have sustained by reason thereof. Because it is a death case, the burden is upon the defendant to establish the contributory negligence on the part of Judy Spart. The same rule applies. The burden is upon the defendant to establish to your satisfaction, by a fair preponderance of the evidence, that Judy Spart was guilty of contributory negligence that led to the accident and resulted in her death.

As applied to both sides, relating to the burden of proof, fair preponderance of evidence means simply evidence which is more convincing to you. It does not necessarily mean more witnesses. It does not mean the volume of evidence. It means evidence which to your minds more nearly speaks the truth and that overbalances the evidence to the contrary. Applying those simple rules to the facts in this case, as you heard them from the witnesses and from the exhibits, you will determine whether or not the plaintiff is entitled to recover.

In determining how much weight you will give to any portion of the evidence, let me say to you that is solely your province. You have seen the witnesses. You should consider everything surrounding their testimony, such as their appearance or manner on the stand, whether they appeared to you to be telling the truth or not, their interest or lack of interest in the outcome of this case, any reason they may have or might have for exaggerating or seeing things differently, and their opportunities to see and observe the things about which they testified. You may consider the reasonableness or unreasonableness of the stories told. You may decide how much weight any portion of the testimony is entitled to.

In that connection, you have a right to draw logical inferences from any facts that are established to your satisfaction. That is, once a fact has been established and you are convinced that it is true, you may, if you wish, draw such inferences as flow naturally and logically from the fact. If a certain thing to your mind would logically and naturally have happened, you may assume or infer that it did happen. . . .

If you reach the conclusion from applying these rules to the facts in this case, and you will find them to be that Harold Halpern was not negligent in the manner in which he operated his automobile on the roadway in question, then that is the end of this lawsuit and your verdict would be no cause of action. If you reach the conclusion that he was negligent and that Judy was also negligent in a manner which contributed to the accident and to her death, your verdict would likewise be no cause of action. If you reach the conclusion that the defendant Halpern was negligent and that Judy was not, then your verdict would be in favor of the plaintiff and you would pass to the question of damages. . . .

NOTES

Excerpts from the charge in this case are provided as a guide to preparing an argument. Judges do not charge juries, of course, until counsel have finished their presentation of the case. But lawyers would understand the doctrine of negligence thoroughly and, therefore, have a general notion of the charge before it was delivered. It would be anachronistic to refer to the charge in the argument, but both the point of view and the statements of law which it contains should be carefully considered.

THE PEOPLE V. BLAISDELL

QUESTION: *Is John Blaisdell guilty of the murder of John Wadleigh?*

The indictment is for first-degree murder, but under New Hampshire law a jury may convict of manslaughter even though the indictment is for first-degree murder. Trial was held at Exeter, New Hampshire, on September 24, 1822.

TESTIMONY

NATHANIEL WEEKS. I was in company with Blaisdell and Wadleigh on the afternoon of the 18th of February. It was so dark that I had just lit a candle. Blaisdell and Wadleigh came into my shop, which stands near the bridge; Wadleigh brought with him an axe and a rough axe handle, which he laid upon a barrel. The handle was of white oak and very large. They left my store together, one taking the axe and the other the axe handle; which either of them took I know not; and I saw nothing more of them. They were both perfectly sober.

Cross-examination: While in my store they drank perhaps a glass apiece. Wadleigh bought a pint of rum and put it in his bottle and afterward told me to put a half pint more in the bottle. The bottle held a little more than a pint. How much they drank I cannot certainly say. They appeared friendly.

LARKIN TAYLOR. I was at Weeks' store at the time he mentions and saw Blaisdell and Wadleigh there. Saw the axe handle, which Blaisdell took up, and Wadleigh took the axe when they went away. Saw nothing further. They were both sober. Cannot tell at what time they went.

Cross-examination: Did not see that they were unfriendly.

JOSIAH G. SMITH. I saw the prisoner and Wadleigh pass my house on the 18th of February about half-past five. They were going toward Kensington. My house is opposite the Stratham road about thirty rods from Weeks'. Blaisdell carried the axe handle on his shoulder and Wadleigh the axe. It was between sunset and dark, and there was a violent snowstorm. They were both apparently sober.

WILLIAM DOLLOFF. I saw the prisoner and Wadleigh the same evening about halfway between J. G. Smith's house and Lane's shop, five rods perhaps from Smith's. Wadleigh had an axe and Blaisdell an axe handle. It was near dark when they passed, and the night was very stormy.

NANCY Y. FOLSOM. On the evening of the eighteenth, I saw two persons pass by my father's house, one of whom I knew to be Wadleigh; Blaisdell I did not know. Wadleigh carried an axe and the other man an axe handle. I have no doubt that the prisoner was the man who passed with Wadleigh. My father was absent, and I was looking out for him. They went together toward Kensington.

JUDE HALL. Between eight and nine on the evening of the eighteenth, somebody knocked at my door. My house is near the Exeter line and about a mile and a quarter from Folsom's. Told my children to open the door. Blaisdell came in, appeared frightened, and asked where the captain was (meaning me). He said he wanted me to help him lead Wadleigh in; that Wadleigh was drunk and had been fighting with a sleigh. Blaisdell said that he would not have carried him into his (Wadleigh's) house for ten dollars, that he would have died if he had not taken him up, and that he led him from the Cove bridge. Wadleigh's house is between the Cove bridge and mine, about thirty rods from mine. I heard heavy groans and found Wadleigh lying on his side. I lifted Wadleigh up and led him home. He appeared to shudder with cold. I got a fire, which he seemed to need. Blaisdell offered to take his hat — he drew back. Then his handkerchief — he still drew back. Blaisdell next offered him a chair, but he stood stiff.

Blaisdell went to take Wadleigh's hat, and Wadleigh showed great horror whenever Blaisdell came near him. After about five or ten minutes, Blaisdell went away and wanted me to go home with him. I said, "Don't go," and Blaisdell said he must go to take care of his cattle. Wadleigh died about three-quarters of an hour before day. I was with him at that time. Blaisdell's house is in Kensington, about half a mile from mine.

PROSECUTING ATTORNEY. Did Wadleigh say anything?

A. After Wadleigh got over his chill and shuddering he said, "Captain, how long have you been here?" Then he gave another deep sigh and was gone again. (Further questions along this line were prohibited on the ground that it was not in evidence whether the deceased was in that state of mind which rendered his declarations admissible.)

Q. Did you ask Wadleigh any questions?

A. I was flustered but remember that Blaisdell said that Wadleigh would say he had done it.

MRS. JOHN WADLEIGH. Jude Hall and Blaisdell brought my husband home between eight and nine o'clock. I was alone. My husband seemed faint and overcome and so was I. I could not for some time come near him or speak to him. I asked Blaisdell where he had found him. He said near the Cove bridge. Blaisdell turned to go, and I asked him to stay. He said he had to go; I asked him a second time, but he said he had to go and take care of his cattle. He then left us. I went to my husband and took off his neck cloth; it was very bloody. The blood began to run dreadfully, and I exclaimed to Jude, "Here is something more than a fall; here is a blow and somebody has given him his death wound." My husband then appeared to hear me speaking and groaned out, "Oh Lord, I'm done," then was gone, but in a minute groaned again, "Oh, that fellow." He then asked, "Where's a bed?" We laid him on a bed and in a few moments he said, "Oh Lord, I'm done." These were the last sounds he uttered. Blaisdell stayed in the house from five to ten minutes, not longer than ten at the farthest.

JAMES ROBINSON. On the evening of February 18, I was coming from Newbury to Exeter in a sleigh with Richard Smith. It was quite stormy. Near the Cove bridge and on this side of it we saw two men standing by the roadside. I said to them, "It is very stormy." One of them agreed, and then I asked, "How far is it to Wedgewood's?" I was not answered. I was acquainted with John Wadleigh and think the voice was not his. This was between seven and eight o'clock. We had no difficulty or quarrel with anyone on the road. We met but one sleigh before we reached Eastman's tavern (about six miles from Cove bridge) and none after that.

RICHARD SMITH. I was with Mr. Robinson as he mentions, and his account is correct except that it seemed to me we met the two men the other side of the Cove bridge. I did not know either of the men. I think we met a sleigh at the foot of the hill near Wedgewood's going toward the bridge and about a quarter of a mile this side of the bridge.

JOSEPH BROWN. I was traveling from Exeter to Kensington on the evening mentioned and saw two men standing by the roadside near Cove bridge. Before I got up to them one said, "Drive on," and when I came up to them, the same voice said, "Take this man aboard, he is drunk and has been fighting with a sleigh." I asked his name, and the man said, "It is John Wadleigh." I knew where Wadleigh lived and then said, "Come, John, get in, I am going by your house and will carry you home." He gave no answer. I put my hand on his shoulder and asked him again to get in. He said nothing, but I observed he breathed very hard. I then said to the other, "He don't seem to care about getting in, and I'll go along if you will take care of him." He said he would, and I drove on. This was about one-third of a mile from Wadleigh's house. It was quite dark, stormy, and slippery. We had no quarrel on the road. Philip Cheney was with me walking by the side of my sleigh.

RICHARD SMITH (recalled). I was on the left side of the sleigh with Mr. Robinson.

JAMES ROBINSON (recalled). I observed no other person on the road and no other sleigh than the one I mentioned before. I did not know either the sleigh or the horse.

JOSEPH BROWN (recalled).

DEFENSE ATTORNEY: Had you come up to the two men when one of them asked you to drive on?

A. No, we stopped when he said the man was drunk. It was I who first proposed to drive on without him. It was so dark that about two rods off we thought the two men were a double sleigh. It was slippery although a new snow had fallen on the ice. I was not driving very fast.

RICHARD SMITH (recalled). I think it was a little beyond the bridge that we met the two persons standing together, and it was about a quarter of a mile this side of the bridge that we met a sleigh, which was probably Mr. Brown's. I did not particularly observe anything in the hands of either of the two men but think one of them held something. I heard no wrangling. I think we met them between seven and eight o'clock. We were traveling at the rate, I should think, of about six miles an hour.

JAMES ROBINSON (recalled). I was on my return home from Newburyport. I did not observe the crossroads particularly. There were, I think, several roads that turned off this side of Eastman's tavern; one, I believe, about a mile beyond the place where we met Wadleigh. There were houses all along the road for some miles beyond the place. It was two days after Wadleigh's death before I heard of it. I did not attend the examination of Blaisdell before the justice.

PHILIP CHENEY. I was with Joseph Brown on the evening of the eighteenth of February. I was walking by the side of the sleigh. We met another sleigh, but I cannot say exactly where, being a stranger in that quarter, but I think it was near the foot of the hill just out of Exeter toward Kensington. We did not meet or pass any other sleigh. We came up to two men who appeared to be standing in or near the road. When we were within one or two rods, Brown said, "Who is there?" One of the persons asked us to take the other in on the sleigh, saying that the man was drunk and that his name was John Wadleigh. Brown asked him to get in. I think this was about thirty rods beyond the bridge. We met no other person on the road that evening. I saw nothing in the hands of either of the persons.

JAMES ROBINSON (recalled). We did not meet any other sleigh near the place where we came up with the two men. We were coming from Newburyport. We passed some sleighs in the farthest part of Kensington, but none between Eastman's tavern and the place where we met the prisoner. There are roads that turn off between that place and Eastman's, and one perhaps a mile from that place. There are several crossroads in that quarter. This matter was not recalled to my memory till about two days after. I think it was not Wadleigh who spoke to us, as I knew Wadleigh's voice and should have recognized it.

DANIEL PERVERE. I was at Wadleigh's house on the night of his death. Wadleigh's boy came for me about eight o'clock to go for the doctor. I went to the house to see if it was necessary and found Wadleigh in bed. I spoke to him but he made no answer. I searched for wounds but could find none right away because he was so bloody. I soon found one on the temple. Wadleigh seemed insensible. Afterward I went home, and about four o'clock I heard Wadleigh was dead.

DR. WILIAM PERRY. I was called to see Wadleigh on the evening of the eighteenth of February. From the representation of the messenger, I supposed it to be a case of intoxication. As I had just recovered from a fever and the night was very stormy, I declined going. Being called again the next morning, I went over and found Wadleigh dead. His shirt and bedding were quite bloody. I observed a contusion on the left side of his forehead, but immediately perceived that this was not sufficient to have caused his death. On examining further I found another contusion on the same side of his head, with fracture and depression of the bone. Blood was still running from the ear. I divided the scalp and found a collection of blood between it and the bone. The depressed piece of bone commenced under the temporal muscle between the hollow of the temple and the ear, extending upward and backward over the ear three inches, its breadth one inch. The upper end of the fractured piece was rectangular and its edges, as well as those of the skull from which it was broken, were straight and well defined. The scalp was cut at the upper end of the wound, and appeared to have been done by the end of the instrument used and the edge of the bone from which the piece was broken. This was the only injury done the skin.

PROSECUTING ATTORNEY. What was the appearance of the wound on the forehead?

A. It was a circular swelling larger than a dollar, with the cuticle raised in the center.

Q. Could the larger wound have been produced by a fall?

A. It could not.

DEFENSE ATTORNEY. What is the particular appearance of a wound produced by a fall?

A. The skin has often the appearance of being scratched.

Q. Have not wounds, generally, a more aggravated appearance after death, and do not contusions then grow darker?

A. They have not, and I do not think they have relatively a darker appearance.

THE COURT. Would the appearance of a wound from a fall on the ice be more ragged or scratched than one from a blow from an axe or other instrument?

A. It would frequently, but if the blow was fair on the ice I do not think it would.

DEFENSE ATTORNEY. Had the principal wound any appearance of one given by a sleigh shoe?

A. It had not.

THE PEOPLE V. BLAISDELL [115

Q. Was not the fracture about the width of a sleigh shoe, or why could not a sleigh runner have produced such a wound?

A. The wound was an inch wide. I could not place a sleigh shoe on a person's head so as to produce such a wound as that on Wadleigh.

THE COURT. Would not a club or a cane have produced a wound of the shape you describe?

A. I think neither of them would; a round instrument would probably have broken the bone in the center and carried in the edge, or split off pieces, but not have cut out a piece like the one in question.

Q. Did you examine the hat, so as to recollect its thickness and discover any fracture?

A. I did. It was a firm wool hat and was not injured. The wound on the side of the head could not have been produced with the hat on.

Q. Would not a blow on an empty and dried skull produce a square fracture?

A. I think not.

DEFENSE ATTORNEY. Is not the part of the skull on which you describe the principal wound to have been, the thinnest?

A. It is.

AUGUSTUS WADLEIGH (son of the deceased). I know this (an axe produced by the Prosecuting Attorney) to have been my father's axe. I have not seen it since my father carried it away from the house the morning before his death. I have no doubt this is the same axe.

DAVID WEDGEWOOD. I found this axe near the Cove bridge a few days after Wadleigh's death. This is the same axe; I marked it at the time. I found it thrown over the fence by the roadside; it was about one hundred rods from my house and twenty-five rods from the bridge. The spot where I found it was about two rods from a place in the road which was stained with blood, and this bloody spot was about six feet from the fence, about eight feet from the middle of the road and about four feet from the outside of the path. The place was as bloody as if a hog had been killed there. I saw no blood on the axe.

CHARLES PARKS. I found this axe handle (shown to him by the Prosecuting Attorney) about a week after Wadleigh's death, on the roadside, close under the fence; it was about seven or eight rods from the bloody place mentioned by Wedgewood. The snow round the spot was still very much stained with blood.

JOHN F. MOSES. After prisoner was arrested he was brought to my house and I, as one of the constables of Exeter, took him into my custody. Prisoner at that time declared to me that after Wadleigh left Weeks' store he did not see him till he found him near Cove bridge. I asked prisoner what he had done with the axe handle he took from Weeks' store; he said that he had no axe handle. Some days after that I told Blaisdell in prison that the axe handle was found; he made no reply. I then reminded him that he was not obliged to make confessions and cautioned him not to tell falsehoods. While at my house, I asked prisoner where the axe was. He said he threw it over the fence. The axe was not at that time found.

NATHANIEL WEEKS (recalled). I think this is the same axe handle that was taken by the prisoner from my store.

ENOCH ROWE. I conversed with Blaisdell on the evening of his arrest. I heard no one advise him to make confessions. He said he threw the axe over the fence because it was heavy, and he could not well carry it and Wadleigh at the same time. He denied having had the axe handle. The distance from Wedgewood's house to the place where blood was found is about one hundred rods, and the distance from this place to the nearest house on the other side, Mr. Dow's farmhouse, is about half a mile.

JOSHUA PIKE. In December, 1821, I purchased some trees of Edward Blaisdell which he agreed to cut for me. In January he told me he was ready to go about it. I went to see him on the subject. Edward Blaisdell, John Wadleigh, and the prisoner were present, chopping wood. Wadleigh asked me what I would give him to cut the trees. I made him an offer, and at last agreed to give him five dollars for the job. Wadleigh then said to the prisoner, "Will you help me?" Prisoner declined, and Wadleigh observed that his brother would assist him, and accordingly he and his brother came next day to haul the trees.

Cross-examination: I heard no bargain between the prisoner and the deceased in the matter and never heard prisoner say anything afterwards on the subject.

JUDE HALL (recalled). Last January I heard the prisoner threaten Wadleigh. He was talking about cutting Pike's trees and said he would give Wadleigh a licking for taking away the job after promising to go halves with him. Blaisdell appeared to be in a passion.

DAVID WEDGEWOOD (recalled). The morning of Wadleigh's death, as soon as I heard of it, I rode over to his house. There was a great collection of people there. Captain Rowe asked me if I would go with others in pursuit of Blaisdell. I consented, and went first to Blaisdell's home, which was about a mile off. His grandmother told me that he had gone out nearly an hour before. We proceeded to search the barn and found a pair of mittens under some flax, which were carried to Wadleigh's house and discovered to be the mittens he had worn. We next searched the prisoner's yard. We found his brother, who told us that the prisoner had borrowed a dollar of him and said he was going over to Esq. Healey's. We proceeded in that direction and soon found the prisoner's tracks in the snow, which we followed about thirty-two hours through woods and crossroads, in Kensington, Southhampton, and Kingston; and after a pursuit of about forty miles, we caught him about six miles from Exeter, in a remote place on the Beech

Road, so called, near Epping. He submitted to us without resistance. There were perhaps a dozen people who went on the first search to Blaisdell's house, and this was about nine o'clock in the morning. Many people were collected about Wadleigh's house. The rumor of his sudden death spread very soon and wide. It was David Kelly who found the mittens (mittens produced). These are the same.

DAVID KELLY. I found these mittens in Blaisdell's barn during our search. They were on the scaffold under some bundles of flax. I carried them to Mrs. Wadleigh, who said they were her husband's.

Cross-examination: I went to the barn in a sleigh with Mr. Wedgewood to search for Blaisdell. The hay was pitched over by some others of the party. I was the first who got up where the flax was.

MRS. WADLEIGH (recalled). I know these mittens to have been my husband's. He wore them away the morning before his death. I observed he had no mittens on when he was brought home, and I asked Jude Hall where he thought they could be. Jude made no answer but shook his head.

(The Prosecuting Attorney asked if there was any objection to the admission of evidence as to the character of the deceased. No objection was offered.)

ENOCH ROWE (recalled). I was very friendly with Wadleigh. He worked several years for me. He was rather remarkable for a mild temper and peaceful deportment.

Cross-examination: I have heard that the deceased sometimes drank heavily but was always good-natured when in that state. Deceased married my sister. He was a stout and strong man.

JOSHUA PIKE (recalled). I knew the deceased. I worked with him a good deal. His temper was pleasant and peaceable. I never saw him drunk.

JOSIAH ROWE. I knew Wadleigh for a long time. He was thought a good-tempered and very peaceable man. I never knew him to be very intemperate.

JUDE HALL (recalled). I saw no bottle near the defendant that night, nor did I see any rum or mittens in his house at that time. Mrs. Wadleigh asked me where I thought her husband's mittens could be. I did not see that either Wadleigh or Blaisdell had mittens on in the road. After I heard that a broken bottle was found in Wadleigh's pocket, I perceived a strong smell of rum about his clothes which I thought at first came from his breath. His surtout and coat were wet on one side.

MRS. WADLEIGH (recalled). I found the pieces of a broken bottle in my husband's coat pocket. His coat was very wet and had a strong smell of rum about it.

(For the defense, the following witnesses only were called.)

MARY POOR. I remember that some time about the latter part of January last, about a fortnight before Wadleigh's death, he was at my house with the prisoner and Mr. Rowe. The prisoner and the deceased appeared perfectly friendly and social. They went away, I think, in the same sleigh.

ABRAHAM ROWE. I remember being at Mrs. Poor's at the time she mentions, with the prisoner and deceased. They appeared then on perfectly friendly terms. We were there about one hour.

THE PEOPLE V. DELANEY

FACTS

ON JUNE 12, 1956, at approximately 1 P.M., an automobile driven by Thomas R. Delaney failed to stop for a stop sign on Yates Street at the intersection of Yates and North Aurora Streets, Ithaca, New York, and collided with an automobile operated by Arthur Pope. Delaney was accompanied by William Prize; Pope had his wife, Margaret Ann Pope, with him. Immediately after the collision Pope approached Delaney, identified himself as a member of the Ithaca Police Department, and asked to see Delaney's license. Pope then placed Delaney under arrest and subsequently issued a summons charging (1) failure to stop for a stop sign and (2) reckless driving.

On June 13, Delaney was arraigned in the Court of the City of Ithaca before City Judge John Masey on the above-stated charges. He pleaded guilty to the charge of failing to stop for a stop sign and was fined five dollars. He pleaded not guilty to the charge of reckless driving. Bail on the second charge was set at $250, and a jury trial was scheduled for July 10, 1956.

Reckless driving is defined in Section 58 of the Motor Vehicle Traffic Laws of New York State thus:

Reckless driving shall mean driving or using any motor vehicle, motorcycle, or any other vehicle propelled by any power other than muscular power or any appliance or accessory thereof in a manner which unreasonably interferes with the free and proper use of the public highway, or unreasonably endangers users of the public highway. Reckless driving is prohibited. Every person violating this provision shall be guilty of a misdemeanor.

On July 10, the case of the *People* v. *Delaney* was tried in the Court of the City of Ithaca, and the testimony which appears below was elicited.

TESTIMONY

The City Prosecutor opened the case for the People by calling Donald Beckenwall to the witness stand.

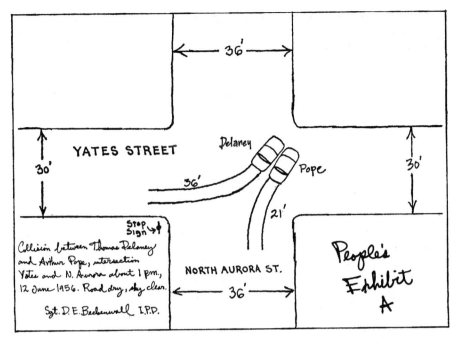

CITY PROSECUTOR. Please state your name, address, and occupation.

BECKENWALL. Donald E. Beckenwall, 710 North Tioga Street, Ithaca, sergeant in the Ithaca Police Department.

Q. To what division of the police department are you assigned?

A. Traffic.

Q. Did you investigate an automobile accident at approximately 1 P.M. on June 12, 1956?

A. Yes. About 1:10 P.M. on June 12, I investigated an automobile accident at the intersection of Yates and North Aurora Streets.

Q. Who was involved in that accident?

A. Officer Pope and Thomas Delaney.

Q. The complainant and defendant in this trial?

A. Yes.

Q. Of what did your investigation of the accident consist?

A. I took the names and addresses of the drivers and of witnesses to the accident. I took pictures of the scene and made a sketch of it. I measured the widths of the streets at the scene of the accident and the length of skid marks made by the automobiles.

Q. I hand you a piece of paper marked "People's Exhibit A," on which there is a drawing and some writing, and ask you whether or not this is the sketch which you made at the scene of the accident (see above).

A. Yes, it is.

Q. Did you make the sketch yourself?

A. Yes.

Q. At the scene of the accident?

A. Yes.

Q. Does it fairly and accurately represent your observations at the scene of the accident with respect to the position of the automobiles after impact and the position and length of skid marks which they made before impact?

A. Yes.

CITY PROSECUTOR. Your Honor, I offer this paper in evidence as People's Exhibit A.

DEFENSE ATTORNEY. No objection.

JUDGE. It may be admitted in evidence.

CITY PROSECUTOR. Sergeant Beckenwall, refreshing your memory with this sketch, will you tell the jury about the position of the cars and the length and position of the skid marks which you found upon examining the scene of the accident?

A. The two automobiles were side by side, diagonally across the intersection, and pointed in a northeasterly direction, with their front ends about three or four feet from the northeast corner of the intersection. The left front fender and left side of the grill of Pope's car were smashed in, and the bumper was displaced to the right about one foot. The right front fender and entire grill of Delaney's car were smashed in. Pope's skid marks began about even with the point where the sidewalk on the south side of Yates Street intersects the east side of North Aurora Street and were about twenty-one feet long. Delaney's skid marks began about even with the stop sign on Yates Street and measured thirty-six feet to the point of impact.

Q. How did you determine the length of the skid marks?

A. I measured them with a steel tape.

Q. And the skid marks from Pope's car were only twenty-one feet long, but those from Delaney's car were thirty-six feet long?

A. That's right.

Q. How long has Officer Pope been a member of the Ithaca Police Department?

A. About six years, I think.

Q. To what division is he assigned?

A. He works with all divisions. He's a patrolman.

Q. Does he perform traffic-control duties?

A. Yes.

CITY PROSECUTOR. No further questions.

DEFENSE ATTORNEY. No questions.

CITY PROSECUTOR. Will Officer Pope please take the stand?

Q. Please state your name, address, and occupation.

Pope. Arthur Pope, 418 Fourth Street, Ithaca, patrolman in the Ithaca Police Department.

Q. Officer Pope, are you acquainted with the defendant in this trial?

A. I didn't know him until we met on June 12.

Q. Will you please tell the jury what occurred on that occasion?

A. I was driving north on North Aurora Street at about twenty-five miles an hour with my wife in the front seat. As we approached Yates Street I noticed, out of the corner of my eye, that a car was barreling out of Yates from my left. Just then my wife screamed, and I slammed on the brakes.

Q. And you collided with this car?

A. We sure did.

Q. What did you do then?

A. Well, right after the collision, I got out of my car and went over to Delaney. I . . .

Q. Delaney was driving the car which collided with you?

A. Yes. I asked him for his driver's license, but he hesitated a minute so I identified myself as a policeman. After he had given me his license I placed him under arrest.

Q. How long have you been a member of the Ithaca Police Department?

A. Six years.

Q. And in that time you have had occasion to arrest drivers for various traffic offenses, including speeding?

A. Yes, plenty of times.

Q. So it's part of your job to be able to judge speed and detect when a person exceeds the speed limit?

A. Yes.

Q. How fast would you say Delaney was traveling when you first saw him?

A. Well, he must have been going at least thirty-five to forty miles an hour.

Q. Upon what evidence do you base that statement?

A. The look I had at his car, the length of the skid marks, and the damage to the two automobiles which resulted from the impact following the skid.

Q. And based upon your experience as a police officer, do you believe Delaney was guilty of reckless driving?

Defense Attorney. Objection, your Honor. That is a question for the jury to decide.

Judge. Sustained.

City Prosecutor. No further questions.

Defense Attorney. Officer Pope, you stated that you saw Delaney's car out of the corner of your eye, that just then your wife screamed, and that you immediately put on the brakes, is that right?

A. Yes.

Q. Where was Delaney's car with reference to the stop sign shown in People's Exhibit A at the time you first saw him?

A. About abreast of the stop sign.

Q. And where was your car at that time?

A. I was just about at the crosswalk.

Q. And you stated that in your opinion Delaney was traveling at thirty-five to forty miles per hour while you were going twenty-five miles per hour?

A. Yes.

Q. Officer Pope, tell the jury how many feet a car traveling at 40 miles per hour covers in one minute?

A. A car going over twenty-five miles an hour leaves skid marks longer than twenty-five feet.

Q. That's not what I asked you. How many feet does a car traveling at forty miles an hour cover in one minute?

A. Well, I don't know offhand.

Q. How many feet away from you was Delaney's car when you first saw it?

A. I don't remember that very clearly.

Q. You stated that you saw his car, heard your wife scream, and put on your brakes almost simultaneously, did you not?

A. Yes.

Q. How long would you say you had to look at Delaney's car — a second, a split-second?

A. Not longer than a second, I guess.

Q. And on the basis of that brief, fleeting glance you decided that Delaney must be speeding and arrested him for reckless driving, is that right?

A. But his skid marks were thirty-six feet long.

Q. When did you arrest Delaney? Right after he handed you his driver's license, did you not?

A. Yes.

Q. Had Sergeant Beckenwall arrived yet?

A. No.

Q. And it was Sergeant Beckenwall who measured the skid marks, wasn't it?

A. Yes.

DEFENSE ATTORNEY. No further questions.

CITY PROSECUTOR. I have a few questions on re-direct, your Honor. Officer Pope, you made some reference to a relationship between the speed of an automobile and the length of skid marks which it leaves. It that a relationship which you normally make use of in your work as a police officer?

A. Yes.

Q. Will you explain it to the jury?

A. Well, the faster a car is going, the longer the skid marks it will leave.

Q. And from the length of the skid marks you can determine the approximate speed of the car?

A. Yes.

Q. According to the rule which you normally use in your work as a police officer, how fast must a car be moving to leave skid marks thirty-six feet long?

A. Well, I don't remember that exactly, but a car going more than twenty-five miles an hour will leave skid marks longer than twenty-five feet. I have a chart from an insurance company which has all the figures worked out.

Q. And you estimated that Delaney's car was traveling thirty-five to forty miles an hour based on your look at his car, on the length of the skid marks he left, and on the damage to the automobiles in the collision, is that right?

A. Yes.

Q. And this is the way you usually estimate speed in your work as a police officer?

A. Yes.

CITY PROSECUTOR. No further questions.

DEFENSE ATTORNEY. No further questions.

CITY PROSECUTOR. Your Honor, at this point the People would normally call Mrs. Margaret Ann Pope to the witness stand, but in the interest of saving time, counsel for the defense has agreed to stipulate that Mrs. Pope was injured in the accident.

DEFENSE ATTORNEY. The defense so stipulates, your Honor.

JUDGE. The record will show that Mrs. Pope was injured in the accident, and jurors will note that the attorneys have stipulated, or agreed, that Mrs. Pope was injured in the accident.

CITY PROSECUTOR. The prosecution rests, your Honor.

DEFENSE ATTORNEY. Will William Prize please take the stand?

Q. Please state your name, address, and occupation.

PRIZE. William Prize, R.D. 2, Ithaca, student at Ithaca High School.

Q. Bill, are you acquainted with the defendant in this case, Tom Delaney?

A. Sure I am. He's a good friend of mine. We go to school together.

Q. Were you with Tom on June 12 about 1 P.M.?

A. Yes.

Q. Will you explain to the jury why you were with him and what happened?

A. Well, it was a hot day, and during noon recess from school we decided to take a ride to cool off. We got in Tom's father's car and drove around for awhile.

Q. And did you drive on Yates Street?

A. Yes. When we got to Yates and North Aurora, I guess Tom didn't see the stop sign. I hollered to him, and he put on the brakes, and we slid into the other car.

Q. Officer Pope's car?

A. Yes.

Q. How fast were you traveling when you saw the stop sign?

A. Between twenty and twenty-five miles an hour.

Q. How do you know that?

A. Because I looked at the speedometer a short time before.

Q. How far from the stop sign were you when you saw it and shouted to Tom?

A. About ten feet, I guess.

Q. And you were traveling between twenty and twenty-five miles an hour?

A. Yes.

DEFENSE ATTORNEY. No further questions.

CITY PROSECUTOR. Do you ride with Delaney very often?

A. We go out for rides once in awhile, and sometimes when I forget my lunch he drives me home at noon.

Q. What route did you take on the day of the accident?

A. Well, I don't remember all the streets.

Q. Well, where did you start? Where was Delaney's car parked?

A. I . . . I don't remember just now.

Q. Did you drive out Cayuga Street? (See page 125.)

A. Yes.

Q. And then over to Tioga?

A. Yes.

Q. And did you turn left from Tioga to Yates?

A. Yes.

Q. Do you know Gaylord Sash?

A. Yes.

Q. Does he own an automobile?

A. Yes.

Q. Did you engage in a race with him on North Cayuga Street on the day of the accident?

A. A race? No, we didn't race with him.

Q. Did you make a left-hand turn from North Tioga into Yates?

A. Left from North Tioga into Yates? Yes, that's right.

Q. Were all four wheels on the ground when you made that turn?

A. Yes.

Q. Do you remember talking with Sergeant Beckenwall at the scene of the accident?

A. No. I didn't speak with him.

Q. Didn't have any conversation with him?

A. No.

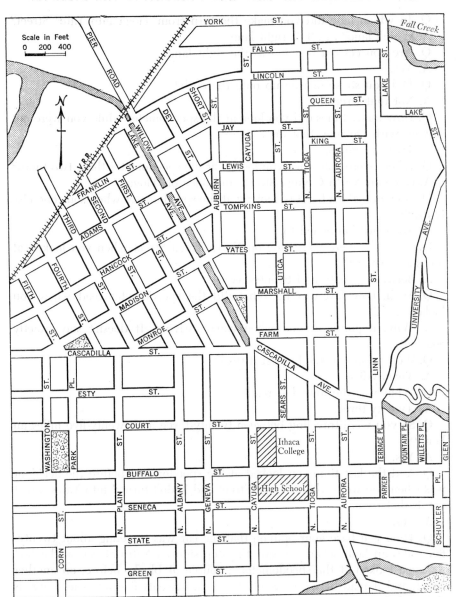

Part of the City of Ithaca, New York. The area shown is chiefly the northern
sector of the city. Ithaca High School is near the center. Court, Buffalo, and Seneca
Streets are generally through east-west arteries without stop signs; North Cayuga,
North Tioga, North Aurora, and Linn are generally through north-south streets
without stop signs. Traffic at virtually all the intersections of these streets is controlled by signals. There are no traffic signals in Ithaca north of the intersection
of Willow, Cascadilla, North Cayuga, and Farm Streets.

Q. In which lane did you make the turn from Tioga into Yates Street?

A. Which lane? . . . The right lane.

Q. Are you certain that it was the right lane?

A. Yes.

Q. Did you strike or ride up onto the curb?

A. Not that I recall.

Q. How many times did you look at the speedometer while you were out driving with Delaney that day?

A. Twice, I guess.

Q. Where were you when you looked at the speedometer those two times?

A. Once on North Cayuga Street, and once on Tioga.

Q. Do you make a habit of looking at the speedometer when someone else is driving?

A. No, I just happened to.

Q. How fast were you going on North Tioga Street when you looked at the speedometer?

A. Between twenty and twenty-five.

Q. Well, how fast was it? What did the speedometer read when you looked at it?

A. Why, it jumps around when you're driving. It doesn't stay exactly constant.

Q. Well, what was the highest it read?

A. Twenty-five.

Q. What was the lowest it read?

A. Twenty-three.

Q. So you were traveling between twenty-three and twenty-five miles an hour?

A. Yes.

Q. And the last time you looked at the speedometer before the accident was when you were still on Tioga Street and hadn't turned into Yates Street yet, is that right?

A. Yes.

Q. Then you base your opinion that the car was traveling about twenty-five miles an hour when you saw the stop sign on Yates Street on the fact that you looked at the speedometer a couple of blocks before, on another street, and it read between twenty-three and twenty-five miles an hour, is that right?

A. Well, the speed stays pretty constant; you can tell by the feel of the car.

Q. Did you turn the corner from Tioga into Yates at twenty-five miles an hour?

A. No, we slowed down to turn the corner.

Q. Then you sped up again, is that right?

A. Yes.

Q. But you could tell by the "feel" of the car that the speed increased to only twenty-five and stayed constant after that?

A. About twenty-five.

Q. How old are you?

A. Fifteen.

Q. Then you don't drive?

A. No.

Q. So all of your experience in determining the speed of a moving vehicle by its "feel" has been as a passenger in cars?

A. Yes.

Q. How long have you been riding in cars — all your life?

A. Yes.

Q. And you said you were fifteen?

A. Yes.

CITY PROSECUTOR. No further questions.

DEFENSE ATTORNEY. No further questions. Will Tom Delaney please take the stand.

Q. Please state your name, address, and occupation.

DELANEY. Thomas R. Delaney, R.D. 2, Ithaca, student at Ithaca High.

Q. How old are you, Tom?

A. Sixteen.

Q. You attend Ithaca High?

A. Yes, sir. I'll be a senior next year.

Q. How did you happen to be out driving the day of the accident?

A. Well, it was awfully hot that day, and Bill and I . . .

Q. "Bill?" Is that William Prize?

A. Yes. Bill Prize and I decided to take a drive during school recess to cool off.

Q. Are you allowed to leave school at noon hour?

A. Yes, sir.

Q. Whose car were you driving?

A. My father's.

Q. With his permission?

A. Yes, sir.

Q. How long have you held a driver's license, Tom?

A. Since last February, sir. About six months.

Q. Have you ever been involved in any accidents or received any tickets from the police for driving infractions?

A. No, sir.

Q. Tom, tell the jury in your own words what happened on June 12.

A. Well, Bill and I were driving like I said. We were going down Yates Street when all of a sudden Bill yelled: "Look out!" I slammed on the brakes and we slid into Mr. Pope's car.

Q. Did you see the stop sign at Yates and Aurora either before or after Bill called out?

A. No, sir.

Q. Did you see Officer Pope's car when Bill called out?

A. Well, I saw it about the same time.

Q. How fast were you traveling when Bill called out?

A. Just about twenty-five miles an hour.

Q. How do you know that?

A. I had glanced down at the speedometer about half a block before.

DEFENSE ATTORNEY. No further questions.

PROSECUTING ATTORNEY. Did you say, Mr. Delaney, that you have never been involved in a motor vehicle accident before?

A. Never.

Q. Never struck and killed anything with a motor vehicle.

A. No, sir.

Q. Did you ever kill an animal with a motor vehicle?

A. No, sir.

[City Prosecutor asked for, and was granted, a short recess during which he conferred with an unidentified member of the Ithaca Police Department.]

Q. Let me ask that question again. Did you ever kill an animal with a tractor?

A. Yes, sir.

Q. You killed an animal with a tractor? When was that?

A. About a year ago.

Q. Mr. Delaney, I hand you a "Report of Motor Vehicle Accident" form and ask you to identify the signature which appears at the bottom of the last page.

A. It's my signature, sir.

Q. Is this the report which you filled out and gave to the police in connection with the accident on June 12?

A. Yes, sir.

Q. Are the answers to questions one and two on that report in your own handwriting?

A. Yes, sir.

Q. Will you read aloud questions one and two and the answers which you wrote to those questions?

A. Question one: How long have you been driving? Six months. Question two: Have you ever been involved in a motor vehicle accident before? No.

Q. Now, you have testified here under oath that you killed an animal with a motor vehicle about a year ago, and you stated on this accident report that you have never been involved in an accident, is that right?

A. Yes.

Q. And one of these answers cannot be true, is that right?

A. Well, if you consider killing an animal with a tractor a motor vehicle accident, yes.

Q. And you testified here that you killed an animal with a tractor about a year ago, but on the report form you stated that you had been driving for only six months, is that right?

A. Yes.

Q. And one of those answers cannot be true, is that right?

A. If you consider a tractor a motor vehicle, yes.

Q. Mr. Delaney, are you acquainted with Gaylord Sash?

A. Yes.

Q. Did you engage in an automobile race with Sash on the day of the accident?

A. No, sir.

Q. You did not race your car against Sash's car?

A. No, sir.

Q. You stated that you glanced at your speedometer just before the accident. Did your eyes come to rest on the speedometer or was that just a fleeting glance?

A. Just a glance.

CITY PROSECUTOR. No further questions.

DEFENSE ATTORNEY. No further questions. Your Honor, the defense rests.

NOTES

Punishment for reckless driving is fixed by Section 70 of the New York State Motor Vehicle Traffic Law thus:

Any person violating any of the provisions of any section of this chapter, which violation is stated separately to be a misdemeanor, except where other punishment is specially prescribed therein, is punishable by a fine not exceeding one hundred dollars or by imprisonment for not exceeding thirty days or by both such fine and imprisonment for conviction of a first offense; by a fine of not less than fifty dollars nor more than two hundred dollars or by imprisonment for not exceeding ninety days or by both such fine and imprisonment for a conviction of a second offense committed within a period of eighteen months; by a fine of not less than one hundred dollars nor more than five hundred dollars or by imprisonment for not exceeding one hundred eighty days or by both such fine and imprisonment for conviction of a third or subsequent offense committed within a period of eighteen months....

In addition to punishment as such for reckless driving, conviction may result in the suspension or revocation of one's driving license or certificate of registration for an indeterminate period.

Possible penalty is not made known to the jury, for punishment is the province of the court alone and has no relevance to the question of fact which the jury must decide. As a practical proposition, however, possible penalty is something which the defense is more often than not anxious to bring to the jury's attention for quite obvious reasons, and it often succeeds in doing so in general if not specific terms. To counteract this, the judge in his charge will caution the jurors to disregard the matter of punishment, leaving it entirely to him.

THE PEOPLE V. WEEKS

QUESTION: *Is Levi Weeks guilty of the murder of Elma Sands?*

FACTS

ELIAS AND CATHERINE RING, Quakers, lived in Greenwich Street, New York City. Their family consisted of Hope Sands, Mrs. Ring's sister; Elma Sands, her cousin; Levi Weeks and his apprentice, boarders; and some other boarders. Weeks was a brother of Ezra Weeks, a respectable and wealthy citizen. On the evening of Sunday, December 22, 1799, Elma left the house and never returned. Two days later a muff she carried was found by a boy in the Manhattan Well. Elma's body was recovered from the well, which was located in Lispenard's Meadows, on January 2. The corpse was taken to the house in which she had resided and exposed for a day to public view in the street. On January 6 the Grand Jury returned an indictment for murder against the young carpenter, Levi Weeks, who was known to have shared in the young lady's possibly somewhat generous affections; and in a few days the town was flooded with handbills condemning Mr. Weeks and sacrificing him to the popular hysteria.

The trial opened on March 31, 1800, before Chief Justice Lansing, Mayor Varick, and Recorder Harrison. The Assistant Attorney, General Cadwallader Colden, directed the prosecution, and Weeks was defended by an illustrious team of lawyers: Brockholst Livingston, Aaron Burr, and Alexander Hamilton.

TESTIMONY

CATHERINE RING. In July last Levi Weeks came to board in our family and soon after began to pay attention to Margaret Clark until the twenty-eighth of August, when she went into the country. Elma lived in our house about three years as our child. After Margaret Clark left, Levi became attentive to Elma. They were left in the house with my husband about the tenth of September when I was in the country. Elma slept in the front room, second story.

After I had been absent about four weeks, I received a letter from my husband, desiring me to come home as he was very lonesome, and I came home six weeks to a day. After my return I paid strict attention to their conduct and saw an appearance of mutual attachment but nothing improper; he was frequently in her room when she was sick. During her illness he paid her the strictest attention and spent several nights in her room, saying he did not like to leave her with Hope, my sister, fearing she might go to sleep and neglect her; and in the night he wanted to go for a physician but I discouraged him, thinking she would be better in the morning.

Not a day passed but convinced me that he was paying his attentions to her; I often found them sitting and standing together, once sitting on her bed. On the twenty-second of December, my sister Hope went to meeting, and Levi went to his brother's; in a short time he returned, having fallen and hurt his knee. Elma dressed his knee for him. It was not much of a hurt, and after she dressed it he went upstairs; she followed him and was gone, I should suppose, considerably more than an hour. This was about noon. Between twelve and one o'clock Elma came down into the room where I was preparing dinner, with smiling countenance, and seemed calm and happy. Her appetite was remarkably good. I left her a short time and went into another room; when I returned, I found Levi sitting by the fire with her, appearing fully composed and happy, but he soon left us and went upstairs. After tea she went to a neighbor's and borrowed a muff; a while later she went to the front door and looked out. She came in and we sat together with my husband and two of the boarders until Levi came in. Then I went to the front door and looked out. Soon after the two boarders came into the hall and went upstairs, at which time I heard the clock strike eight.

I shut the door and came in saying, "The clock has just struck eight." I sat down, and in the course of a minute or two afterward Elma got up and went out. I observed Levi's eyes fixed upon her, and I thought he looked at her for her to go. In the course of a minute, I believe not more, I took the candle and went upstairs; she had on her hat and shawl and was holding her muff. She looked paler than usual. I went down and she was just ready to follow. I came in where Elias and Levi were sitting; no other person was up in the house but we four. Levi instantly took his hat and went out into the entry. The moment the door opened I heard a walking on the stairs; directly I heard a whispering near the door at the bottom of the stairs for nearly a minute, so near the door I thought I might understand what was said, and I listened for that purpose; soon I heard them step along, and the front door opened and the latch fell. I took up the candle and ran to the door to see which way they went; it was moonlight, but having the candle made it darker.

DEFENSE COUNSEL. Are you sure you had shut the door before?

A. I am positive; it stuck and was very difficult to shut. I then ran upstairs to see if they might not be there; why I did it I don't know, but somehow I felt agitated on the occasion. But she was not there. About ten o'clock Levi came home. The moment he came in I saw he was pale and much agitated. He sat down and asked, "Has Hope come home?" I answered, "No." Then he asked, "Has Elma gone to bed?" I said, "No, she has gone out; at least I saw her ready to go out and have good reason to think she went." He said, "I am surprised that she would go out so late at night and alone." I replied, "I have no reason to think she went out alone"; to which he made no reply but looked earnest and thoughtful and leaned his head down on his hand.

PROSECUTING ATTORNEY. Had anything passed to lead him to believe that she went out alone?

A. No, there had not.

Q. Did you express any alarm to him?

A. No, I thought she had gone to the neighbor's to leave the muff. After waiting until about twelve o'clock, I lit the candle and searched the house, except where the two boarders were sleeping and Levi's room.

Q. Was anything said about Elma at breakfast, by anybody?

A. No. Nobody mentioned her. After Levi had gone out, I heard some person enter the house and run softly upstairs. I intended to go and see, thinking it was her, but soon after Levi came in saying, "Is Elma got home?" I answered, "I expect she is upstairs. I heard someone go up." He replied, "It was me you heard." I said, "I'm sure I thought it was her step." I did not believe him, and went up myself. When I returned he was standing at the front door. I don't recollect his saying anything, but he went away. Some time after he came in again and said, "Is Elma returned?" I answered, "No." "Have you sent anywhere for her?" I answered, "No." He said, "Why haven't you?" I answered, "I did not think of sending, expecting her in every minute." He said, "I am surprised at her going out so late and alone." I said, "Indeed, Levi, to tell the truth, I believe she went with thee. She told me she was to, and I have good reason to think she did." He looked surprised, and said, "If she had gone with me she would have come with me, and I never saw her after she left the room."

THE COURT. Was there anything uncommon in his manner?

A. Indeed there was, more than I can express.

DEFENSE COUNSEL. Do you mean that this was after you expressed your surprise?

A. I had observed his look fixed upon me before.

THE COURT. Did you tell him you saw a difference in his look?

A. I did not then. A short time afterward, the owner of the muff called for it, as Elma had promised to return it the night it was borrowed, or early the next morning. I told her I would send for it, as I expected Elma was at Henry Clement's. She sat down with me, and soon after Levi came in and sat until the girl — who had gone for the muff — returned saying Elma had not been there. I was struck with astonishment; although my uneasiness had been great, yet I fully expected she was there. Levi said nothing, but sat with his head down and then went out. Soon after this my sister returned, and a short time after Levi came in. She immediately attacked him saying, "Where is Elma? I know thee knows. Tell me, for Caty is uneasy and says Elma told her she was going with thee, and she is sure she did." He looked surprised and said, "She told Caty so? Why, if she had gone with me she would have returned with me. I never saw her after she left the room, and I am surprised you would think of my keeping you in suspense." The day passed without much more being said, except of my saying that I had been to the door fifty times to look for her; he answered he had looked more than fifty times.

The next afternoon, when I and my sister were so distressed we determined to stand it no longer and were about to send for him, he came in and laid down his hat, but seeing our agitation, he turned around and was going out. I said, "Stop, Levi, this matter has become so serious, I can stand it no longer." He said he was sorry to see us distressed and was willing to do what he could. I then proceeded, "On Sunday after twelve o'clock, she came downstairs, after being with thee, and told me that night at eight o'clock you were going to be married." I had not proceeded much farther, if any, before he turned pale. He trembled, was much agitated, and began to cry, "I'm ruined, forever, unless she appears to clear me. My existence will be only a burden — I'd rather die than live under it." Then he proceeded to clear himself, saying he would never marry without his brother's approval. I replied, "She told me thee had talked to him twice on the subject." He said, "My brother can answer for himself."

On Thursday, the twenty-sixth of December, about ten o'clock, Margaret and Deborah Clark being in the room with me, Levi came in. Seeing us much distressed, he sat down and tried to comfort us, saying, "Give her up; she is gone, no doubt, and all our grieving will do no good." With an earnest look I turned to him, saying, "Levi, give me thy firm opinion from the bottom of thy heart; tell me the truth, what thee thinks has become of her." He replied, "Mrs. Ring, it's my firm belief she's now in eternity; it certainly is. Therefore, make yourself easy, for your mourning will never bring her back." I answered, "Why does thee say so? What reason has thee to think it?" "Why, from things I've heard drop." "What were they?" I said. "Why, I heard her say she wished she never had an existence." I asked, "What other reason has thee?" "Why, I have heard her say if she had laudanum, she would swallow it."

I said, "Why, Levi! As it was always easy for her to get that, it doesn't bear the weight of a straw with me, and the circumstance thee alludes to, I believe I was present, as well as several others." This he did not deny, nor mention any other time. The circumstance was this: my sister was ill; the doctor had left a small bottle with her, and she had put it in her hand, clapped it to her mouth. He said, "Elma, don't do that." She replied, "I shouldn't be afraid to drink it if it was full." My husband answered, "Why, it would kill thee." She said, "I shouldn't be afraid." I thought she spoke not thinking, though she was used to taking large quantities when sick, and this made her think light of it.

PROSECUTING ATTORNEY. Mrs. Ring, I wish you would be particular as to her temper and disposition on the twenty-second. Was it composed that afternoon?

A. Very much so, I never saw her pleasanter in my life — she was more so than usual.

Q. Has she not always borne a good character — I mean that of a modest, discreet girl?

A. Very much so.

Q. Would not the conduct between the prisoner and her have been thought improper if it was not supposed that they would soon be married?

A. Yes.

Q. How old was she?

A. About twenty-two.

Cross-examination: Levi's character while boarding in the house gained the esteem of everyone. His moral conduct was good. After the twenty-second he ate his meals as usual. On the twenty-second Elma looked rather paler than usual. For a year past she had been rather unwell. There was no other woman in the house when I went to the country. She slept in the third story before I went to the country, but for three weeks before her death she slept in the back room in the second story, next to Mr. Watkin's bedroom. I never asked Levi if he was engaged to Elma until Tuesday after her death, nor said a word about it to him. I had no reason to think that anyone but Levi had any undue intimacy with her.

HOPE SANDS. The first time I knew Levi and Elma to be together in private was about two weeks after Elma and I came to town. I found Levi and Elma together in her bedroom. I was there when Levi came in. Elma gave me a sign. I immediately went out. He followed me to the door, shut and locked it. I went downstairs, took my shoes off, went back softly to listen if I could hear their conversation. I heard whispering but could not understand anything. I stayed at the door at least an hour and finally went downstairs. Margaret Clark went up to the room and, finding the door locked, returned much surprised, asking if I knew who was there. We went up to the next room, the door of Elma's room was unlocked, and Levi came out and went downstairs.

On Monday, the day after Elma was missing, about 10 or 11 A.M., I met Levi upstairs alone. I attacked him about her; he denied knowing anything, though by his looks I was confident he did. He soon began to use all possible means to convince me of his innocence. I replied it was hard to judge one I had so good an opinion of, but he was certainly the person who could give information if he chose. He said, "Do you think if I knew where she was I would not tell you?"

The Sunday evening after she was missing, he came to me saying, "Hope, if you can say anything in my favor, do it, for you can do more good than any friend in the world to clear me." He pressed me very hard to go to the police with him. I refused. Then he gave me a paper he had drawn, asking me to sign it. The purport of the paper was that he had paid no more particular attention to Elma than to any other female in the house; that nothing had passed between them like courtship, or looking like marriage. I refused, saying, "Levi, if I was to do it, thee knows it would be positive lies." He said it would be of no service to me, and reached out and took it out of my hand.

Cross-examination: Levi and Elma were locked up together at the time about an hour. He was liked very much; all spoke well of him. He once went to the museum with me and Elma. He went once to church with me in the evening; Elma was to have gone but she was sick. I never knew him to walk out with her but that time. I heard him say one evening that he believed she despised him for she would never go in the street with him. He once asked me to go to his brother's with him but I could not. Elma was present and said, "Why don't you ask me?" He replied, "I know you wouldn't go if I did."

ELIAS RING. While my wife was in the country, Levi and Elma were constantly together in private. I was alone and very lonesome and was induced to believe from their conduct that they were shortly to be married.

Cross-examination: The partition between Watkins' house and ours is a plank partition, lathed and plastered. Mr. Watkins is a good neighbor. On December 22 Elma was as cheerful and gay as I've ever seen her. About 8 P.M. Elma went out; I saw her go out of the room and heard the front door open and shut about three or four minutes thereafter. My wife took the candle, went out, and was gone about two minutes. The two boarders, Lacey and Russell, came in, and one of them pulled out his watch and observed that it was eight o'clock. I am not certain that I heard anyone go upstairs. When my wife returned, I asked her who went out; she said, "Elma and Levi." I answered that she would get sick. About ten o'clock, Levi came in. He asked if Hope had got in; my wife answered, "No." He asked, "Is Elma gone to bed?" She answered, "No, she is gone out." He observed it was strange she should go out so late and alone. I never threatened Levi that I know of; I told him I believed him guilty, and he appeared as white as ashes and trembled all over like a leaf. His character was always good, and he was generally esteemed. I never spoke to Elma about her improper intimacy with Levi. I heard no whispering in the entry or anybody come downstairs. I sat in the corner and was not attentive to these things.

MARGARET CLARK. I lived at Mr. Ring's about six months before Levi Weeks came to board there. I can't say that I thought there was anything that looked like courting Elma, but they appeared intimate. I know once of their being locked up together in her bedroom. Another time I saw him standing in her room when she was sick, but I thought nothing of this because he was always attentive to anyone who was sick.

Cross-examination: Did Levi not pay as much attention to Hope Sands as he did to Elma?

A. Yes, I think he did, and more too. (Corroborates previous testimony concerning Elma's cheerfulness on the twenty-second.)

RICHARD CROUCHER. I was a lodger but not a boarder in Mr. Ring's house. I remained at the house all the time of Mrs. Ring's absence in the country and paid particular attention to the behavior of the prisoner and the deceased, and I was satisfied from what I saw that there was a warm courtship going on. I have known the prisoner to be with the deceased in private frequently and at all times of night. I know him to have passed two whole nights in her room. Once, too, at a time when they were less cautious than usual, I saw them in a very intimate situation. I did not tell anyone about it.

Cross-examination: Where were you on the night of December 22?

A. I supped that night at Mrs. Ashmore's, 884 Bowery Lane; it was the birthday of her son. It was my agreement with Mrs. Ring to be home at ten o'clock nights, but on this occasion I stayed out till eleven or half-past eleven.

Q. Do you know where the Manhattan Well is?

A. I do.

Q. Did you pass by it that evening?

A. I did not. I wish I had — I might perhaps have saved the life of the deceased.

Q. Have you ever had a quarrel with the prisoner?

A. I bear him no malice.

Q. But have you ever had any words with him?

A. Once I had — the reason was this, if you wish me to tell it: going hastily upstairs, I suddenly came upon Elma who stood at the door. She cried out, "Ah!" and fainted away. On hearing this the prisoner came down from his room and said it was not the first time I had insulted her. I told him he was an impertinent puppy. Afterward, being sensible of his error, he begged my pardon.

Q. And you say you bear him no ill will?

A. I bear him no malice, but I despise every man who does not behave properly.

Q. How near to the Manhattan Well do you think you passed that night?

A. I do not know what road I took. I go sometimes by the road, sometimes across the field.

Re-direct examination: Mr. Croucher, have you ever heard any noise in the prisoner's room at an uncommon time of night since this affair happened?

A. Yes, I have. The night the deceased was missing, and the next night, and every succeeding night. I heard him up whenever I waked at all hours from eleven at night till four in the morning — a continual noise, almost.

Re-cross examination: What kind of noises were these?

A. The noise of chairs being moved about, tongs thrown down, and the like.

Q. Were you ever upon any other than friendly terms with Elma?

A. After I offended the prisoner, who she thought was an Adonis, I never spoke to her again.

HENRY REYNOLDS and JOHN BENSON (neighbors) testified that Elma was modest and discreet, and of a cheerful disposition.

WILLIAM ANDERSON (the prisoner's apprentice). I did not think Levi was more attentive to Elma than to Margaret or to Hope. Levi said to me one day that he kept Elma's company neither for courtship nor for dishonor, but for conversation. He always slept with me, but one night he went downstairs in his nightshirt and did not return until morning. He slept as usual the night Elma was missing and the next two, but on the fourth night he sighed out in his sleep, "Oh, poor Elma."

SUSANNA BROAD. I live opposite Ezra Weeks' lumberyard, and on the night the deceased was lost I heard the gate open and a sleigh or carriage come out of the yard about eight o'clock. It rumbled, had no bells on it, and returned again before long. I am sure as to the hour and date.

CATHERINE LYON. On Sunday night a little after eight, before Christmas, I saw Elma Sands in Greenwich Street at the pump near the door of the new building. A good many people were passing; I could not see that anyone was with her. She spoke to me, and I heard someone say, "Let's go." She bade me goodnight and went on. I did not see Elma's face, but I knew her form. I did not see any sleigh.

BUTHRONG ANDERSON. On Sunday night before Christmas I was driving on Broadway about 8:30 in the evening and saw a one-horse sleigh at full gallop with two or three men and a woman in it. The horse was dark-colored. Have seen Ezra Weeks drive a horse of the same size and color.

JOSEPH STRINGHAM and JOSEPH CORNWELL (who accompanied Anderson in his sleigh) corroborated Anderson's testimony but thought the Sunday was December 8, just after Thanksgiving.

ARNOTTA VAN NORDEN. I live near the well. About eight or nine o'clock in the evening, my husband heard a noise and said it was from the well. I looked through my window, and we heard a woman cry out, "Lord have mercy on me. Lord, help me!"

LAWRENCE VAN NORDEN. I am the husband of the preceding witness. I heard the cry; got up and looked out the window. It was a clear night. I saw a man walking near the well. In a little while the cries stopped, and I went back to bed again.

Cross-examination: I live one hundred yards from the well. There was snow on the ground. I did not see a sleigh. I did not go to the well the next morning to examine it, nor mention what I heard and saw to anybody the next day.

RICHARD SKINNER (a surgeon). I saw the body after it was taken from the well. There were several bruises on it but the neck was not broken. Marks on the neck might have been made by a hand; they were spots looking like a chain. I do not know Mr. and Mrs. Ring. I cannot say what caused the spots.

JAMES LENT. On January 2 I went with Mr. Watkins and Elias Ring to drag the Manhattan Well. We found the body of a woman. As soon as Ring saw her calico gown, he said it was Elma — he knew the gown. We drew her up gently; she slewed around but not a thread of her clothes touched either side of the well. When she was drawn up, we laid her on a plank. Her hat was off; her gown was torn open just above the waist; and her shoes were gone. Her hair hung over her head. I saw on her right hand something like a kick; scratches of sand were on her skin — some skin was knocked off. Her stockings were torn at the toes, and the right foot was bare and scratched on the upper part as if she had been dragged on the ground. I did not see any bruises on her face. I went to the police and then with the officer to find the defendant. I told him I was very sorry for his situation. He turned around and said, "It is too hard," and he dropped his head and said, "Is it the Manhattan Well she was found in?"

Q. Was any mention made of the Manhattan Well in the presence of the prisoner before he asked the question?

A. I did not hear any; I don't believe there was.

DR. JAMES SNEDEKER (a physician). I examined the body the second day after it was taken from the well. I thought the left collarbone was broken and that the neck was not injured.

ELIZABETH OSBORN. I was slightly acquainted with Elma Sands. On the twenty-second of December I lent her my muff; she came to borrow it herself, and I observed that she was very neatly dressed and seemed to be a very lively and happy girl.

MR. WILLIAMS. At the request of the Attorney General I made an experiment to see in what time a man might drive a horse by the usual route from Ring's to the Manhattan Well, and from there back again to Ezra Weeks'. Although the roads were bad, it was done once in fifteen minutes and once in sixteen, without going out of a trot.

ALEX BUSKIRK. I was with Mr. Williams when he made the test and agree that he stated our findings correctly. Ezra Weeks' horse was a good horse in appearance.

MR. CROSS. I am acquainted with Ezra Weeks' horse. He is a very good horse and will go a mile in five minutes.

DEMAS MEED. I am an apprentice of Ezra Weeks and live with him. I take care of his horse and sleigh. On the Sunday night I locked the gate as usual and put the key in my pocket or on the mantel. I did not miss it in the morning, nor was anything mislaid. The eight harness bells were tied on as usual. I would have known if anyone had taken the horse and sleigh even for half an hour. It would take five or six minutes to take the bells off and put them on, and ten or fifteen minutes to harness up. After Mr. McCombs left, a little before nine, I went upstairs and saw Levi Weeks in his room.

LORENA FORREST. I live next door to Mrs. Ring. About twelve o'clock on January 2, Levi Weeks came into our house to buy some tobacco. I asked him if he had any news of Elma. He answered, "No." I told him I thought the Ring's family had, for they seemed very agitated. He went away and came back in about half an hour. I told him that Mrs. Ring said the muff had been found in a drain. He did not seem to change countenance. Nothing was said about the Manhattan Well. I heard Mr. Croucher say that he came near the well on the evening she was missing.

JOSEPH WATKINS. I was present at the finding of the body. About the middle of September, Mrs. Ring being in the country, I heard a man's voice in the bedroom on the second story where Elma slept. I am very positive it was not Levi's voice. I said to my wife: "It is Ring's voice, and the girl will be ruined." I did not mention this to anybody else until after Elma was missing. My room is next to hers. The partition between is plank, lathed and plastered. I was not certain that it was Ring's voice, but thought it was. Often heard that voice in Elma's room. Did not hear it after Mrs. Ring came back from the country. Mrs. Ring came into our house one morning and said Elma was so sick since she was at your house last night. My wife said she was not there. Mrs. Ring often said that Levi was kind and friendly to everyone, not more so to Elma than to any of the rest. I once said to Croucher that I believed Ring had a hand in it, and asked Croucher where he had been that night. He did not answer. The day she was laid out I saw Croucher busily trying to make people believe the prisoner was guilty. Ring has a high-sounding voice. Weeks has a low, soft voice.

LORENA FORREST (recalled). A day or two after Elma was found, Croucher was at our house and said it was a very unfortunate thing he had not come that way at just that time, as he might have saved her life. He said he had come by that night.

MRS. WATKINS. I live next door to Elma. Mrs. Ring came into our house one morning and said her boarders had gone out without breakfast; that Elma had been sick all night, ever since she came from our house, and she thought it came from her sitting over our stove. I replied that she had not been at our house. Have heard Mrs. Ring say Levi was very kind to the family.

DAVID FORREST. On the twenty-sixth of December, Croucher came into my store to buy a loaf of bread. Said Ring's family was in great distress; his opinion was that the girl had killed herself. On Friday after the body was found, Croucher came running into the store and said, "What do you think of this innocent young man now; there is material evidence against him and he'll hang."

EZRA LACEY. I am a lodger in Ring's house. Was there the night Elma was missing. Levi Weeks was there about eight o'clock when I came away. Left Mr. Ring, Elma, and him together. Do not know whether Mrs. Ring was there or not. Noticed no change in his countenance after Elma was missing. Thought he was more attentive to Hope than to Elma. After the disappearance, I heard Ring say one night that if he should meet Levi in the dark he would not think it wrong to put him out of the way.

HUGH M'DOUGALL. I have been acquainted with Croucher for some time, but never liked his looks. On January 2, the day the body was found, he was extremely busy among the crowd spreading insinuations against the prisoner.

JOHN B. McCOMBS. Between six and seven on the night of December 22, my wife and I went to Ezra Weeks' house. We found Levi sitting there, and he remained until eight o'clock. I am sure of the time.

MRS. EZRA WEEKS. On Sunday night, December 22, I and my husband were at home. McCombs and his wife came in, and Levi was there and stayed until about eight. Saw nothing peculiar in his conduct.

EZRA WEEKS. On Sunday, December 22, Levi came to my house in the morning about nine o'clock. I went to church and left him there. I dined at my father-in-law's that day and did not return until about five. Just as we had had tea, my brother came in, and I believe in about half an hour Mr. and Mrs. McCombs came in. My brother stayed until about eight o'clock. McCombs and his wife stayed about twenty minutes, as near as I can judge, after my brother went out. I lighted them downstairs to the street and all the way to the corner, it being very dark and slippery. Then I came back again and just as I set the candle down, before I had time to sit down myself, Levi came in to inquire about the business of the next day, as he had charge of my shop. He stayed until about ten o'clock and,

I suppose, went home as usual. About 2 P.M. on January 2, Levi came and told me Mrs. Forrest had told him that the muff was found in a well near Bayard's Lane. I told him I supposed it must be the Manhattan Well. This place came to my recollection because I had furnished the wood materials for the well and, as my business often called me that way, I rode past the well almost every day.

CHARLES THURSTON. I have worked for Ezra Weeks as foreman for about two years. From the time the girl was missing, I never saw any difference in Levi's conduct.

Several witnesses testify to Levi's good character. Several witnesses testify to Mrs. Ring's good character and Elma's cheerful disposition. Several witnesses testify that they supped with Mrs. Ashmore on December 22, her son's birthday, that Croucher was in the party, and that he came between four and five and remained until after ten.

TWA 266—UN 826

ABOUT 8:30 A.M. on December 16, 1960, Trans World Airlines Flight 266 left Dayton, Ohio. After a short hop to Columbus, where additional passengers came on board, Captain David A. Wollan, thirty-nine, took his Lockheed Super Constellation to eleven thousand feet and headed slightly north of east for La Guardia Airport, New York, 475 miles or one hour and forty minutes away. In his care were the lives of thirty-nine passengers and four crew members, as well as a million-and-a-half-dollar airplane.

Halfway across Pennsylvania, TWA 266 came under the control of the Air Route Traffic Control Center at New York (ARTCC/NY), which maintains radar and radio contact with all planes flying within two hundred miles of New York City. Just before passing over Allentown, Pennsylvania, ARTCC/NY directed Captain Wollan to approach New York over airway V 6 (see page 142). At 10:26 A.M. Wollan, having by this time been cleared to descend to nine thousand feet, reported that he was passing over Solberg radio beacon. ARTCC/NY then directed him to contact La Guardia Airport Approach Control (LGA A/C). William L. Smith, a radar controller at La Guardia and an employee of the Federal Aviation Agency, cleared TWA 266 to fifty-five hundred feet and directed Wollan to pass without delay through the Linden Holding Pattern.

Linden is one of two areas in which La Guardia holds planes that cannot be landed immediately. Particularly on days like December 16, when inadequate visibility made instrument landings necessary, airports as

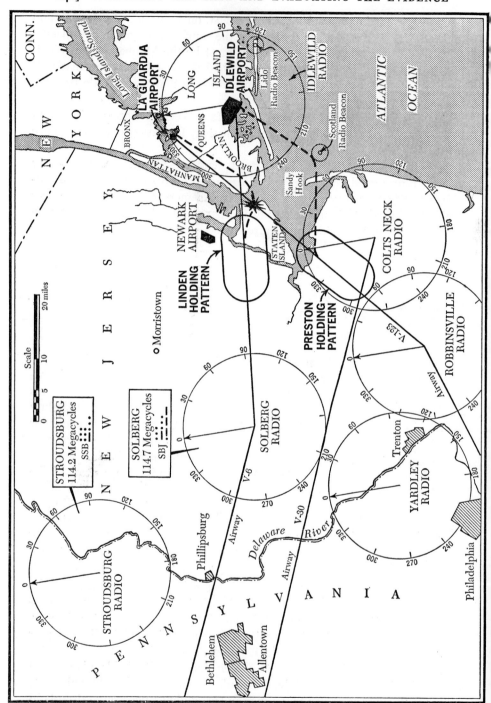

busy as La Guardia frequently have to delay incoming planes by having them fly oval patterns at different altitudes until it is their turn to land. These ovals are about eight miles wide and sixteen miles long, centered on a point at which two or more high-frequency radio beacons intersect. A pilot knows he has reached the center of the Linden Holding Pattern, for example, by tuning one of the two high-frequency receivers with which his plane is equipped to Colts Neck radio and the other to either Solberg or Stroudsburg and noting when the 0° beacon from Colts Neck intersects either the 92° beacon from Solberg or the 125° beacon from Stroudsburg.

But Captain Wollan did not have to worry about this kind of tricky aerial navigation on December 16. Traffic was momentarily light at La Guardia. Smith instructed him to fly on a heading of 150°, which would cause the Constellation to intersect the Instrument Landing System beacon from La Guardia. From this point La Guardia Tower would guide TWA 266 onto the field.

About 10:33 A.M. LGA A/C informed Wollan that the radar screen showed a plane six miles distant and approaching from his right. This was not an unusual situation. Planes frequently pass over or under one another. Since the radar used in 1960 did not show elevation, neither Smith nor Wollan had any definite way of knowing whether the blips approaching one another on the radar screen were on a collision course or safely separated by thousands of feet. But since all planes in the New York air space are supposedly under tight radar control, they made the reasonable assumption that danger was not imminent.

Wollan acknowledged Smith's warning without comment. Smith directed TWA 266 to turn slightly to the left and to begin descending to fifteen hundred feet. About 10:33:30 he told Wollan, "that appears to be jet traffic off your right now, three o'clock, at one mile, northeast-bound."

It was "jet traffic." United Air Lines Flight 826, a five-million-dollar Douglas DC-8 jet, piloted by Captain Robert H. Sawyer, forty-six, had left Chicago's O'Hare International Airport with eighty-four passengers and crew members about the same time that TWA 266 had left Dayton. Flying nonstop at twenty-five thousand feet and at slightly over five hundred miles an hour, UN 826 was scheduled to arrive at Idlewild Airport, New York, at 10:45 A.M., only five minutes after TWA 266 was to land at La Guardia. UN 826 came under the control of ARTCC/NY a few minutes after TWA 266, and passed Allentown four and a half minutes behind the slower piston-engine plane. The flight plan for UN 826 called for the jet to fly southeast across Pennsylvania to Robbinsville radio beacon and then northeast on airway V 123 to the Preston Holding Pattern, from which it would fly first east and then northeast to Idlewild Airport.

Before UN 826 reached Allentown, ARTCC/NY instructed Captain Sawyer to follow airway V 30 to its intersection with V 123. This new routing took Sawyer somewhat north of his planned course and cut several minutes from his flying time, although it gave him very little time after reaching V 123 to orient himself in the Preston Holding Pattern. The center point of Preston is the intersection of radio beams from Solberg at 120°, Robbinsville at 50°, and Colts Neck at 346°. ARTCC/NY cleared UN 826 to descend to fourteen thousand feet over Allentown and to five thousand feet just before entering the Preston pattern. At 10:33 A.M. Captain Sawyer reported that he was leaving six thousand feet for five thousand feet. At 10:33:15 ARTCC/NY, having instructed Sawyer to hold in the Preston pattern, told him to contact Idlewild Airport Approach Control (IDL A/C) for further instructions. At 10:33:28 Sawyer radioed IDL A/C: "Idlewild Approach Control. United eight two six, 'proaching Preston at five thousand." At that instant, unfortunately, UN 826 was not "'proaching Preston." For some unexplained reason on which this case hinges, the plane was already about ten miles beyond the Preston Holding Pattern.

At approximately 10:33:42 A.M. on December 16, 1960 — the eve of the fifty-seventh anniversary of the Wright brothers' first flight — UN 826, in level flight at 378 mph about 5,200 feet above Miller Army Airfield on Staten Island, collided with TWA 266. The right wing of the jet cut into the passenger compartment of the Super Constellation, causing the latter plane to break into several pieces and to fall almost vertically. The outer right jet engine and portions of the right wing were torn from UN 826. It continued about nine miles to the northeast and fell into crowded Sterling Place in the Park Slope section of Brooklyn.

The forty-four persons aboard the Super Constellation, the eighty-four on the DC-8, and six people living on Sterling Place were killed. The accident marked the first mid-air collision of planes controlled by ground-based radar, and resulted in one of the largest death tolls in commercial aviation history. Damage claims resulting from the loss of life and property were expected to total fifteen million dollars.

On January 4, 1961, the Civil Aeronautics Board opened public hearings in Brooklyn to determine the cause of the collision. The cause of the collision was quickly uncovered, and the next question was "Why?" Were the radar or high-frequency radio beacons maintained by the FAA to blame? Had Captain Sawyer made an error? Had equipment in the DC-8 failed? Or was it another factor or combination of factors?

TESTIMONY

Seven of the persons who saw the planes collide disagreed on some inconsequential details but agreed that the point of impact was about half a mile northwest of Miller Field, Staten Island. Both planes appeared to be flying nearly level. No one saw either aircraft maneuver to avoid the collision. Most witnesses said that the jet appeared to strike the right side of the Super Constellation. The jet lost an engine and continued on to the northeast. The piston-engine plane dropped almost vertically, its tail down.

Members of the CAB investigating team reported finding no traces of alcohol or other stimulants, and no excessive amounts of carbon dioxide in the bodies of crew members. No mechanical deficiencies were discovered in either plane, except for one inoperative high-frequency radio receiver in the jet.

WILLIAM L. SMITH, radar controller at LGA A/C, testified that he twice notified the Super Constellation pilot of an approaching radar blip and had waited for the pilot to request a change of course. He explained that controllers were instructed not to give course changes in such situations except at the pilot's request, since radar does not indicate elevation and two approaching blips might be planes separated in altitude by thousands of feet. Smith (corroborated on this point by several other radar traffic-control experts) said that radar blips cross paths all the time and that trying to steer all blips around one another would badly slow the flow of air traffic. A pilot flying in clouds and warned of an approaching blip must assume one of two things: (1) the blip represents an uncontrolled plane flying visually, outside clouds, in which case it could be no threat to the plane in the clouds; or (2) the blip represents another plane in the clouds, in which case the other plane must be under orders of the traffic-control system and have an assigned flight zone safely separated from his own. Asked if he expected TWA 266 to request guidance around the approaching blip, Smith said after a long pause, "If the pilot of 266 had been in a position to see what I observed on the scope, he might have had reason to request a vector [course]." Asked if it would have been normal for the pilot to make such a request, Smith replied, "We have had such requests."

Following are excerpts from the transcript of tape-recorded conversations between radar controllers and TWA 266. Communications involving other planes and other nonessential items are deleted.

(10:25 A.M.) ARTCC/NY. Trans World three seven four, Capital one thirty-two, Trans World two six six: the current La Guardia weather is measured five hundred overcast one mile with — uh — light snow. The winds are from the northwest at one five knots, the altimeter two niner six six. Over.

TWA 266. Two six six.

. . . .

TWA 266. Uh — New York. Two six six. Do you know what the runway is?
ARTCC/NY. Uh — Trans World two sixty-six, they're making approaches from the — uh — southwest — I'll stand — correction — stand by and I'll obtain the active runway. (Pause) Uh — they're using I-L-S to — uh — runway four, La Guardia, sir. Understand the localizer is inoperative.

TWA 266. Uh — roger, thank you.
ARTCC/NY. Roger.

. . . .

ARTCC/NY. Trans World two six six, descend to and maintain niner thousand. Report leaving ten, one zero thousand.

TWA 266. TWA two sixty-six cleared to niner thousand, leaving one zero thousand.

ARTCC/NY. Roger, Trans World two sixty-six.

(10:26) TWA 266: TWA two six six by Solberg two seven.

ARTCC/NY. World two sixty-six, Roger. (Pause) Trans World two sixty-six, radar service terminated. Contact La Guardia approach on one two five point seven.

TWA 266. One twenty-five seven.

ARTCC/NY. Trans World two sixty-six out.

After establishing contact with LGA A/C and being cleared to descend to fifty-five hundred feet, TWA 266 began approaching the field.

LGA A/C. Trans World two six six, make that further right, one five zero.

TWA 266. One five zero. TWA two six six.

(10:32:47) LGA A/C. And Trans World two sixty-six, traffic at two-thirty,[1] six miles, northeast-bound.

TWA 266. Two sixty-six.

TWA 374. TWA three seven four is Dodger inbound.

LGA A/C. Roger, Trans World three seven four. Contact La Guardia Tower now, one eighteen seven. That's runway four, sir.

TWA 374. Roger.

LGA A/C. Trans World two sixty-six, what is your altitude?

TWA 266. Fifty-five hundred.

LGA A/C. Roger, continue your descent to one five hundred.

TWA 266. Descend to one five hundred.

LGA A/C. Roger, and turn left now heading one three zero.

TWA 266. One three zero for two sixty-six.

(10:33:26) LGA A/C. Roger, that appears to be jet traffic off your right now, three o'clock, at one mile, northeast-bound.

The communication was not acknowledged. An unidentified noise similar to that of an open microphone was heard for approximately six seconds.

There was no further communication from TWA 266.

JOHN F. PAHL, chief of the CAB engineering division, testified concerning

---

[1] The plane is envisioned as being in the middle of a horizontal clock dial, pointed at twelve o'clock. The traffic was, therefore, slightly ahead of a point directly to the plane's right.

information gleaned from the flight recorder[2] recovered from the United jet. The recorder showed that the plane passed Preston at 10:32:21 A.M.; altitude, 8,700 feet; speed, 504 mph; rate of descent, 3,600 feet per minute; the jet struck the Constellation at 10:33:42; altitude, between 5,175 and 5,250 feet; speed, 378 mph; rate of descent, nil. The collision occurred about about one mile west of Miller Army Airfield. On the basis of information from the flight recorder and other sources, the CAB prepared a graphic representation of the actual paths followed by the two planes (see page 148).

RONALD DI GIOVANNI, ARTCC/NY radar controller and an employee of the FAA, testified that he had guided UN 826 across Pennsylvania. He said that he had instructed Captain Sawyer to alter his flight program by following airway V 30 rather than flying directly to Robbinsville radio beacon before turning northeast; that UN 826 saved three or four minutes of flight time by following this shorter route; that he, Di Giovanni, had neglected to inform IDL A/C that UN 826 would arrive ahead of schedule; that he had watched UN 826 intermittently as it crossed Pennsylvania; that he had last noted the UN 826 blip on his radar screen as it was from one to three miles southwest of Preston. He said that he saw this blip between 10:33:01 and 10:33:14 A.M.; that he instructed UN 826 to hold in the Preston pattern and contact IDL A/C; that he pressed the button which was supposed to actuate a light in the IDL A/C room, notifying them that ARTCC/NY was handing over a plane for guidance; that in view of statements made to him by controllers in that room he could only surmise that he had not pressed the button hard enough to actuate the light.

IDL A/C RADAR OPERATORS testified that they received a call from UN 826 at 10:33:28 saying that the plane was approaching Preston; that they were not expecting UN 826 for several minutes; that the warning light that indicates imminent transfer of a plane from ARTCC/NY to IDL A/C was not lit; and that they were unable to locate UN 826 on radar. Nevertheless, they responded with a summary of weather and landing conditions then prevailing at Idlewild, meanwhile attempting unsuccessfully to locate the UN 826 blip. UN 826 did not acknowledge their communication regarding the weather.

Following are excerpts from the transcript of tape-recorded conversations between radar controllers and UN 826. Communications involving other planes and other nonessential items are deleted.

---

[2] A flight recorder is a 7 × 5 × 2-inch container built to withstand 2,000° Fahrenheit, a shock ten times the force of gravity, and immersion in sea water for thirty-six hours. Lines etched on a metal tape by a diamond stylus provide moment-by-moment data on speed, altitude, direction, and gravity forces. This evidence marked the first time precise information had been obtained from the flight recorder of a crashed plane.

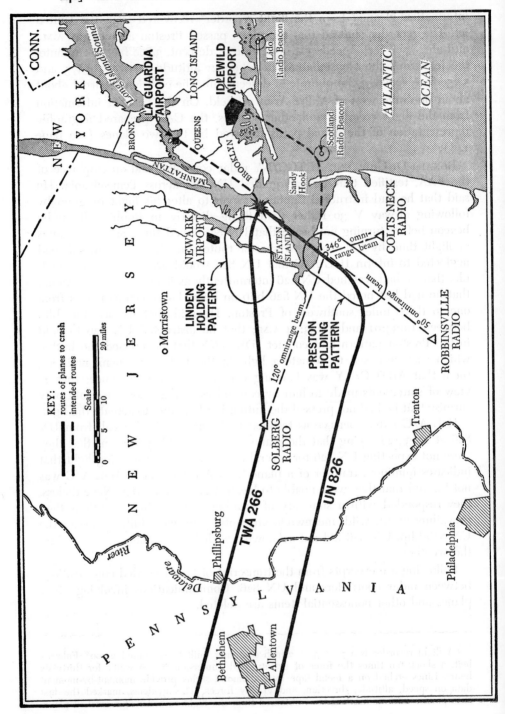

(10:30) ARTCC/NY. United eight twenty-six, now descend to and maintain five thousand.

UN 826. Maintain five thousand. We're leaving fourteen, United eight twenty-six.

ARTCC/NY. Roger. Look like you'll be able to make Preston at five?

UN 826. Er — will head it right on down. We'll dump it.

CAB investigators later testified that the words following "down" were so blurred as to be nearly unintelligible and that "We'll dump it" was at best an uncertain guess as to what was said.

. . . .

(10:32) ARTCC/NY outlined the waiting pattern UN 826 was supposed to fly at Preston.

. . . .

(10:33) UN 826. "United eight twenty-six out of six.

ARTCC/NY. Er — is that eight twenty-six leaving — er — five, correction, leaving six?

UN 826. (Garbled)

ARTCC/NY. Eight twenty-six. I'm sorry I broke you up. Was that you reporting leaving six thousand for five?

UN 826. Leaving six for five, United eight twenty-six, affirmative.

(10:33:15) ARTCC/NY. Eight twenty-six, roger, and you received the holding instructions at Preston. Radar service is terminated. Contact Idlewild Approach Control one two three point seven. Good day.

UN 826. Good day.

(10:33:28) UN 826. Idlewild Approach Control. United eight two six, 'proaching Preston at five thousand.

(10:33:33) IDL A/C. United eight twenty-six. This is Idlewild Approach Control. Maintain five thousand. Little or no delay at Preston. Idlewild landing: runway four, right. I-L-S in use. Idlewild weather: six thousand scattered; estimated ceiling, one thousand five hundred overcast; visibility one-half a mile; light rain and fog. Wind is north-northeast at seven knots; the altimeter, two nine six three (10:33:54)

This message was not acknowledged. There was no further communication from UN 826.

GLENN A. ALFRED, United Air Lines flight training manager, testified that Captain Sawyer had flown for United since 1941 and had logged 332.2 hours in jets since May 17, 1960, when he completed DC-8 ground school with a final examination grade of 93 per cent and a 99 per cent quiz average; that Sawyer had flown the Chicago—New York run many times and was highly regarded by United as a pilot; that United pilots were trained to stay within the FAA maximum speed of 180 knots (about 205 mph) when flying in holding patterns below 15,000 feet; that it was well within the capacity of a DC-8 entering Preston at the speed and altitude indicated by the flight recorder of the UN 826 to stay within the pattern at the proper speed and altitude; that UN 826 had reported to a United Air Lines communications center in New York (on a frequency not monitored by the FAA) that one of its high-frequency radio receivers was inoperative; that it is, of course, more difficult to locate the intersection of two radio beacons with one receiver than with two, but it was entirely possible to do so by tuning from one frequency to the other; that, in fact, many planes were equipped with only one high-frequency receiver.

DAVID D. THOMAS, director of the Bureau of Air Traffic Management of the FAA, testified that radar traffic control systems could not maintain a constant watch on every plane in their control. Only jet aircraft flying above 24,000 feet, where speeds were greatest and human eyesight was least reliable, were under constant surveillance. Controllers were therefore required to offer only as much surveillance as possible to planes at lower altitudes. To function safely, the system requires that pilots follow the traffic instructions given them from time to time. He said there was no provision in air traffic-control procedures for "radar hand-offs" of planes from an air route traffic control center to an airport approach control facility, although this had been an objective of the FAA since March, 1960. In a radar hand-off the center would keep a plane under radar surveillance until the airport picked it up. "This objective has not been met either here, in New York, or in any other section of the country," Thomas said in answer to a question. He said furthermore that radar hand-offs had been made in the New York area, but they did not occur "as a matter of routine."

ROYS JONES, chief of the Program Planning Board of the FAA's New York region, testified that the United jet was not under radar surveillance as it flew northeast out of the Preston Holding Pattern; that an attempt had been made to pass control of the plane from ARTCC/NY to IDL A/C about four minutes before the crash, but the tower did not pick it up; that the center, in transferring control of UN 826, failed to inform the tower that the plane had been cleared to take a short-cut into the Preston pattern that would reduce flight time by several minutes; that the plane was no longer under radar surveillance by the center at 10:33:15 A.M., when the control center transmitted its last message to the plane. Asked how long before that transmission radar service was actually terminated, he answered, "I don't know. I can't answer that question."

CAPTAIN W. J. PICUNE, United Air Lines pilot, testified that he approached Preston on December 16, about 2:30 P.M. When he picked up the 346° beacon from Colts Neck, he noticed that he was off the Staten Island shore, four to five miles from Miller Field and five or more miles beyond Preston. IDL A/C told him he was outside the Preston Holding Pattern and requested him to circle "as tightly as possible." He said that he had flown this course frequently and had never before been told he was outside the pattern. Picune had not reported this incident to the FAA.

CAPTAIN P. L. WALLACE, United Air Lines pilot, testified that during a flight on the evening of December 16, Colts Neck radio indicated that he was still some distance from Preston when IDL A/C informed him that he had reached Preston. He had not reported this incident to the FAA.

CAPTAIN JOHN F. MORAM, American Airlines pilot, testified that he was approaching Preston at about 3:30 P.M. on December 16, when the radio which he had tuned to Colts Neck flashed an automatic warning that something was wrong; that he received clearance to double back and try again; and that the warning signal appeared again. He then tuned to Solberg radio and successfully located Preston. Moram had not reported this incident to the FAA.

CAPTAIN W. S. McCORMICK, American Airlines pilot, testified that he had flown in the vicinity of Colts Neck radio during the morning of December 16. He said his copilot's radio had flashed a warning indicating trouble when tuned to Colts Neck, but had worked properly on other radio stations. McCormick had not reported this to the FAA.

CAPTAIN R. J. GOSNELL, Capital Airlines pilot (Capital 132—see transcript), testified that he landed at La Guardia just ahead of the scheduled arrival of TWA 266, that his copilot took bearings from Colts Neck during his approach to La Guardia, and that they jibed with his plane's course.

Testimony from other pilots showed that at least two other flights on December 16 used Colts Neck radio without difficulty. (The law requires that pilots report to the FAA any malfunction of navigation equipment. That no one reported a malfunction of Colts Neck suggests that they were not convinced on the sixteenth that anything was wrong.)

ERNEST L. GOYLE, electronics expert employed by the FAA, testified that careful tests had produced no indication that Colts Neck radio was putting out faulty signals, and that if the radio beacons were off by more than one degree, automatic warning horns would have sounded. (These radios are of the type known as "very high frequency omnidirectional." They actually send out 360 beacons — one for each degree of the compass — any one of which can be used as a navigational guide.)

Goyle's testimony closed the first hearing. On July 20, 1961, in Washington, D.C., the CAB reopened public hearings briefly to hear new evidence.

JOHN F. PAHL, chief of the CAB engineering division, testified that trajectory studies had placed the collision six thousand feet northwest of Miller Field; that investigation revealed that ARTCC/NY, LGA A/C, and IDL A/C each checked their timing devices with a different source; and that it was therefore impossible to determine how closely the time at one installation matched that at the others on December 16; the presumption was that they were at least very close.

WILLIAM E. JACKSON, chief of the CAB Research and Development Division, testified that exhaustive tests had failed to reveal any malfunction of Colts Neck radio.

WILLIAM L. KISER, FCC engineer in charge of the district office covering New Jersey, testified that some factories in the area used machines which emitted high-frequency oscillations or electronic vibrations similar to those put out by very high-frequency omnidirectional radio stations; that these industrial transmissions in the area were known to have interfered with airplane navigation equipment on at least 275 occasions; that it was impossible to tell if this happened on December 16 because industrial installations typically emitted the oscillations only sporadically.

SUGGESTIONS

A specific question is not offered for this case because there are so many possibilities; it is better to have the student frame the question that seems most interesting. In doing so, however, care must be taken in handling the matter of legal liability. In some interpretations of the case, the person, organization, or circumstance that caused the collision will also be legally liable. But this need not be so. It may be argued that ARTCC/NY made the collision possible, for example, but it probably could not be shown that ARTCC/NY is legally liable, since personnel at that installation apparently performed their duties as required by law. The question must be phrased so that it is clear whether attention is to be focused on legal liability or the actual cause.

Some possible interpretations of the case are suggested by the facts and testimony presented here; others are not. To put the hint more broadly, the evidence available will support arguments which it in no way suggests.

TEXAS TOWER NUMBER 4

BY THE YEAR 1952 the necessity for radar detection of hostile aircraft at least three hundred miles from their intended targets within the United States had become apparent to all those who had studied the problems associated with the air defense of the continental United States. Shore-based radars did not fill the need, so studies were made to determine whether there were particular regions off our shores where a cheaper and more reliable substitute for radar picket ships might be installed. Five locations were found off the northeast coast of the United States where structures patterned after the oil-drilling rigs in the Gulf of Mexico off the coast of Texas could be erected so as to provide proper radar coverage. They were to become known as the Texas towers. However, only three of the five were actually built, these being identified as Texas towers Nos. 2, 3, and 4.

Tower No. 4, the last one to be built, toppled into the sea in 185 feet of water at 7:25 P.M. Sunday evening, January 15, 1961, during a North Atlantic storm, taking with it the lives of twenty-eight persons, fourteen of whom were military personnel of the Air Force, the remaining fourteen being civilian construction workers engaged in the further repair of the structure.

The day after the tragedy the Preparedness Investigating Subcommittee of the United States Senate[1] announced that it would conduct an inquiry into the tragedy to determine whether or not a formal investigation might be warranted. Similarly, and on the same day, the commander of the Air Defense Command of the Department of the Air Force established a fact-finding Board of Officers to investigate the tower's collapse. Although this board was somewhat delayed in its deliberations by the illness of a material witness, it completed its field investigation late in February and presented its report to Air Force Headquarters.

Meanwhile, discussions had taken place between the chairman of the Preparedness Subcommittee and Air Force officials concerning the extent to which information acquired by the Board of Officers might be made available to the subcommittee in aid of its inquiry. It appeared from those discussions that the Air Force would be reluctant to reveal any of its information until all Air Force proceedings concerning the tower's collapse were terminated. Consequently, the chairman directed the staff to conduct its own field investigation, which took place during the early part of March, 1961.

Then, on March 20, 1961, the Department of the Air Force announced publicly that Major General Viccellio, Commander of the 26th Air Division, with headquarters in Syracuse, New York, had preferred charges of culpable negligence (under article 119 of the Uniform Code of Military Justice) and dereliction of duty (article 92) against Colonel William Banks, USAF, Acting Commander of the Boston Air Defense Sector, Stewart Air Force Base, Newburgh, New York, and charges of dereliction of duty against both Major William Sheppard, USAF, Commander of the 4604th Support Squadron, with headquarters at Otis Air Force Base, Falmouth, Massachusetts, and Major Reginald Stark, USAF, Acting Commander of the squadron during a portion of the time prior to the collapse of tower No. 4.

[1] The senators on the subcommittee were John Stennis, Mississippi, Chairman; Stuart Symington, Missouri; E. L. Bartlett, Alaska; Henry M. Jackson, Washington; Styles Bridges, New Hampshire; Leverett Saltonstall, Massachusetts; and Margaret Chase Smith, Maine. The subcommittee is an adjunct of the Senate Committee on Armed Services.

Since these officers had been given no prior opportunity to cross-examine the witnesses who appeared before the Board of Officers and whose testimony presumably gave rise to the charges against them, an investigating officer was appointed to determine which of the charges, if any, should be made the basis of possible courts-martial proceedings. During that investigation the right was extended to those charged to confront the witnesses who had appeared earlier before the Board of Officers and whose testimony was presumably damaging to those charged.

The Preparedness Subcommittee unanimously agreed that in order to avoid any interference with or prejudice to the judicial rights of those military officers, it would restrict its investigation, for the time being, to matters relating to the design, construction, and repair of Texas tower No. 4, leaving to a properly constituted judicial forum the determination of the guilt or innocence of those officers in properly discharging their responsibilities as military commanders.[2]

Accordingly, the subcommittee held open hearings on May 3, 4, 10, 11, and 17, which were limited to the design, construction, and repair of Texas tower No. 4, and took testimony from sixteen witnesses. Many persons other than those who were actually subpoenaed to testify were contacted and interviewed during the course of the subcommittee's inquiry. Moreover, many documents and exhibits from various sources became part of the official files of the subcommittee but do not appear in the official transcript of the hearings. Such information and documentation is incorporated into this report whenever it is applicable and relevant.

Having, then, restricted its inquiry to matters relating to the design, construction, and repair of the tower, the subcommittee noted the emergence of three significant issues:

1. Was there a deficiency in the design of the tower?
2. Was there a deficiency in the construction of the tower?
3. Was there a deficiency in the repairs which were designed to restore to the tower its intended structural integrity?

It is with these issues that this case is concerned. The following is a summary of the subcommittee's findings.

---

[2] After further investigation, the Air Force announced on June 9, 1961, that the charges against Major Sheppard and Major Stark, as well as the charge of culpable negligence against Colonel Banks, had been dropped, but that the colonel would face a court-martial on the dereliction-of-duty count. Colonel Banks was tried at Stewart Air Force Base from August 21 to 23, 1961. When the evidence had been heard, the three generals and five colonels who comprised the court accepted without objection the opinion of its law officer that the case against Colonel Banks had not been proved — in effect, he was acquitted. (See footnote 9.)

PRELIMINARY BACKGROUND

The concept of the Texas towers originated from the award of an Air Force contract to the Lincoln Laboratory of the Massachusetts Institute of Technology to determine whether cheaper and more reliable substitutes might be found for the picket ships which served as a seaward extension of the early warning radar system. In a report of August 1, 1952, entitled "Preliminary Report on the Substitution of Off-Shore Towers for Picket Vessels in the Continental Air Defense System," it was concluded that it was both feasible and practical to construct such platforms off the northeast shore of the United States at five locations out in the Atlantic Ocean that would provide proper radar coverage. More specific geographic information concerning their locations is as follows:

Tower No. 1 was to have been located on Cashes Ledge, 106 miles northeast of Salem, Massachusetts.

Tower No. 2 was placed on Georges Bank, 174 miles southeast of Salem, Massachusetts.

Tower No. 3 was erected on Nantucket Shoals, 113 miles southeast of Wickford, Rhode Island.

Tower No. 4 was erected 80 miles east of Barnegat Inlet, New Jersey, but was referred to as the "location off New York," bearing 84 miles southeast of Coney Island, New York.

Tower No. 5 was to have been erected on Browns Bank, 75 miles south of Yarmouth, Nova Scotia.

The Lincoln Laboratory report also contained recommendations for constructing the towers and conclusions on oceanographic considerations, two of which are set forth verbatim as follows, because they bear on subsequent events:

All authorities that have been consulted agree that the maximum storm wave in the area considered will be 40 feet high. . . . From the point of view of wave damage, there are no serious problems.

In design, the wave problem is twofold. The structure must be high enough to prevent wave action from reaching the flat horizontal platform, and the structure, necessarily subjected to wave action, must be strong enough to avoid failure.

Having preliminarily determined feasibility, the Air Force conducted negotiations and discussions with the Department of the Navy's Bureau of Yards and Docks, and agreement was reached early in 1954 that the Bureau would act as the design and construction agency for the Air Force in the Texas tower project.

Ultimately, the District Public Works Office of the First Naval District, with headquarters in Boston, Massachusetts, took charge of the program and on April 9, 1954, a selection board convened for the purpose chose from a list submitted to it an architectural and engineering firm to conduct a more detailed feasibility study and report of the proposed offshore radar platforms. The board decided to select a firm or firms which possessed no "pet" or patented features for this type of construction on the theory that such firms could better suit their designs to the field conditions prevailing at the various sites.

Although this decision eliminated from consideration at least three corporations having considerable experience in the design and construction of offshore platforms, i.e., DeLong Corp., Merritt, Chapman & Scott, and the Frederick Snare Corp., these firms were permitted to bid for the construction of the towers designed by others.

The selection board[3] recommended, and the then district public works officer concurred, that a joint venture composed of the firms of Anderson-Nichols Co. of Boston, Massachusetts, and Moran, Proctor, Mueser & Rutledge of New York City be selected for the feasibility study and report. A letter of intent was duly issued on June 18, 1954, and subsequently implemented by the award of BuDocks contract NOy–82761.

Conflict developed in the testimony as to the contemplated division of responsibility between the two firms in the conduct of the feasibility study and, subsequently, in the design of the towers themselves. On the one hand, Mr. E. Ross Anderson, president of Anderson-Nichols Co., testified that when it appeared that his firm was seriously being considered as the architectural and engineering firm for the Texas towers, he invited the participation of the Moran, Proctor firm in the program for what he termed the submarine foundation or footings only, the footings being that portion of the foundation structure which is embedded in the ocean floor and on which the legs of the tower rest. Moran, Proctor had more extensive experience and an enviable reputation as designers of that type of foundation. The design of the heavy structural components, such as the legs, the braces, if any, and the platform would, in Mr. Anderson's contemplation at least, remain the responsibility of his firm. However, since the design of the footings was most directly concerned with such oceanographic considerations as ocean floor composition, soil-bearing intensities, velocities of underwater tidal currents, bottom scour, bathymetry profiles, and the like, it was agreed on June 1, 1954, that the studies of these factors would be undertaken by the Moran, Proctor firm, including the determination of probable maximum wind velocities and wave heights likely to be encountered at the various sites.

On the other hand, on July 22, 1954, then Commander, now Captain, J. J. Albers (CEC), USN, assigned to the Moran, Proctor firm the investiga-

[3] The members of the board were Commander J. J. Albers, Commander F. L. Biggs, Lieutenant La Porte, and D. Y. Taylor, with S. S. Swindells as recorder.

tion of factors leading to the design of all the heavy structural components of the five towers, including the footings, the legs, the braces, if any, and the structural frame of the platform as its responsibility under the joint venture with the Anderson-Nichols Co., the latter being relegated to the architectural layout of the interior of the platforms and engineering for the utilities systems. Captain Albers testified that the reasons for dictating this division of responsibility were that

1. the entire structure functions as a unit and its three components should, therefore, be designed by one organization;

2. the Navy wanted to utilize the experience of the Moran, Proctor firm in the designing of heavy marine structures; and

3. this was the most feasible manner in which to expedite the work.

It is uncontroverted, however, that Moran, Proctor's participation in the project was brought about through the invitation of Mr. Anderson; that Navy had neither approached the Moran, Proctor firm nor solicited their participation prior to the invitation extended by Mr. Anderson; and that the Navy initially left the determination of the division of responsibility for the work up to the two firms comprising the joint venture. While the edict by the Navy on July 22, 1954, specifying the division of work applied at the time it was made only to the feasibility study and report, it was followed by the two firms later in their actual design of the project.

THE FEASIBILITY STUDY

On the recommendation of the Moran, Proctor firm, the First Naval District awarded a contract to the Woods Hole Oceanographic Institution of Woods Hole, Massachusetts, a nongovernmental, nonprofit research organization, for the purpose of aiding in the determination of the environmental forces of wind velocities and wave heights to which the towers would be exposed during their twenty-year anticipated life and thus arrive at some criteria of forces to be incorporated into the design. The Woods Hole Institution also had the responsibility for positioning the towers and determining the water depths at the various sites. In the case of Texas tower No. 4:

a. Loran type A navigation equipment, accurate to within half a mile, was used for position determination. It was found several years later through a survey conducted in October, 1960, by the U.S. Coast and Geodetic Survey that the tower was actually 0.6 of a nautical mile from where it was thought to be all that time.

b. The water depth was actually found to be 185 feet instead of the 180 feet thought at the time of marking the spot by a buoy. This error could be attributed either to an error in positioning as placing it within a deeper fathom line or to bottom sand ripples 5 feet in height, the high point in roughly an acre of coverage being the return received by the echo sounding equipment.

Other aspects considered in the feasibility study included the configuration, or size and shape, of the towers, which would be governed in large measure by the prevailing environment of natural forces. The aspects of configuration most immediately affected by these forces were the height of the platform above mean sea level, the number and size of the legs, and braced legs as opposed to unbraced legs for a water depth of 185 feet.

The platform elevation

The maximum intensity of a wave force occurs close to the maximum elevation of the wave crest. If these large intensities of wave force should be applied to large areas such as the platform, excessive total forces would result. Therefore, safety and integrity of the platforms requires that the platforms themselves always be definitely above the crests of any waves.

This criterion is confirmed by the loss of two oil-drilling rigs in the Gulf of Mexico which succumbed to waves striking the platforms.

The Woods Hole Institution also made a study of the weather reports for the preceding twenty years and found that the maximum wind velocity of 128 miles per hour occurred during a hurricane in 1938, and that the average height of the 10 per cent highest waves was 66 feet, as computed during an easterly storm in November 1945. According to theory, the height of one wave in every thousand will be one and a half times higher than the average 10 per cent highest waves. This theory has been fairly well substantiated for waves up to 20 feet high but not higher, because of the difficulty of observing and measuring higher waves. However, the theory is presumed to hold true for waves of greater heights than 20 feet. The measurement is from trough to crest which, as a rough rule of thumb, means that approximately 60 per cent of the wave would be above and approximately 40 per cent below mean sea level.

A large and unresolved uncertainty remains concerning the maximum height of waves that may strike the platform supports during its useful life. While the maximum possible height is uncertain, there seems to be a definite probability that one such wave (gigantic) may strike the platform supports within a period of 20 years. Our design has proceeded on the basis that the occurrence of one such wave may cause stresses in the structural elements of the platform supports into the plastic range of stress for the structural materials. However, if the platform itself is not struck by such a wave, the ultimate safety of the platform and the personnel on it will not be endangered, and it is believed that repairs or replacements of overstressed elements can be made if such a wave occurs.

After considerable study, it was decided that the probability of 60-foot waves occurring several times during a period of 20 years at any of the locations definitely exists. . . . Such waves are associated with northeasterly or easterly storms rather than with hurricanes, and the wind velocities associated with such waves are those of storms. . . . Under hurricane conditions with high wind velocities it is not probable that waves over 40 feet will occur. It is, however, definitely possible under these high-wind conditions that the waves will be unstable and will be breaking due to wind forces and independently of bottom drag conditions.

These considerations give rise to design criteria of 125-mile-per-hour wind in combination with a breaking wave 35 feet high, and this was concurred in by the scientists of the Woods Hole Oceanographic Institution.

Preliminary evaluations indicated that a height for the lowest elements of the platform above mean sea level of 67 feet was desirable. In view of all uncertainties concerning maximum waves, a single wave with a height of 90 feet seems possible in deep water. If the bottom of the platform is at elevation 67 feet, a 4.5-foot clearance for the crest of such a wave is provided. Further, . . . bottom of platform at elevation 67 provides clearance for a 96-foot wave.[4]

The number of the legs

The need for minimum interference to the passage of waves led to a design configuration of a three-legged structure, the minimum number to support a platform, and to the use of legs of a minimum diameter consistent with the load-carrying capacity and the elimination of any auxiliary legs since "additional supporting members increase wave forces as rapidly as increased resistance is obtained." A three-legged configuration for an offshore structure is rather unusual in that most, if not all, of the oil-drilling rigs in the Gulf of Mexico use legs in multiples of two. A three-legged structure contains no factor of safety because

an inherent characteristic of the three-legged structure is that loss of one leg by any accidental means will result in complete and immediate loss of the platform and personnel. Therefore, accident protection in the form of increased size and strength of the main legs or supplementary legs which will not contribute to vertical support of the platform under normal conditions, but which will prevent complete loss in case of an accident, is strongly recommended.

The recommendation was not adopted on the ground that the tower could be evacuated before any vessel out of control could strike the platform supports and topple the tower.

Testimony by Mr. L. B. DeLong, president of the DeLong Corp., a pioneer in the design and construction of offshore platforms, supported the

---

[4] These computations apparently assume that 70 per cent of the wave would be above mean sea level rather than the 60 per cent mentioned earlier as a "rough rule of thumb."

use of the three-legged structure as proper for the purpose of keeping the resistance to wave passage to the minimum consistent with load-bearing capacity.

The hydrodynamic forces of the waves were found to be of far greater significance than the aerodynamic forces of winds acting against the tower. Keeping the resistance to these forces to a minimum outweighed the safety factor inherent in the incorporation of a greater number of legs and the recommendation for the installation of auxiliary legs.

The braced underwater foundation

Generally speaking, a water depth of 100 feet is treated as the point where legs must be braced to insure the integrity of support of an off-shore platform. It was found in the feasibility study that

1. The bending moments under design wave forces in cylindrical legs approximately 250 feet in length between ocean bottom and bottom of platform without bracing required unreasonably large diameter legs.
2. Even with large diameter cylindrical legs the deflections of the platform without bracing were greatly in excess of the design criteria.

It was, therefore, concluded that tower No. 4, in a water depth of 185 feet, would require braced legs.

The feasibility study and the report thereon were completed in October 1954 at a cost of $130,000, of which the Anderson-Nichols Co. received $60,000 and the Moran, Proctor firm $70,000. The feasibility report established that it was both feasible and practical to erect such offshore platforms in the Atlantic Ocean for the purpose intended.

THE DESIGN OF THE TEXAS TOWERS

Following the completion of the feasibility study, the district public works officer, by a letter of intent dated December 7, 1954, and subsequently implemented by BuDocks contract NOy–86107, awarded a contract for the design and preparation of specifications for all five Texas towers. This, too, was awarded to the joint venture of Anderson-Nichols Co. and Moran, Proctor, Mueser & Rutledge. However, in contrast to the original contemplation of the person who invited their particiaption in the venture, the Moran, Proctor firm undertook the responsibility for the design of all the heavy structural components, with the Anderson-Nichols Co. relegated to the layout of living quarters, equipment rooms, and utilities systems engineering.

Physical description

In general, the towers took the form of a multidecked platform in the

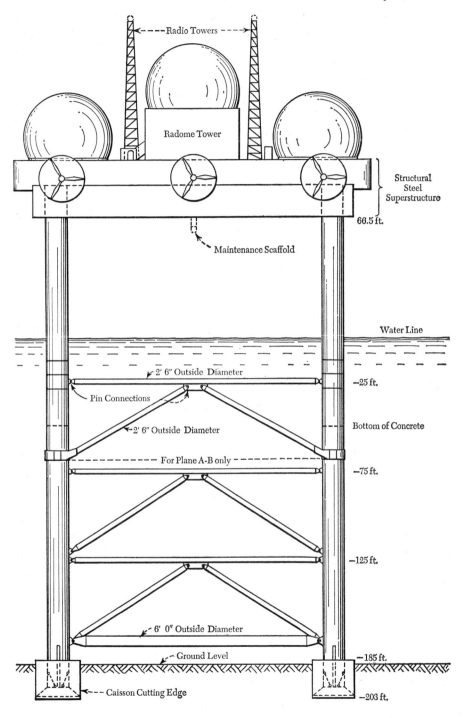

Radio Towers

Radome Tower

Structural
Steel
Superstructure

66.5 ft.

Maintenance Scaffold

Water Line

2′ 6″ Outside Diameter

−25 ft.

Pin Connections

2′ 6″ Outside Diameter

Bottom of Concrete

For Plane A-B only

−75 ft.

−125 ft.

6′ 0″ Outside Diameter

Ground Level

−185 ft.

Caisson Cutting Edge

−203 ft.

shape of an equilateral triangle 155 feet on a side attached to three legs, the diameters of which differ somewhat from tower to tower. The platform in its various decks contained equipment rooms, living quarters, radomes, radio antennas, and a heliport for the helicopters, a principal means of rapid transportation to and from the tower.

After all the equipment, such as radars, diesel generators, evaporators, and the like, had been installed, the gross weight of the platform was some 5,000 to 5,500 tons. Without the equipment its structural gross weight was about 4,300 tons.

The legs were lettered for identification purposes A, B, and C, and the sides between the legs were called the A–B plane, the B–C plane, and the A–C plane. In tower No. 4, the B leg was the most northerly, the A leg the most southerly, and the C leg the most easterly or seaward, so that the A–B side became the side closest to the shore. The hollow A and B legs were used for the storage of fuel oil while the C leg was used as the intake for sea water from which the evaporators made fresh water. Other fuel storage tanks were installed inside the lowest deck of the platform. As installed, the A–B side of the tower was on a bearing of N. 26° E.

The legs themselves, in tower No. 4, consisted of a ring of steel $1\frac{3}{16}$ inch thick with a diameter of 12½ feet. (See page 161.) An inner ring or core of 8 feet in diameter extended from the base of the platform to 50 feet below the surface of the water, and between those two rings of steel cement was poured to provide greater rigidity.

The pin-connected bracings of tower No. 4 were installed underwater at depths of −25 feet, −75 feet, and −125 feet, the horizontal braces being affixed to the legs at those levels with the diagonal braces extending from the midpoint of each down to the legs and next lower horizontal brace.

The footings beneath each leg were 25 feet in diameter, filled with cement, and sunk or embedded into the ocean floor to a depth of 18 feet.

Design specifications

Structural engineers use the term "static" and "dynamic" in differentiating between types of forces applied to a structure. While there is some difficulty in precisely defining the differences between the two, the term "dynamic" is generally used where the forces are instantaneously variable in either magnitude or direction, thus subjecting a structure to instantaneous fluctuations of force. Mr. Brewer, chief engineer of Brewer Engineering Laboratories, Inc., used the analogy of a diver at the end of a diving board. If he remains still, his weight will exert a static force on the board. If he jumps up and down, he will impart an impulsive dynamic loading to the board by which, although there is no change in his weight, he will exert stresses on the board some three or four times his inert static-weight stress. Although the sea is in constant, unrelenting random motion, in the design of the towers merely the static force of a single breaking wave 35 feet high was taken as the basis for computing the stress exerted against the tower by the sea. In a motion study conducted by Mr. Brewer on tower No. 4, at a time when the upper braces on the A–B side were admittedly not functioning, he found that a series of waves 10 to 11 feet high caused greater stress and greater movement of the platform than did waves 30 feet high. This was due to the peculiar spacing between 10-foot waves, roughly the dimension of the tower, so that these waves could strike all three tower legs simultaneously. The peculiar spacing between 30-foot waves, however, was such that only one wave would strike the legs at one time.

No model studies for the exposure to such hydrodynamic forces were conducted, on the grounds that

1. it was impossible to duplicate the random nature of the sea waves in an artificial basin; and

2. the design engineers were told that a Reynolds number, by which the miniature model is magnified through mathematical multiplication to the actual size of the tower itself, would not be applicable in this case.

The K-type brace with pin connections, as opposed to welded connections, was incorporated into the design for the underwater bracing system on tower No. 4 on the ground that the pin connection would eliminate secondary bending stresses because of its lesser rigidity. In the original design the clearance or tolerance between the 8-inch diameter of the pin and the hole into which it was to be inserted was $\frac{1}{64}$ inch.

All the towers were designed to withstand the forces of a 125-mile-per-hour wind coupled with a breaking wave 35 feet high.

Shortly after the award of the contract for the design and specifications of the Texas towers to the Moran, Proctor firm, the services of a Mr. Theodore Kuss were engaged as an employee of that firm. Mr. Kuss was the inventor of a method of erecting offshore structures in deep water. His patent provided, in essence, that the template, consisting of the legs and their braces, would be completely fabricated in a shipyard, towed to the site in a horizontal attitude, and, through the flooding of buoyancy chambers, upended or tipped up to a vertical position. (See page 164.)

Up until the time of his employment with the Moran, Proctor firm, the patented Kuss method of erecting towers had not been considered by the Navy's Bureau of Yards and Docks as a process to be utilized in erecting tower No. 4. This method had never actually been used before its adaptation for tower No. 4 and has reportedly been used but once since then. In the Kuss patent it is stated:

Another object of the invention is the provision of a structure of such a shape that it may be built economically and still have the required strength to resist stresses due to floating the same on water and those due to erection of the structure underwater.

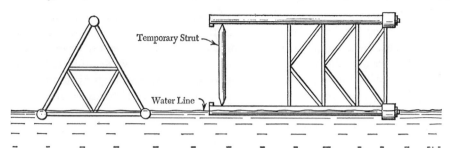

Temporary Strut

Water Line

Ground Level

a. (end view)   b. (side view)

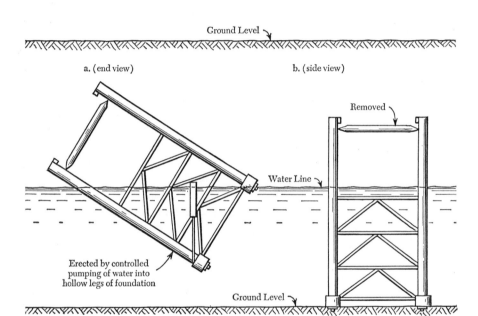

Removed

Water Line

Erected by controlled
pumping of water into
hollow legs of foundation

Ground Level

c. (side view)   d. (side view)

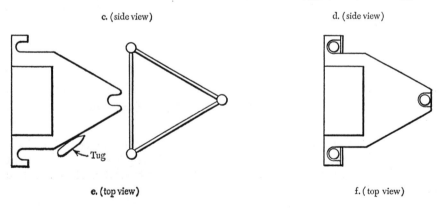

Tug

e. (top view)   f. (top view)

The patent also contains a statement to the effect that a sudden swinging about the horizontal axis of the template might set up undesirable stresses in the caisson and create dangerous conditions. In the actual process of tipping up the tower No. 4 template, it rotated, through unequal flooding of the buoyancy chambers, 17° in one direction, then 34° in the opposite direction about the horizontal axis before being brought under control. The design of the template did not allow for the stresses that might be exerted on the structure during the towing and tipping up operations.

In tower No. 4,

The design contemplated that the separate foundation structure would be provided with a temporary construction platform which was limited in weight to 375 tons by the flotation and upending requirements of the horizontally constructed foundation structure. The design planned that the temporary construction platform would be used for the operations of securing the foundation structure to the ocean bottom by means of steel pipe piles driven through skirts at the bottoms of the foundation legs and for concrete filling of the bottom portions of the foundation structure and the placing of concrete linings in the upper portions of the foundation legs.

Then the permanent platform would be floated into position between the legs after their embedment and strengthening through concrete lining.

The contract price for the design and specifications of the five towers amounted to $600,000, of which the Moran, Proctor firm was to receive $450,000 and the Anderson-Nichols Co. $150,000. Contract administration costs and change orders increased the total cost to $953,000.

THE CONSTRUCTION OF THE TEXAS TOWERS

By a letter dated December 29, 1954, the district public works officer of the First Naval District requested an acceleration of the design of Texas tower No. 2 on Georges Bank. The shipyard construction of tower No. 2 was begun only one month after the design was completed. Tower No. 2 was constructed under a cost-plus-fixed-fee BuDocks contract NOy–88201 by the DeLong Corp. in a joint venture with Raymond Concrete Pile Co. and was completed in November 1955.

The initial design for tower No. 2 called for installation of I-bar link bracing. DeLong objected to the bracing on the ground that from his experience as a pioneer in this field, he knew that it could be built differently by eliminating the bracing and increasing the depth of the embedment of caissons, and the design engineers permitted this to be done.

The DeLong method of constructing tower No. 2 consisted of the platform being first supported by auxiliary legs from which the permanent legs were lowered, embedded, and stiffened before the weight of the platform was transferred to the permanent legs. The construction of tower No. 2 in the use of the DeLong method proceeded without incident. It is located in 56 feet of water, possesses legs 10 feet in diameter with a 15-foot diameter for embedment purposes which extends from a depth of 48 to 50 feet below the ocean floor to 15 feet above for abrasion protection. Its platform is at an elevation of 61 feet above mean sea level.

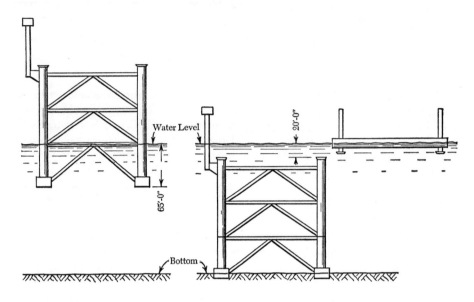

a. Template floating out with control towers

b. Template sunk to bottom and leveled with temporary platform approaching

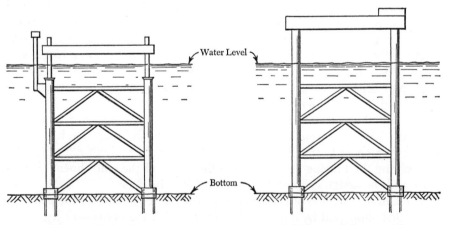

c. Temporary platform floated over template and jacked up; piling driven

d. Temporary platform removed; permanent platform floated over template with deckhouse complete, jacked up, and welded off.

On November 20, 1955, tower No. 2 was subjected to a severe storm with sustained winds from the northeast of 75 miles per hour and waves of 45 to 50 feet in height. Breaking waves from opposing seas caused by tidal currents or shifting winds threw water against the bottom of the platform four times during the course of the storm. The "flying bridge" or rotating maintenance platform suspended 14 feet below the tower platform suffered some damage from wave action. However, there was no structural damage to the tower itself.

Invitations to bid for the construction of towers Nos. 1, 3, 4, and 5 were issued by the district public works officer on July 5, 1955. During the bidding period tower No. 5 was eliminated because of fund limitations. Under the bidding procedure the prospective builders were permitted to bid on each tower separately and on any combination of the towers. The DeLong-Raymond joint venture was the low bidder on all the towers individually except tower No. 4 and all combinations of towers except combinations where tower No. 4 was involved. Accordingly, it was the recommendation of Captain Albers that the DeLong-Raymond joint venture be awarded the contract for the construction of towers Nos. 1 and 3 and that the J. Rich Steers–Morrison–Knudsen joint venture be awarded the contract for the construction of tower No. 4. Dr. Charyk, undersecretary of the Air Force, testified that fund limitations required the elimination of tower No. 1. This had the effect, as well, of eliminating the DeLong Corp., which had directed the successful construction of the first of the towers, from any further participation in the construction of any of the remaining Texas towers.

Mr. DeLong testified that his corporation, through his chief engineer, Mr. Suderow, since deceased, had an agreement with the design engineers that if his corporation were the low bidder on tower No. 4, it would be permitted to construct it in accordance with a method proposed by DeLong and referred to as scheme B. (See page 166.) This was emphatically denied by both Captain Albers and the design engineers. However, as proof of his contention, Mr. DeLong testified that if he had been required to build a pin-connected tower under the horizontal tow and vertical tip-up of the Kuss method he would not have submitted a bid and, in fact, "would not have wanted any part of it." His testimony that there was an implied or tacit agreement with the design engineers was substantiated by documentation furnished pursuant to a *subpoena duces tecum* served on Mr. DeLong requiring him to furnish all plans, drawings, proposals, submissions, contracts, and agreements prepared or made by the DeLong Corp. in connection with, in contemplation of, or in the solicitation of bids for, the construction of Texas towers Nos. 1, 3, and 4. The documents produced included the instructions by the DeLong Corp. to its possible subcontractors in preparing their bids, a memorandum of agreement and joint venture agreement with Raymond Concrete Pile Co. for the disposition of barges proposed for use in construction of tower No. 4, and a drawing dated October 17, 1955, similar to scheme B. The DeLong plan essentially called for welded connections for the braces, and a vertical tow of the template to the site. His objections to the use of pin connections were that "the sea never gets tired"— its constant random motion would only serve to wear the pin connections – and that there would be no means by which to evaluate the stresses imposed on the template during a horizontal tow to site and tip-up, and there would be the danger that one or two legs might touch bottom first, resulting in even greater stress. He also objected to the time during which the tower would be at the mercy of the sea in floating the permanent platform into position between the three legs after they were upright.

On the other hand, there was introduced into the record a memorandum which Dr. Rutledge, of the design engineering firm, prepared of a conference with Captain Garner Clark, USN, Assistant Chief of the Bureau of Yards and Docks, at which Captain Clark stated that he had denied DeLong permission to submit a bid based on an alternate design for the construction of Texas tower No. 4. Moreover, Dr. Rutledge testified that the design engineers had no authority to make any agreement such as Mr. DeLong alleged, nor did they do so.

The J. Rich Steers, Inc.–Morrison–Knudsen bid for tower No. 4 was almost identical to its bid for tower No. 3 even though tower No. 4 was to be erected in far deeper water, would require a great deal more work in the fabrication and installation of the bracing, and, generally, was a far more ambitious undertaking. Mr. Rau, Vice-President and Chief Engineer of J. Rich Steers, Inc., testified that his corporation had had a great deal of experience in marine construction but lacked experience in the use of jacks and jacking assemblies for elevating the platforms upon the legs. Mr. Rau stated:

Therefore we associated ourselves with Morrison–Knudsen in September of 1955 because they had with them a man named Lucas, who was a former partner of DeLong's for a number of years, and had experience, a number of experiences, in jacking up the platforms.

Mr. Lucas was then under a prohibition by agreement with the DeLong Corp. not to compete or assist anyone to compete in the type of enterprise in which the DeLong Corp. was engaged. The DeLong Corp. brought suit against Lucas and was awarded damages of $647,000 plus interest for breach of the agreement as constituting the proximate cause of the loss of the contracts by DeLong for the construction of Texas towers Nos. 3 and 4.[5]

A lump sum contract NOy–88202 for $16,431,000 was awarded to J. Rich

---

[5] *DeLong Corporation* v. *Lucas* (1959), 176 Fed. Supp. 104 affirmed on appeal (1960), 278 F. 2d 804.

Steers, Inc.–Morrison–Knudsen as a joint venture for the construction of towers Nos. 3 and 4 in November 1955.

Steers owned the greater percentage of the joint venture and assumed construction management and responsibility for the project with Morrison–Knudsen furnishing primarily support personnel. Continental Copper & Steel Industries, Inc., received the subcontract for fabrication from Steers and leased the South Portland, Maine, basin for the prefabrication work.

The construction of Texas tower No. 3 proceeded by utilizing temporary legs to bear the weight of the platform until the permanent legs were lowered, embedded, and stiffened. It was placed on Nantucket Shoals in 82 feet of water. Its legs have a constant diameter of 14 feet and are embedded into the ocean floor to a depth of 60 feet. Its construction appears to have progressed without incident except that one permanent leg became tilted in being lowered to the ocean bottom, and this was not corrected. Tower No. 3 was completed late in 1956.

During the fabrication of Texas tower No. 4 Steers requested several change orders which deviated from the original design, and these were approved by the design engineers and the Navy's Bureau of Yards and Docks, the latter also having previously approved the design specifications. These changes had several major consequences:

a. In permitting the substitution of a permanent platform for the originally contemplated temporary one, it meant that the permanent platform would be jacked up above the water before the legs had been embedded into the ocean floor and before any concrete stiffening had been placed in the legs.

b. Without the legs first being embedded, there was insufficient draft (water depth) above the upper panels of bracing to float the platform into position between them. For this reason the upper panels of bracing had to be folded down in the initial stages of construction to be connected up later underwater.

c. In order to fold down the upper panel of bracings, an increase in the tolerance between the size of the pin and the holes into which they were to be inserted was granted. Difficulty in fabrication had required an increase in tolerance from the $\frac{1}{64}$ inch called for in the design to $\frac{1}{16}$ inch. For the upper panels of bracing this was further increased to ⅛ inch.

The design engineers had first approved, then later disapproved, the method proposed by Steers for lashing down the diagonal struts during the tow to site and transmitted to Steers certain required modifications. It is inferred from the testimony of Mr. Rau that the modifications required by the design engineers reduced the strength of the lashings from that in the Steers proposal.

The template (consisting of the three legs and their permanent and temporary bracings) and, as a separate element, the permanent platform were towed to sea from Portland Harbor on June 28, 1957. The template was floated in a horizontal position resting on the A–B plane in accordance with the Kuss patent.

Mr. Kuss had granted a royalty-free license to his employers, Moran, Proctor, Mueser & Rutledge, who, in turn, granted an identical license to the United States government for the construction of tower No. 4.

A storm, which did not exceed the criteria for the towing operation, occurred at the site and delayed the tip-up process. It was discovered that the two diagonals in the upper panel of braces on the A–B side had broken loose from their lashings and were damaged. During the tip-up process these diagonals sheared off their connecting pin plates and were lost.

The Navy's officer in charge of construction, Commander Edmund Foster (CEC), USN, the designers, and the contractor held various discussions over the action which should be taken in view of this structural mishap. The two alternatives were to return the template to port to effect repairs or to attempt repairs at sea. Commander Foster declined to assume responsibility for the decision. Conversely, the contractor denied making the decision and testified that the responsibility had to rest with the Navy. The design engineers disclaimed any responsibility for the decision. All the parties concerned, however, agreed that the other party's decision in attempting repairs at sea was correct.

The platform was towed into position between the three legs (now in a vertical position), and sea swells of about 3 feet in height caused it to dent the three legs, the indentations being an average of 10 feet high, 6 to 8 feet wide, and about 10 to 12 inches deep. The plating of the legs exposed to the crushing action of the platform framework was $1\frac{3}{16}$ inch thick, which was too thin, since it was not supported by the concrete stiffening, to resist the force. It was agreed that the contractor's operations were carried out in accordance with the erection procedure contemplated by the plans and specifications. On July 12, 1957, the Bureau of Yards and Docks agreed to finance the direct costs of strengthening the legs at their indentations, which ultimately would end up about 10 feet underwater after the embedment of the footings.

On July 8, 1957, before concrete stiffening was put in the legs, the heavy permanent platform was jacked up clear of the water.

The water depth, as noted previously, turned out to be 185 feet instead of 180 feet as originally contemplated in the design. Also, the total range of tide was measured at $3\frac{1}{2}$ feet instead of the original estimate of one foot. Thus, in order to achieve a safe clearance of the platform above mean sea level, it was necessary to modify the design by

a. reducing the embedment of the footings from 20 feet to 18 feet; and

b. raising the platform to the maximum extent permitted by the design.

These changes resulted in a platform elevation of 66.5 feet instead of the 67 feet called for in the design.

REPAIRS TO TEXAS TOWER NO. 4

Installation of the collar connections

Agreement apparently having been reached to attempt repairs of the tower at sea, the design engineers, under contract with the builder, designed collar connections encircling legs *A* and *B* to secure the replacement diagonals to the legs. (See page 172.) Dardelet bolts[6] were inserted through the collars into the legs to keep the collars from moving vertically. The installation of these bolts required underwater cutting and fitting to close tolerances, and the repair was only as good as the capability and integrity of the divers working under adverse conditions at an underwater depth of 65 feet. Moreover, the repair was made even more difficult by the reactions of the legs to the forces of the sea in that, even at this time, the tower's foundation was in motion. These repairs were completed by November 1957 and the tower was accepted by the Navy from the contractor. The Navy did not conduct an underwater inspection prior to turning the tower over to the Air Force. In the motion picture film of the construction of tower No. 4, which was shown during the hearings, a ball, suspended so as to move freely, was in rather violent motion at the time of Air Force acceptance.

By the summer of 1958 the Air Force personnel operating the tower had complained of sensations of considerable movement of the platform with frequencies of 15 to 18 cycles per minute. Although those who observed the motions had no means of properly measuring their extent, the motions did not occur during severe weather conditions, as the maximum wind velocity and wave height during that period were about 30 knots and 15 feet, respectively. However, the frequency of the horizontal oscillations gave some clue as to the stiffness of the tower (the design frequency was 37 to 46 cpm), and the design engineers made a special analysis to determine whether or not the replaced diagonals on the *A–B* side were functioning. This analysis led to the conclusion that the upper tier of bracing on the *A–B* side was not functioning; this, in turn, prompted an analysis of the

---

[6] A Dardelet bolt is a patented device similar in appearance to an ordinary button-head bolt, except that the shank is serrated rather than smooth. The function of the serrated shank is to hold the bolt tightly in the hole which is prepared for it. Dardelet bolts are always driven, rather than simply slipped, into their holes.

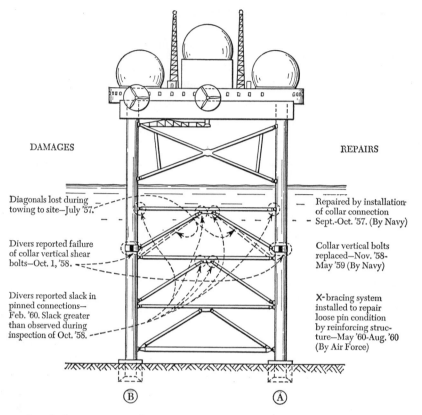

DAMAGES

Diagonals lost during
towing to site—July '57.

Divers reported failure
of collar vertical shear
bolts—Oct. 1, '58.

Divers reported slack in
pinned connections—
Feb. '60. Slack greater
than observed during
inspection of Oct. '58.

REPAIRS

Repaired by installation
of collar connection
Sept.-Oct. '57. (By Navy)

Collar vertical bolts
replaced—Nov. '58-
May '59 (By Navy)

X-bracing system
installed to repair
loose pin condition
by reinforcing struc-
ture—May '60-Aug. '60
(By Air Force)

Ⓑ   Ⓐ

strength of the tower under this condition and the amplitude of motion
which might indicate danger. It was estimated that, if the tower leg steel
were stressed to the yield point, the tower could stand a 125-mile-per-hour
wind combined with a 36-foot wave or an 87-mile-per-hour wind combined
with a 67-foot wave. The horizontal deflection at the same time would be
about 6 inches. Because of this motion and the fact that the tower had not
yet experienced a hurricane, the tower was totally evacuated of personnel
in advance of Hurricane Daisy in August of 1958.

The Brewer Engineering Laboratories, Inc., of Marion, Massachusetts
received a subcontract from Hallicrafters Co. to conduct a motion study
of the tower during the fall of 1958 and winter of 1959. The Brewer study
had as its purpose

a. to experimentally measure the translational (horizontal) and
rotational (twisting) excursions and corresponding frequencies (the
number of times per minute it did each) of the tower platform from
aerodynamic and hydrodynamic forces;

b. to measure the caisson bending stresses at the lower deck; and

c. to investigate the integrity of the subsea truss work (the functioning of the underwater braces).

Prior to undertaking the experiment, two conferences were held, one at the Air Force Cambridge Research Center in Bedford, Massachusetts, where it was revealed that the Air Force was interested in rotational motions and frequencies of the platform because of these influences on radar search equipment; and the other at the offices of Moran, Proctor, Mueser & Rutledge, who were interested in caisson-bending at the lower deck and the integrity of the upper tier of bracing in the A–B plane.

At both of these conferences the integrity of portions of the underwater truss work was questioned.

Mr. Brewer asserted that Mr. Kuss had told him that all he (Kuss) required was a measurement from Brewer of the natural frequency of the tower, and Kuss could then compute all other facets of the tower's functioning.

The matter of the final tolerances authorized on the clevis joints[7] was also unclear. In the meeting of November 12, 1958, Mr. Kuss indicated that tower motions of plus or minus 2 inches could occur without taking up known clearances of the pins in the first truss bay beneath the ocean surface. Commander Foster also stated that his office in Bath, Maine, had found it necessary to approve an increase in tolerance in certain instances greater than those initially called for in the Moran-Proctor structural drawings because of difficulties encountered in fabricating the templates.[8]

During the winter of 1958–59, winds to 65 knots and waves to 30 feet were experienced over a five-month survey. From the Brewer study the following was found:

a. The observed natural tower frequencies (17 to 23 cpm translational and 23 to 24 cpm rotational) were approximately one-third of those predicted by the designer's theoretical calculations.

b. The subsea truss work was essentially ineffective for excursions up to 3 inches and rotations to 0.1°. It was expected that the clearances in the pin connections would be taken up with increasing deflections of the tower platform.

c. Positive evidence of the fact that relative motion between members

---

[7] Clevis joints are the connections by which horizontal and diagonal bracing members were attached to the legs.

[8] The design specified a 1/64-inch tolerance for all pin connections. The pins were 8 inches in diameter and weighed between 300 and 400 pounds. They had to be inserted through five layers of plates, in some instances as much as 125 feet above the ground. The close tolerance and circumstances of fabrication created awkward problems for the builders. Commander Foster therefore approved an increase in the tolerance to 1/16 inch in all pin connections on the tower except the top level of bracing, where the tolerance was increased to 1/8.

of the underwater truss system occurred during the ever-present tower oscillations was provided by hydrophones. The metallic rumbling noises heard beneath the tower were coincident with the frequency of tower motion. They were interpreted to result from the movement of very heavy metal objects.

d. Ten-foot waves produced the greatest tower motions and therefore the greatest stresses of waves up to 30 feet in height experienced during the study.

e. Hydrodynamic forces (waves) were far more important than aerodynamic forces (wind).

Mr. Brewer recommended that, if the extent of the platform excursions and rotations was objectionable, then an investigation should be conducted to determine whether greater rigidity might be achieved by installing bracing above water to reduce the bending moments of the legs. This suggestion was limited to a means by which to reduce platform motion and was not intended as a means of strengthening the tower. Mr. Brewer testified that a complete stress reanalysis would have to be made because such bracing would increase the resistance to wave passage and, therefore, could conceivably have the effect of actually weakening the tower.

From merely a cursory computation which was not required as a portion of his responsibility under his contract, Mr. Brewer found that if the tower legs were to have no bracing, the weight of the platform alone would collapse the legs without any wind or wave force being exerted against the tower.

The design engineers, however, found fault with the Brewer study by the following comment:

During the fall of 1958 a subcontract was given to the Brewer Engineering Laboratories, Inc., to perform motion studies on the tower. These consisted of horizontal acceleration measurements in the vicinity of each of the three legs correlated with strain gage measurements on the legs and simultaneous observations of wind and wave direction and amplitude. These studies were not very successful mostly because it was very difficult to determine the true translations which involved the multiple integration of the curves obtained from rather irregular data.

The suspicions that the upper tier of bracing in the A–B plane was not functioning properly were confirmed by diver inspection by Marine Contractors, Inc., East Boston, Massachusetts, under Navy contract NBY–22027. In a report dated November 25, 1958, they stated in substance the following:

a. The pins in the horizontal brace at −23 feet at the midpoint of the A–B plane were loose on the A diagonal and had withdrawn 9 inches on the B diagonal.

b. The Dardelet keeper plates on the *B* leg were loose and several of the studs and nuts were missing from them.

c. None of the Dardelet bolts on either side of the collar on the *A* leg were in place, either having sheared off or fallen out, and there was evidence of vertical motion of the collar on the caisson.

d. In tightening the collar bolts to a certain torque, they would be found looser within a day or two.

e. The *A* leg developed oil leaks which could not be repaired.

The responsibility for the failure of the Dardelet bolts on the *A* leg was not determinable. Although there was reason to believe that the contractor may not have installed these bolts in accordance with the plans, there was no way to demonstrate this conclusively. Conversely, it was possible that the bolts were correctly installed. As for the Dardelet bolts on the *B* leg, no failure was observed but roughly half were loose and some were not of design dimensions. The failure of the Dardelet bolts on the *A* leg permitted vertical motion of the collar on the *A* caisson. This movement was applying, and had applied for an unknown period of time, exceptional stresses on other bracing members, particularly in the *A–B* plane.

The First Naval District considered this failure of the Dardelet bolts a construction deficiency and required the contractor to replace them with T-bolts. Apparently Dardelet bolts are considered by some as nothing more than a temporary device. In the fall of 1958, after confirmation of the structural deficiency in the collar connections of the upper braces on the *A–B* side, the design engineers issued the first in what was to become a series of warnings on the structural integrity of the tower. In a letter dated September 18, 1958, Mr. Kuss wrote to the officer in charge of construction as follows:

In the meantime and if the collars cannot be tightened and the shear bolts replaced, we are compelled to warn you that a definite hazard exists to the safety of the tower and the personnel aboard in the event of a major hurricane passing directly over the tower location.

Replacement of the Dardelet bolts

The work to replace the Dardelet bolts with T-bolts began in November 1958 but was discontinued when about 50 per cent complete because of weather. None of the T-bolts were installed until the following year, and the entire repair was completed in May 1959. In the meantime, with the tower in this condition, it was exposed to five severe storms with maximum waves of 33 feet in height and winds up to 90 miles per hour. The design engineers certified that upon completion of the T-bolt installation the tower would be restored to its original design strength, and in a report dated June 1959, Marine Contractors, Inc., the diver firm, certified that repairs to the collar connections were satisfactory.

The cost of replacing the Dardelet bolts with T-bolts was taken from the original "Military construction program, Texas tower" appropriation. It was said that this repair reduced the tower movement to a lesser magnitude than at any time since its construction.

In August of 1959, the First Naval District awarded a contract to Moran, Proctor, Mueser & Rutledge for a motion study of the radome bases on towers No. 2 and No. 4. The report, dated September 16, 1959, was prepared at Air Force request to provide information as to whether or not the motion of the tower would be within the limits of acceptable tolerances for operational radar purposes. The study had nothing to do with the structural stability or instability of the tower. The completion of this report in September 1959 constituted the last item of work performed by the Navy for the Air Force in connection with Texas tower No. 4 up to the time of its collapse.

By January of 1960, less than a year after the collars were fixed, the operating personnel again complained of excessive platform motion. Marine Contractors, Inc., performed another underwater inspection in February 1960. In the report of Mr. Alan Crockett, general manager for Marine Contractors, Inc., the following statement appears:

> This concern did a similar survey on tower No. 4 last October [1958], and the results did not show the magnitude of clearance to be found in the pins that we have appreciated during this survey. We feel that there is approximately ¾ inch increase in clearance between the surveys. . . . The tower movement is very erratic in an oscillatory direction. . . . The noise factor heard on the tower in the vicinity of A caisson is resulting from the motion of the tower taking up total clearances in the pins and flanges on one side or the other to bringing the two metal surfaces together at the extremity of motion causing the metallic bang.

The condition of the tower at this time is illustrated on p. 172.

Loose pins and worn connections became a cause for considerable concern. On March 1, 1960, the Engineering Section of the 551st Aircraft Early Warning and Control wing at Otis Air Force Base telegraphed the 26th Air Division in Syracuse, New York, stating in substance that the 4604th Support Squadron had notified the 551st AEW&C wing of the excessive sway in the tower on January 20, 1960; that diver inspection in early February disclosed that pins had loosened from ⅛ inch tolerance to as much as one inch in some cases; that this prompted a meeting with the design engineers, Moran, Proctor, Mueser & Rutledge, on February 25, who recommended the installation of above-water bracing; that such bracing would cost from $400,000 to $500,000; and that these repairs must be accomplished on an emergency basis not later than August 1, 1960.

A copy of this teletypewriter exchange (TWX) was mailed to the First Naval District and is identified as unclassified message No. 0979.

Captain Thomas J. White (CEC), USN, the district public works officer of the First Naval District, had received a copy of the telegram from the Air Force personnel at Otis Air Force Base and had discussed with a Colonel Cipolla of the Air Force the motion difficulties being experienced at tower No. 4. The Bureau of Yards and Docks within his naval district had passed on the design and construction of this tower and, although it was obviously in further difficulty of an emergency nature, he took no action to ascertain the cause of the trouble. In a letter dated March 15, 1960, to Colonel Stephany of the Air Force, he advised that he did not want the Navy to become involved in what he had orally termed nickel and dime maintenance and repair, but that since "the motion difficulty appeared to be related to the original design," he would look favorably upon a request for the Navy to administer the engineering and repair contracts to correct the difficulty. In his testimony during the hearings he stated in substance that by "original design" he also included the collar connections for the replacement diagonals.

The Air Force did not accept the offer he profferred on behalf of the Navy and dealt directly this time with the original designers, Moran, Proctor, Mueser & Rutledge and the original builder, J. Rich Steers, Inc.

The design engineers issued another warning concerning the structural integrity of the tower and the safety of personnel on board. In his letter of April 1, 1960, Mr. Kuss stated as follows:

The loose pin connections are a very serious matter since there seems to be no way of satisfactorily remedying the condition. Furthermore, the condition is one which will tend to worsen at an increasing rate with time. This is because the looseness induces impact stresses in the pins and pin plates which are greater than for the nondynamic design assumptions and will become increasingly greater as the play in the joint enlarges.

. . . We have concluded that the only practical cure for the situation is the addition of new above-water braces which we have advocated and designed.

. . . Time is of the essence in the program for erecting new braces. The hurricane season has been pretty well established as beginning after the first week of August and the schedule for construction to be reasonably sure of accomplishment should be essentially complete by that time.

Installation of the X-bracing

The installation of the X-bracing above water was a matter of emergency because a condition existed which would result in the probable loss of the tower if it was not corrected. This bracing was installed at elevations of 9 feet to 58 feet above water in the area presenting maximum resistance to the passage of waves, and represented a scheme which was diametrically opposed to the original concept of keeping resistance to wave passage to a minimum. No effort was made to rectify the admittedly serious conditions of loose pins and worn connections underwater but, nonetheless, the design engineers on August 10, 1960, certified that the above-water X-bracing had restored the tower to its original design strength.

About a month later, on September 12, 1960, Hurricane Donna passed through the area. The actual maximum wind velocities and wave heights experienced at tower No. 4 from the effects of Hurricane Donna have not been clearly substantiated, other than admittedly having exceeded the original design criteria of 125 miles per hour for wind velocity and 35-foot breaking wave height. Some sources claim winds of 132 miles per hour and breaking waves of at least 50 feet in height. Others claim winds of 115 miles per hour and breaking waves of 65 feet in height, while still others claim waves of 75 feet in height, the latter purportedly being a measurement above mean sea level and not from trough to crest. Light structural steel for the exhaust vents, 8 feet above the base of the platform, which was 66.5 feet above mean sea level, was dented from wave action.

Repair of the flying bridge

The "flying bridge" or rotating maintenance scaffold suspended beneath the tower was torn loose (see page 179) and had to be repaired before divers could ascertain the damage to the underwater foundation.

J. Rich Steers, Inc., the original builders under contract with the Air Force, completed repair to the "flying bridge" on November 1, 1960, and inspections on November 11, 12, and 13 revealed the following damage:

a. The above-water X-bracing was cracked and fractured in its primary and secondary members.

b. The upper tier A diagonal was fractured.

c. The two diagonals in the second tier of bracing at the midpoint of the horizontal at elevation −75 feet had torn loose from their attachment and were moving freely. These damages were all on the A–B side.

Figure 5 illustrates this damage with the exception that at this time the lowest diagonal brace, shown as being fractured, presumably was still intact.

By item 4 of the contract between Steers and the Air Force of September 27, 1960, for repair of the scaffold and underwater inspection, Steers was requested to give the Air Force a report, if possible —

concerning the tower's present structural capacity or incapacity to withstand future storm conditions within the limits set by the original design criteria of winds up to 125 miles per hour in combination with breaking wave action having a crest height of 35 feet. This statement of the present structural stability and "storm worthiness" will be of key importance to the Air Force personnel evacuation procedures for Texas tower No. 4 to prevent the loss of life in future.

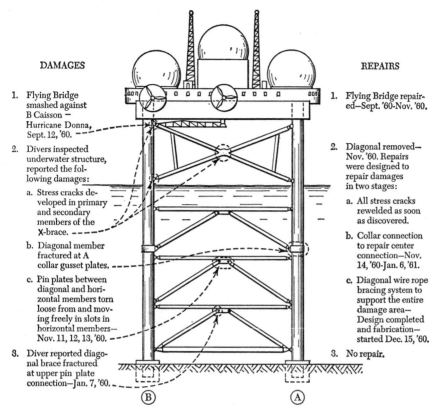

DAMAGES

1. Flying Bridge smashed against B Caisson — Hurricane Donna, Sept. 12, '60.

2. Divers inspected underwater structure, reported the following damages:

   a. Stress cracks developed in primary and secondary members of the X-brace.

   b. Diagonal member fractured at A collar gusset plates.

   c. Pin plates between diagonal and horizontal members torn loose from and moving freely in slots in horizontal members— Nov. 11, 12, 13, '60.

3. Diver reported diagonal brace fractured at upper pin plate connection—Jan. 7, '60.

REPAIRS

1. Flying Bridge repaired—Sept. '60-Nov. '60.

2. Diagonal removed— Nov. '60. Repairs were designed to repair damages in two stages:

   a. All stress cracks rewelded as soon as discovered.

   b. Collar connection to repair center connection—Nov. 14, '60-Jan. 6, '61.

   c. Diagonal wire rope bracing system to support the entire damage area— Design completed and fabrication— started Dec. 15, '60.

3. No repair.

At a meeting on September 28, 1960, Steers informed them that it would not attempt this work and referred the Air Force to the design engineers Moran, Proctor, Mueser & Rutledge for such a report.

On or about October 3, 1960, the Moran, Proctor firm agreed to do this work, but did not confirm it in writing until January 4, 1961. In their confirming letter, the design engineers agreed to

a. examine the results of the findings of damage;

b. evaluate any structural deficiencies that may be found; and

c. make recommendations as to repairs or modifications to be made, but the fee of $2,500 would not include the design or preparation of specifications for any new work required.

When the extent of the damage to the tower caused by Donna was reported to him on or about November 12, 1960, General Elder, commander of the Boston Air Defense Sector, became very much concerned because, throughout all the discussions over the tower's troubles, no one had advised him of the actual remaining strength of the tower. On November 16, 1960, General Elder called Mr. Kuss, asking him as the person probably best qualified, to advise him as to the tower's remaining strength. Mr. Kuss would not do so. Whereupon General Elder ordered the evacuation of as many of the personnel from the tower as possible, consistent with maintaining Air Force custody of expensive and classified equipment and providing the necessary support to the construction workers. The minimum necessary was determined to be fourteen military personnel, an insufficient number to operate the radar equipment as well, so General Elder ordered an operational stand-down of the radar equipment.

General Elder also established a continuing weather watch with orders to notify him of any weather forecasts predicting wind velocities of 50 knots or more in the tower No. 4 area.

Several meetings and discussions took place between the design engineers, the contractor, and representatives of the Air Force at which the damage was reviewed and the method of repair established with an estimated completion date of April 1, 1961.

Further repairs

The permanent repairs decided on at those meetings consisted of the installation of three strands of crossed cable bracings on the A–B side from the −125-foot level to the −25-foot level to be in virtual substitution of the upper two tiers or panels of K-braces, it being assumed that the lowest tier of bracing still possessed structural integrity. It was also decided to repair, through the installation of a sleeve, the attachment of the two diagonals on the horizontal brace at the −75-foot level, and this was completed on January 1, 1961, after much difficulty from winds and waves. To strengthen the legs at the lower level where the cable bracing was to be attached, concrete would be poured in, the materials for which would be delivered to the tower by the supply ship, *AKL–17*, a Military Sea Transportation Service vessel under lease to the Air Force and engaged solely in supplying the towers.

On December 12, 1960, the tower was subjected to another severe storm with high seas and winds of 87 knots. Then, on January 7, 1961, the divers discovered that the B diagonal in the lowest panel of bracing was broken.

A meeting was held in Steers' office in New York City on January 12, 1961, the initial purpose of which was to negotiate costs for repair of the tower.

Mr. Rau said that the cost analysis would have to be revised because of additional work required to fix the B diagonal in the lowest panel. He said that the broken diagonal was a very grave problem and that its loss would reduce the over-all structural integrity of the tower to approximately 55 per cent of its original design criteria even after the cable bracing had been installed, having learned this from Mr. Kuss by telephone earlier in the morning. Therefore, he stated, with the diagonal broken, the installation of the cross cable bracing alone would not of itself restore the integrity of the tower.

When Mr. Kuss joined the meeting in the afternoon, he stated that the tower was in critical condition with the lowest diagonal broken, and that it would require an entirely new scheme of repair and modification to bring the tower back to its original strength, at a probable cost of more than one million dollars.

It was at this same meeting that Mr. Kuss was again, and repeatedly, requested to advise as to the tower's remaining strength in accordance with the responsibility his firm had assumed within the meaning of item 4 of the Steers contract with the Air Force, namely:

This statement of the present structural stability and "storm worthiness" will be of key importance to the Air Force personnel evacuation procedures for Texas tower No. 4 to prevent the loss of life in the future.

In response to these requests Mr. Kuss would only say that he had made an analysis predicting what the structural integrity of the tower would be after the newly designed cable bracing was installed, and with the lowest diagonal considered ineffective. He estimated that the over-all integrity of the structure would be 55 per cent of its design strength, but he said that his figure could not be applied in direct proportions to the wind and to the wave criteria of the original design because these forces vary with the square of the wind velocity and only approximately with wave height.

Mr. Kuss testified before the subcommittee that a complete evaluation of the tower's strength would take about a week.

As a result of the meeting of January 12, 1961, it was decided to completely evacuate the tower by February 1, 1961. This was the date at which Steers would have used the grouting (sand, gravel, and cement) supplies and rewelded the X-bracing above water. Then the Air Force would have time in which to winterize and preserve equipment which would be left on board pending a return in the spring to resume repair under more favorable weather conditions.

The cable bracing had not been installed.

Three days later, January 15, 1961, at 7:25 on a Sunday evening, during a winter storm, Texas tower No. 4 collapsed. There were no survivors of the twenty-eight men on board.

The maximum prevailing weather at the time the tower disappeared, from the radar scope of the supply ship, consisted of winds of force 11 (approximately 55 knots) and waves 35 to 40 feet high.

The tower platform now rests on the ocean floor 200 yards from its original location on a southwest bearing of 242°. It rotated in a counterclockwise direction through 35° so that the A–B plane is now on a bearing of N. 9° W. rather than N. 26° E.

The platform still has affixed to it 115 feet of the *A* leg, the other two legs having broken off at the base of the platform. Each of the legs fractured at their footings with the possible exception of the *B* leg, which appears to have bent over at the footing without splitting. The footings are apparently in good condition without any evidence of fracture, movement, or scour.

DIRECT TESTIMONY

The testimony before the subcommittee of Mr. Philip Rutledge and Mr. Theodore Kuss of Moran, Proctor, Mueser & Rutledge, particularly concerning the final acts of this tragedy, is of special interest and is reproduced below from the transcript of the subcommittee hearings. A few repetitions and other inconsequential remarks have been deleted. The questioning is by Mr. James T. Kendall, chief counsel to the subcommittee. Mr. Rutledge and Mr. Kuss later amplified their answers to Mr. Kendall in response to questions by Senator Stennis, but no new or different information was elicited.

MR. KENDALL. Well, going to the early part of 1960, I believe that there was a report that a diver examination had revealed loose pins and worn connections in the underwater bracings at elevations −25 feet and −75 feet; is that right?

MR. RUTLEDGE. Yes, sir; Mr. Kuss attended a meeting at Otis Air Force Base where that report was presented.

MR. KENDALL. Did you consider that a — possibly I should direct this question to Mr. Kuss.

Mr. Kuss, did you consider that a serious consideration?

MR. KUSS. Well, it looked quite serious, for the reason that this looseness had developed in such a short time since the last diver inspection. It was quite mysterious to me and somewhat alarming. If it had happened over the four-year period that the tower was up, it wouldn't have been so puzzling. But there was about an 8-month gap between the diver's report that everything was tight and this report that designated loose pins.

MR. KENDALL. Was it your opinion, Mr. Kuss, that the situation was so serious that if it wasn't corrected, it would worsen at an accelerating rate and raise a serious question as to the safety of the tower?

MR. KUSS. As I said, because of the uncertainty of what was causing this apparent rapid loosening of the pins, it could have been quite serious. We were alarmed.

MR. KENDALL. Well——

SENATOR STENNIS. Pardon me, let's put a date on that. You perhaps did already, Mr. Counsel.

When was it, now, that you are talking about there, Mr. Kuss, when you say, "We were alarmed"? An approximate date?

Mr. Kuss. This is February 1960. I don't have the day; February 1960.

Mr. Kendall. You did write two letters with reference to the problem, didn't you, Mr. Kuss, one dated April 1, 1960, to Major Phelan?

Mr. Kuss. Yes, sir.

Mr. Kendall. And you stated in that letter that the "loose pin connections are a very serious matter since there seems to be no way of satisfactorily remedying this condition." Is that right?

Mr. Kuss. That's right.

Mr. Kendall. And furthermore, "that the condition was one that would tend to worsen at an increasing rate with time?"

Mr. Kuss. It couldn't do anything but increase; yes. The condition could not get better. It would increase, if anything.

Mr. Kendall. You also wrote a letter, I believe, dated August 10, 1960, to the base procurement office, Otis Air Force Base. That is a letter in which you enclosed your report on your analysis of the existing damage. And in that report you again stated:

The looseness of the pins will in all probability continue to worsen, at perhaps an accelerating rate, since the sloppiness contributes to the magnitude of the impact stresses on the connections, and the increased impact in turn aggravates the wear in the joints. It was therefore concluded by our office that it would be hazardous to permit the conditions to remain uncorrected through any more winter seasons, with the ultimate loss of the tower being the possible result of such neglect.

Mr. Kuss. Yes, sir; that's in the report.

Mr. Kendall. Is that when you recommended the installation of the above-water braces?

Mr. Kuss. Yes, sir.

Mr. Rutledge. Sir, this was a confirmation of the recommendation which had been made in May or June.

Mr. Kendall. And they were installed in August 1960?

Mr. Rutledge. Installation was completed shortly after the first of August 1960.

Mr. Kendall. Was a complete stress reanalysis made before making that recommendation?

Mr. Kuss. Oh, yes, sir.

Mr. Kendall. Weren't the braces and the pin connections at the −25-foot and −75-foot level in bad shape at that time?

Mr. Kuss. They looked to be, sir.

Mr. Kendall. Well, wasn't it considered necessary to effect a repair of those braces?

Mr. Kuss. Yes, sir, if possible.

Mr. Kendall. Was it done?

Mr. Kuss. No, sir. I would like to give you a little history of this, right here.

Mr. Kendall. Yes, sir, go right ahead.

Mr. Kuss. At our meetings with the Air Force, when it was decided to put the above-water bracing on, we all agreed that something would have to be done to the pins ultimately; but the way the tower stood, it would have been impossible or very dangerous to remove the pins, as, for instance, to put in larger ones. We felt if we could secure the tower with the above-water bracing, then, when the weather was suitable, we could go after the pins and do something to them.

Now, along those lines, when the contractor was erecting the above-water bracing, it was provided in his contract that he examine those pins, re-examine them well — that is, better than they had been examined before. That meant taking off the washers at the ends of the pins so that you could actually see the relationship of the hole to the pin. That was part of the contract he had. We had no information on the true condition of the pins, because the previous divers had always had to contend with the fact that there was a plate which covered the hole. So although we knew the pins were loose, we did not know the exact conditions. We couldn't combat it until——

Mr. Kendall. You knew the braces were ineffective, didn't you, Mr. Kuss?

Mr. Kuss. They were not ineffective.

Mr. Kendall. Well, they were not working properly.

Mr. Kuss. Yes, they were not working properly.

Mr. Kendall. I take it you do not agree with the statements that have been made in the record that the installation of this above-water X-bracing, without correction of the difficulties in the undersea bracings, caused the tower to act like a huge hinge?

Mr. Kuss. No, sir, I don't understand that.

Mr. Kendall. You don't understand it or you don't agree with it, which, or both?

Mr. Kuss. I don't agree with it.

Mr. Kendall. How long would it take to make a stress reanalysis of this tower?

Mr. Kuss. Of the stress in the various members, you mean?

Mr. Kendall. Yes, sir; such as you made in connection with the installation of the above-water X-bracings.

Mr. Kuss. Well, for each different condition, each different problem, it might take a week.

Mr. Kendall. How long did the analysis that you made take?

Mr. Kuss. I would say a week.

Mr. Kendall. That is a complete stress reanalysis?

Mr. Kuss. Yes, sir.

Mr. Kendall. Of the entire tower?

Mr. Kuss. Yes.

Mr. Kendall. Now, as to installation of this above-water X-bracing, did you certify that the tower had been restored to the original design strength?

Mr. Kuss. Yes.

Mr. Kendall. Well, how could it have been restored to the original strength when you admittedly had the deteriorated pin connections below water, and braces were not functioning correctly?

Mr. Kuss. Our analysis took in the fact that the pins were loose.

Mr. Kendall. You considered, then, that it had been restored to the original design strength?

Mr. Kuss. Yes, sir.

Mr. Kendall. As a matter of fact, you put that X-bracing in the area where the impact of the waves was the strongest?

Mr. Kuss. Yes, sir.

Mr. Kendall. And that was a complete departure from the original design concept?

Mr. Kuss. From the original design, yes.

Mr. Kendall. And each storm that hit that X-bracing resulted in cracks in it, didn't it?

Mr. Kuss. I don't know that.

Mr. Kendall. Well, were there cracks in the X-bracing after——

Mr. Rutledge. While the X-bracing was being installed, when it was partially installed, the contractor was facing the difficulty that occurs in every welded connection, that with a partial welded connection, if a storm hits, the connection isn't strong enough to take the forces imposed and cracks occur. These occurred at least once, and possibly twice, during the installation of the above-water bracing, and these are in the record of our resident engineer who was supervising this work. When this entire bracing was completely installed, there were no cracks in any of the connections. The contractor corrected all of the cracking.

Mr. Kendall. That bracing was completely installed in August?

Mr. Rutledge. In the early part of August the work was completed.

Mr. Kendall. Well, after Hurricane Donna in September were there any cracks?

Mr. Rutledge. Yes, sir; but that was a different situation.

Mr. Kendall. After the storm in December 1960, were there any cracks?

Mr. Rutledge. We have no report on that, sir.

Mr. Kendall. Those were the only two storms of major consequence, I believe, until the one on January 15, is that right?

Mr. Rutledge. We have no specific information on that, sir.

Mr. Kendall. All right, Mr. Kuss, about the middle of November 1960, did anyone in the Air Force ask you to tell him what the remaining strength of the tower was at that time?

Mr. Kuss. Yes.

Mr. Kendall. Who was it, sir?

Mr. Kuss. Captain Grassfield.

Mr. Kendall. What about General Elder?

Mr. Kuss. Let me get these dates straight.

Mr. Kendall. About the middle of November 1960, isn't it true that General Elder called you on the telephone and asked you to tell him what the remaining strength of the tower was?

Mr. Kuss. Yes, sir.

Mr. Kendall. What did you tell him?

Mr. Kuss. This was — at that time, I refused to estimate the strength of the tower.

Mr. Kendall. You gave him no estimate at all?

Mr. Kuss. No, sir.

Mr. Kendall. At that time, your firm had agreed with J. Rich Steers, Inc., and the date of the agreement was October 3, 1960, to evaluate the remaining strength of the tower in terms of its original design criteria, isn't that right?

Mr. Kuss. That's right, sir.

Mr. Kendall. Why couldn't you give him an estimate in November 1960?

Mr. Kuss. This damage was so extensive that it came completely outside the terms of what we expected to find.

Mr. Kendall. You just told me that it would take about a week to make a stress reanalysis, and you had here about six weeks.

Go ahead, sir.

Mr. Kuss. I have considerable knowledge of this tower, sir, having worked with it a long time. From the conditions that were discovered, I knew without making any figures that it was very dangerous. It wasn't a matter of figuring.

Furthermore, we had no knowledge that we had a report of the total damage. It could have been more, so I didn't want to encourage anybody that it was safe in any way. Even though I had made an analysis, it might have been based on the wrong premises.

Mr. Rutledge. May we put it on the record that we were first informed about the damage by Mr. Koch of J. Rich Steers Co. on November 14, in our office. He had received a radio call from the tower and he transmitted this information to us, and the telephone call from General Elder was on the morning of November 16.

Mr. Kendall. From the date of October 3, 1960, until November 14, your firm had made no stress reanalysis?

Mr. Rutledge. We had no information, sir, on the damage except that the maintenance bridge had been destroyed. We hunted up the drawings for the maintenance bridge so that they could replace that.

Mr. Kendall. Mr. Kuss, were there any other occasions when you were asked by anyone in the Air Force as to what the remaining strength of the tower was?

Mr. Kuss. I——

Senator Stennis. Pardon me, Mr. Counsel. I want to be sure I understood Mr. Kuss.

Mr. Kuss, as I understand your testimony, you say that about November 16, 1960, when you got this additional information about the condition of the tower, even without having to make any calculations, you knew from that incomplete report, although you were not certain that you had the full picture as to the damage — but from that incomplete report, you considered the tower highly unsafe and dangerous; is that right?

Mr. Kuss. With the damage reported to me, it was very serious, and it may have been more.

Senator Stennis. Very serious. Well, now, could we make that more specific? I am not trying to put words in your mouth at all. You are the witness and you are an expert witness. But as I have understood the tenor of your testimony, it is based on this knowledge that you had, even though it might not have been complete as to all the conditions — you considered it highly dangerous; is that correct?

Mr. Kuss. Yes, sir; yes, sir.

Senator Stennis. All right, I just wanted to be certain.

Mr. Kuss. I so told General Elder.[9]

Senator Stennis. And that was November 16?

Mr. Kuss. Yes, sir.

Senator Stennis. All right, now, Counsel, you have another date in mind. Will you proceed?

Mr. Kendall. I'll ask you this, Mr. Kuss. At any time prior to the collapse of the tower did you report to anyone an estimate of the remaining strength of the tower as it then stood?

Mr. Kuss. No.

Mr. Kendall. Wasn't it possible to make an analysis between October 3, 1960, and January 15, 1961? Or from November 14, 1960, to January 15, 1961?

Mr. Kuss. I don't know as I was asked to make any analysis.

---

[9] During the court-martial of Colonel William Banks, his immediate superior, General Elder, was reported to have testified that "no civilian engineers had ever told him the tower was unsafe." (New York *Times,* August 24, 1961, p. 59.)

MR. KENDALL. That is what your contract was for, Mr. Kuss. You had a contract with J. Rich Steers, Inc., dated October 3 to evaluate the remaining strength of the tower. That is true, isn't it?

MR. KUSS. Yes.

MR. KENDALL. And up to January 15, you hadn't given an evaluation, had you?

MR. KUSS. Yes, sir; I had given an evaluation that it was very dangerous.

MR. KENDALL. Is that what you call an evaluation of the remaining strength of the tower?

MR. KUSS. Under the circumstances, that was it.

MR. KENDALL. That is a good engineering evaluation, that it was very dangerous?

MR. KUSS. Yes, sir.

MR. KENDALL. But you never came up with a detailed analysis such as you have in this report, did you?

MR. KUSS. No, sir.

SENATOR STENNIS. Pardon me again. While you are on this point, you used the term "very dangerous," and I think that is understood. But as I interpret it, you mean that it was just dangerous for human habitation, and that it was likely to collapse under any additional strain, is that correct?

MR. KUSS. Yes, sir. I don't see any need for adding any figures to that. That is a conclusion.

SENATOR STENNIS. I understand your testimony, but I wanted to be certain I understood the element of danger to humans and the likelihood of collapse.

MR. KENDALL. If you had given some figures, Mr. Kuss, wouldn't the Air Force have been in a better position to evaluate the weather forecasts in relation to the strength of the tower?

MR. KUSS. I didn't want to have them do that. That would be highly dangerous and misleading, because I did not know the total damage, or couldn't be sure that I knew the total damage.

MR. KENDALL. Finally, I believe a figure of 55 per cent of the original strength was attributed to a statement made by you. What did you mean by that statement, and when was it made?

MR. KUSS. This was made on January 12 in the Steers office.

MR. KENDALL. What did you mean by the statement?

MR. KUSS. We were discussing the installation of the rope bracing.

MR. KENDALL. That is what we have been referring to as the cable bracing?

MR. KUSS. The cable bracing, here in red [indicating]. In order to evaluate whether even with the installation of that in, it would be worthwhile. I was asked to evaluate the strength of the tower after the rope bracing was in.

MR. KENDALL. In other words, you said that after that cable had been installed but without the replacement of the lower diagonal, it would be 55 per cent as strong as its design criteria.

MR. KUSS. Yes.

MR. KENDALL. At the time of the collapse, since the cable bracing had not been installed, the tower was even weaker than that?

MR. KUSS. Much weaker. It was worse than the time I told them it was dangerous.

MR. KENDALL. It had gotten worse all the time, because you had some more damage in the December storm, or you discovered some after the storm?

MR. KUSS. Yes, sir.

MR. KENDALL. Do you have any judgment as to the per cent of strength at that time?

MR. KUSS. After Donna?

MR. KENDALL. After the December storm.

MR. KUSS. You see——

MR. KENDALL. As of January 12, 1961, say, Mr. Kuss?

MR. KUSS. Sir, I was almost surprised the tower stood up.

SENATOR STENNIS. What was that, now? You were surprised that it stood up?

MR. KUSS. Yes, sir.

MR. KENDALL. During what period?

MR. KUSS. During any of the moderate weather periods that they had.

MR. KENDALL. So you made no estimate in figures of the remaining strength of the tower and have none now?

MR. KUSS. No, sir. You see, the percentage of residual safety is, when you are getting down to 95, you are on——

MR. KENDALL. But the intensity of the storm during which the tower ultimately collapsed was nowhere near the design criteria, was it, Mr. Kuss?

MR. KUSS. We don't know.

MR. KENDALL. What is your information on that? It was an ordinary winter storm, was it not?

MR. KUSS. I suppose, but we had no figures on that.

MR. KENDALL. Well, it was not a storm involving winds of 125 miles an hour and breaking waves of 35 feet, was it?

MR. KUSS. No, I don't think so.

MR. KENDALL. We are faced now, Mr. Kuss, with the tower collapse, and we have several alternatives — faulty design, possibly; faulty construction; faulty repair; or a combination of all of these things.

Can you or Mr. Rutledge tell us now what made this tower collapse?

MR. RUTLEDGE. If I may answer, sir, from information that we have heard, and I believe it was part of the testimony here, the tower during Hurricane

Donna was subjected to forces that were very much in excess of the design criteria forces.

MR. KENDALL. Does that conclude your observation on that?

MR. RUTLEDGE. These forces of Hurricane Donna, as has been testified, broke two of the panels of bracing in the tower. With two panels of bracing completely gone, the tower was in a very dangerous condition. It definitely did not have strength to resist the design criteria, and it could resist only something very much smaller.

As Mr. Kuss has testified, it was essentially impossible and extremely dangerous to say what it could resist.

NOTES

Work on this complex case should probably be assigned to teams of students. Alternatively, it is possible to single out one or more questions for attention and to exclude others from consideration.

The subcommittee limited its inquiry to possible deficiencies in the design, construction, and maintenance of the tower. The Air Force having now ruled that no officer was guilty of dereliction of duty, it is appropriate to add a fourth major question: Was the Air Force derelict in its duty to safeguard the lives of the military and civilian personnel and to protect the equipment on the tower? It is better to consider the manner in which the responsibility of the Air Force as a whole, rather than the responsibility of an individual, was discharged since the chain of command and the division of duties among individuals was very complicated and adequate information is not available.

Below are listed some of the subordinate questions which arise in connection with one or more of the four major topics noted above, and which may be pursued either as part of a more elaborate investigation or as limited inquiries.

1. Was it wise to utilize the Kuss tip-up method in this project?
2. Who was responsible for approving the repair at sea of the braces damaged before and during erection?
3. Was this decision wise?
4. Should the use of pin connections have been approved?
5. Should the pin tolerances have been increased?
6. Should the Navy have approved and accepted the tower when it did?
7. Should the Air Force have accepted the tower when it did?
8. Was the reliance placed on the efficacy of the X-bracing reasonable?
9. Did Moran, Proctor, Mueser & Rutledge discharge the obligations it incurred by reason of its agreement with the Air Force on October 3, 1960?

CUSTER'S LAST STAND

INTRODUCTION

IN FEBRUARY, 1876, Lieutenant General Philip H. Sheridan, commandant of the Missouri Division of the United States Army, was ordered to crush recalcitrant Sioux and Cheyenne Indians. The Indians had refused repeated offers by the Federal Government to provide financial assistance and guaranteed land reservations if the Indians would abandon the nomadic life which brought them into conflict with white settlers then entering the Montana, Wyoming, and North and South Dakota Territories in steadily increasing numbers. Sheridan believed that the Indians were wintering in southeastern Montana. He devised a simple plan to bring them to heel.

Colonel John Gibbon was to move east from central Montana with four hundred men. Gibbon's mission was to prevent the Indians from escaping north of the Yellowstone River and to link up with Brigadier General Alfred H. Terry who would march west from Fort Abraham Lincoln in western North Dakota with nine hundred men. Brigadier General George Crook was to move north from southeastern Wyoming with another nine hundred men. As the strategists saw it, the great problem was to corner the Indians. It was assumed that they would make every effort to escape rather than fight, and further, that any one of the three bodies of troops could defeat any Indians they might encounter. As it turned out, both assumptions were incorrect.

Crook marched north according to plan and was thrashed by a large war party under Crazy Horse, chief of the Oglala Sioux, south of Rosebud Creek on June 17, 1876 (see map on page 192). He retreated about thirty miles to his base camp and licked his wounds for the rest of the campaign. Neither Gibbon nor Terry learned of Crook's defeat until after the battle on the Little Big Horn. Aside from this brief appearance, therefore, Crook plays no role in our story.

Terry set out from Fort Lincoln on May 17, with 150 mule-drawn wagons, a Gatling gun platoon, 3 companies of infantry, and the Seventh Cavalry Regiment under the command of Major General George Armstrong Custer, probably the best-known regiment and certainly the best-publicized soldier in the United States Army.

Terry moved west to the Little Missouri River in thirteen days. Finding no sign of Indians there, he continued westward, systematically searching the valleys of the Powder and Tongue Rivers, as well as a number of smaller streams. On June 9 he established a camp at the junction of the

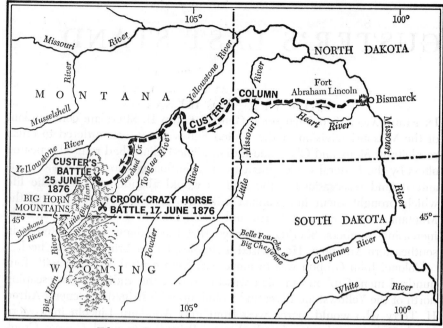

Edgar I. Stewart, *Custer's Luck* (University of Oklahoma Press, 1955).

Custer's Route from Fort Abraham Lincoln to the Little Big Horn River,
May 17 to June 25, 1876.

Tongue and Yellowstone Rivers. Thirteen days later he had joined forces
with Gibbon and learned that a sizable group of Indians was camping on
the upper Rosebud or on the Little Big Horn. On June 22, therefore, he
sent the Seventh Cavalry south on the Rosebud with orders to move to
the headwaters of that stream and then to cross over to the Little Big Horn
and move north. Terry, meanwhile, proposed to take the infantry west on
the Yellowstone to the mouth of the Big Horn and then to march south
on the Big Horn and Little Big Horn, eventually joining forces with Custer.
Between the two groups, Terry hoped that one or both could catch and
destroy the Indians.

By this time evidence indicated that the Indian encampment might be
somewhat larger than previously anticipated. Formerly, there were said
to be five hundred to seven hundred Indians. Custer now apparently believed that the village might contain as many as one thousand to fifteen
hundred warriors. In fact, four thousand seems closer to the actual number
of fighters waiting on the Little Big Horn; with women, children, and men
too old to fight, the total group may have numbered close to ten thousand.
It may have been the largest assembly of Indians ever gathered on this

continent. They were, moreover, waiting. Under the prodding of Crazy Horse and Sitting Bull they had determined to stand and fight as never before.

By 8 P.M. on June 24, the third day of his march, Custer had moved 600 men and 175 pack mules to a point on the Rosebud some 50 miles south of the Yellowstone. On June 23 and 24 the column had discovered numerous signs of recent Indian camps and equally numerous indications that the column's progress was under observation by the Indians. Late on the twenty-fourth Custer learned that the Indian trails he was following led over a divide and into the valley of the Little Big Horn. He decided to attempt to cross the divide that night, conceal his troops during the following day, and attack the Indian village at dawn on the twenty-sixth. About 11 P.M. his column began moving to the west, up a small tributary of the Rosebud. By 2 A.M. the next day, however, the first streaks of dawn appeared, and the column was still so far from the top of the divide that it was obvious they could not cross without being seen in the early morning light. Believing that his presence had not yet been discovered, Custer at first resolved to camp where he was, but during the morning it became increasingly obvious that the Indians were watching him and might be preparing to attack the column. Custer decided to attack first. At noon on the twenty-fifth he crossed the divide and began to descend to the Little Big Horn.

Ignorant of the true size of the opposing force and ignorant of their determination not to be routed, Custer divided his command into 4 groups. The pack train, which necessarily lagged behind, was put under the charge of Captain McDougall with 130 soldiers. Captain Benteen was given about 125 men and sent to the west to head off any Indians who might try to escape to the Little Big Horn Mountains in the south. Major Reno, with about 115 troops, was directed to move north along the west bank of the Little Big Horn and attack the village directly. Custer, with 225 men, rode north along the bluffs east of the river, apparently intending to swoop down at the middle or northern end of the village and catch the fleeing Indians from the flank (see map on page 194).

Custer sent back two messengers before encountering a large body of Indians, and no other member of his command lived to explain how he was wiped out so quickly and so thoroughly. Reno with 115 men, attacking a village of perhaps 10,000, stopped short of his goal and retreated to a hilltop. He was later joined by Benteen and McDougall, held off the Indians for two days until Terry relieved him, and lived to face a military court convened to investigate his conduct in the battle. This case is concerned with that investigation.

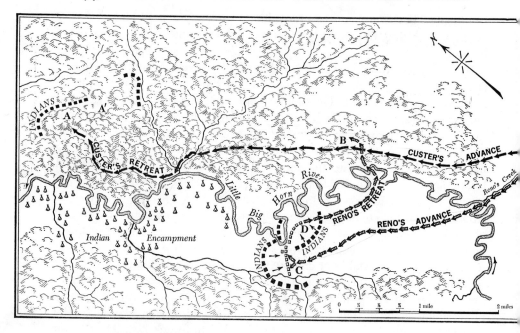

The battle of the Little Big Horn, June 25, 1876. The geographical features shown reflect chiefly the map prepared by the U. S. Geological Survey in 1891. This was the first accurate map of the area, unfortunately, and it does not show the exact conditions which existed in 1876 because the Little Big Horn constantly changes its course. This and all other maps of the battle provide only a general notion of the movements and dispositions of the forces.

A–A': *Area in which most of the bodies of Custer's troops were later discovered. Custer's route to this position, as indicated by the heavy arrows, is uncertain since no one lived to describe it. The route given is according to accounts of Indian eyewitnesses.*

B: *Hilltop on which Reno regrouped his forces after retreating.*

C: *Position of Reno's first skirmish line.*

D: *Position of Reno's second skirmish line at the edge of the timber.*

The central question before the court follows: "Was the conduct of Major Marcus A. Reno at the battle of the Little Big Horn, that of a brave, efficient, prudent, and obedient officer?" The court considered Reno's conduct during the entire period from noon on the twenty-fifth until the morning of the twenty-seventh when he was relieved by General Terry. We are concerned here only with his conduct from the time when he left Custer to attack the village until he reached a hilltop after having retreated. The relevant facts appear in the following testimony.

TESTIMONY

LIEUTENANT GEORGE D. WALLACE

Direct examination: I was assigned to Company G on June 25, 1876. About 12:15 P.M. the regiment was divided among Custer, Reno, Benteen, and McDougall; Reno was given Companies A, G, and M, and twenty-two Indian scouts. Company A was commanded by Moylan; G, by McIntosh; and M, by French. I do not know what orders were given at this time. Benteen soon moved off to the left and disappeared. Custer and Reno moved forward on opposite sides of a small stream [now called Reno's Creek], and McDougall followed behind.

About 2 P.M. — I looked at my watch — when we had gone ten or twelve miles, Reno crossed the stream and marched alongside Custer. After a short time we passed a tepee with dead Indians in it. Shortly thereafter, Cook, the regimental adjutant, came to Reno and transmitted an order from Custer. I was riding to the left of Hodgson, Reno's adjutant, and he was riding to Reno's left. I would estimate that it was about 2:15 P.M. As nearly as I can recall, the order was, "The Indians are about two and one-half miles ahead on the jump. Follow them as fast as you can and charge them wherever you find them, and we will support you." I am not positive about the word "we." I am positive that Custer gave no other order to Reno and did not speak directly to Reno. We moved forward at a gallop. Custer followed at a slow trot for a short distance and then moved to our right. This was the last time I saw him. I supposed that he was following us.

We moved forward at a gallop for about fifteen minutes, recrossing to the left bank of the small stream during this time, and came to a ford in the Little Big Horn. The crossing was about belly-deep to the horses and was not opposed. We halted for a few minutes on the other side and then moved forward with Companies A and M abreast, G to the rear, and the Indian scouts under Varnum and Hare ahead. We went about two miles, first at a trot and later a gallop. No order to charge was given. The bottom land was flat, about two miles wide, and mostly covered with grass that had been grazed off and cut up by many pony hoofs. The river was very crooked so that we were sometimes close to the bank and sometimes quite far away. The Indian village was a little more than two miles from the ford, but there was so much dust in the air that I did not see it until we had dismounted. At first, the Indians seemed to be running away, but later they ran toward us. Part way to the village, G Company was brought up to the left [sic, right] side of the line and remained there.

We dismounted at a place where the river made a big loop to the left, and a stand of trees lined the bank. The horses were put in the timber, and a skirmish line was formed with its right on the timber and its left extending a few hundred yards at right angles to the river. We had been fired on a little during the last quarter-mile of our advance, but we had not returned the fire. It was about 2:30 P.M.

The skirmish line moved forward about one hundred yards. It was then within seventy-five to one hundred yards of the first tepees. There were two hundred or three hundred Indians engaging us at that time and many more began to appear, notably from a ravine some hundreds of yards to our front. The firing was brisk, but the Indians did not make much of an attack on our front. Instead, many passed around our left flank and began to encircle us. The whole space to our rear, for a mile or two, was filled with Indians — not a solid mass, but riding around, yelling and hooting, and those within range were shooting. After a short time, it was reported that they were trying to get at our horses from the other side of the river. Company G fell back to the timber to protect the horses. Soon after, the skirmish line fell back to the edge of the timber. Indians began firing from across the stream, some fifty yards from us, and from our rear in the timber. There was no protection where we were, and on the other side was a bank.

Reno had gone into the timber with Company G, and I did not see him until after the retreat, but I heard his order to get ready to charge. Exactly what the orders were I don't know, but I recognized his voice. The companies were mounted and commenced getting out. I could not find McIntosh, so I mounted what men I could find and led them out. It was about 3:15 P.M. I knew of two men who had been killed at this point.

When I got out of the woods, the troops were moving at a gallop in a column of fours, and Indians were all over the landscape. Some were riding alongside the troops with Winchester repeating rifles set across the pommels of their saddles, pumping shots into the column. It was half- or three-quarters of a mile to the hill where we retreated, and it took about fifteen minutes, including three to five minutes to cross the river. This crossing place was about twenty-five feet wide and belly-deep to the horses. The left bank was four or five feet high, and the right bank probably eight feet. After getting to the top of the hill, we halted, preparing to stand off the Indians. Benteen soon joined us. The pack train came up later.

Reno's losses in the valley were eight killed and five wounded in Company A, eleven killed in Company G, and eight killed and two wounded in Company M.

In my opinion the Indians knew exactly what we were doing from the time we left the mouth of the Rosebud. Their running away after we crossed the stream was only a sham. I do not think there was any defensible position on the left side of the river.

Cross-examination: No announcement that I know of was made to Reno concerning a junction with Benteen. I heard of no plan for reuniting the battalions. Reno crossed the little stream to march alongside Custer's troops because Custer had motioned to him with his hat. I saw no communication between the men. Cook's message was, "The Indians are about two and one-half miles ahead. They are on the jump. Go forward as fast as you think proper and charge them wherever you find them, and he will support you." I am in doubt as to the pronoun, but I understood, and it was the understanding of all the other officers to whom I talked, that Custer was to support Reno. That was the only order I heard. I was near Reno until we crossed the Little Big Horn.

Each soldier was armed with two revolvers and a carbine, which had been loaded. They carried two additional revolver loadings (a total of twenty-four cartridges) and fifty carbine cartridges in their belts, as well as fifty more carbine cartridges in their saddlebags. While some of the men had been in the service for two to four years, a great many were recruits who had never been on a horse until that campaign, and they lost control of their horses when galloping in line.

I first saw the village while on the skirmish line; I looked back but did not see Custer coming. I asked the first officer I saw, Moylan, if we could communicate with Custer. We asked a half-breed scout named Jackson if he would go. He waved his hand to the rear of our position and said there were too many for one man to go through. That was the first time I had seen the Indians to our rear. Till then I had expected Custer and his men to support us.

I think Reno's conduct was all that could have been expected of anyone. The troops could not have been handled any better. They used up most of their fifty rounds, and one company had to get ammunition from their saddlebags. I think he did the only thing possible under the circumstances. If we had remained in the timber, all would have been killed. It was his duty to take care of his command and to use his best judgment and discretion. I saw no evidence of fear in his conduct at any time. Before we retired from the timber, Indians were crossing the river on our right and firing at us from the right bank. It was about 2:20 P.M. when we first crossed the river; 2:30 when we reached the timber; and about 3:15 or 3:30 when we reached the hill in retreat. Many Indians were ahead of us on the hilltop across the river. Hodgson was killed about fifty yards after crossing the stream by a shot from the bluffs, and DeWolf was shot by the Indians on that side. The troops were first dismounted and deployed on the crest and then mounted and moved back about the time we heard that Benteen was coming. He was close to us, about two hundred yards away, and not coming over our trail but to the right of it. The pack train was then about three miles to our rear.

F. F. GIRARD

Direct examination: On June 25, 1876, I was assigned to the Seventh Cavalry Regiment as a civilian scout and interpreter. I was ahead of Custer's and Reno's commands as they advanced down the small tributary of the Little Big Horn. I rode up on a little knoll near a tepee containing some dead Indians. This point was about a mile and a quarter from the river. I could see the Indian village. I waved my hat and called to Custer, "Here are your Indians, running like devils." Reno was ordered forward almost at once. I heard Custer give the order. He called to Reno, beckoning him over. Reno rode over, and Custer said, "You will take your battalion and try to bring them to battle, and I will support you." As Reno was going off, Custer added, "And take the scouts with you." Having heard the order, I joined Reno and instructed the other scouts to do the same. We lost sight of Custer's column when, after going about a mile, we arrived at a knoll next to the river.

Just before we crossed the river, the scouts on my left called attention to a large number of Indians coming up the valley. There seemed to be fifteen hundred Indians about two and one-half miles away. I called Reno's attention to it and thought Custer should know about it. I rode back toward the knoll, and met Cook. I told him. He said, "All right. I'll go back and report." As I returned, I could see Reno's column going down to where they dismounted and threw out the skirmish line. They did not move in a straight line, but skirted the edge of the timber along the river. It was not more than ten minutes from when Reno crossed the river until he halted and deployed his troops as skirmishers. I halted forty-five or fifty yards back from the edge of the timber. Charlie Reynolds, Dr. Porter, George Herendeen, and Bloody Knife were with me. Reynolds asked if I had any whisky. He said he had never felt so depressed and discouraged in his life. We dismounted. Just then the skirmish line was being drawn up, and the Indians were coming toward us. They were about one thousand yards away from the left flank of the line. Reynolds and I fired a few shots at long range and then put our horses in the timber. The Indians were firing at our scouts and the scouts at them. They advanced to within two hundred yards. There were only about fifty or seventy-five of them. I did not see that the skirmish line advanced any; and after a few minutes, while I was in the timber with Reynolds, the line pivoted around so that the left flank became the right.

The village was then a mile or a half mile away. The timber was about seventy-five yards at the widest portion, narrowing to about thirty yards. We stayed in the timber four or five minutes and fired about seven shots. Somebody gave the order, "Men, to your horses. The Indians are in our rear." Reynolds looked at me, and I said, "What damn fool move is this?" He said, "I don't know. We will have to go. We will have to get out of this." We got to our horses, and Reynolds mounted. I cautioned him to walk the horse because Indians were firing at him. The troops were mounted and going by very fast, pell-mell. They were in a great hurry to get out and were completely disorderly. Every man was for himself. There were no Indians in the timber. I asked an officer, "What are you going to do?" and he said, "Charge the Indians." I thought they were going to charge out onto the plain and then return to the timber, so I stayed there. Reynolds galloped after the troops, trying to catch up with them, but the Indians surrounded and killed him. De Rudio, O'Neill, and Jackson were left in the woods with me. We stayed in the timber until about 9 P.M., when it became dark, and then made our way to Reno's position across the river.

All the Indians I saw go to Reno's left and rear numbered about two hundred. The line had been moved into the timber by the time the Indians had come within three hundred yards. The bulk of those I saw at first had apparently left to intercept Custer before he reached the village. The party I was firing at numbered only twenty or thirty.

I think that if Reno had been determined and resolute, he could have held out against all the Indians as long as his ammunition and provisions held out.

Cross-examination: The order I heard was given to Reno by Custer in person. I do not pretend to say that the adjutant did not deliver it first. I can't help what Wallace says.

When we got to the ford, and I saw the Indians, I said, "Major Reno, the Indians are coming up the valley to meet us." He looked at me, looked at the valley, and gave the order, "Forward." The Indians were about two and one-half miles away and coming in large numbers.

I knew that Custer was under the impression that the Indians were running away and that it was important for him to know they were coming to meet us instead. I thought the information might change his plans.

I asked, "What is this damn move?" because I thought that to move out onto the prairie was like running into certain death. I didn't know what the plan was, but when I understood that the troops were to charge, I supposed that they would later return.

Reno dismissed me from my position as interpreter and Custer reinstated me, but I have no unkind feelings toward Reno.

LIEUTENANT CHARLES A. VARNUM

Direct examination: I was in command of the Indian scouts. I was not present when the division of commands was made. When I joined Reno, one of his companies had already crossed the river. Eight or ten Indian scouts were with me, and I was soon joined by Hare, who had been detailed to assist me. We started down the valley fifty or seventy-five yards ahead of the column.

There was a large body of Indians some distance off, running around on the prairie in every direction, kicking up all the dust they could, so that it was impossible to tell their number.

The Indians let us come closer. They didn't uncover the village much, but we could see a large number of tepees. We went down about two miles and the column halted, dismounted, and was deployed as skirmishers. I did not hear any of the orders.

Our skirmish line was about two miles from the first crossing and about eight hundred yards from the nearest part of the village. After we first crossed the river, it was fifteen or twenty minutes before the troops halted; I think it was about 2:30 P.M. then. Thick timber was to the right of the line and then dense underbrush clear to the river, which may have been one hundred yards away. I could not see it and don't know for sure.

I don't know whether the line was ordered to charge before it was dismounted. I was not near enough to hear any commands. A few shots had been fired by the Indians before the deployment. There was a sort of engagement between the scouts and the Indians. Except for those few shots, there was no firing on the line. Those shots were at the left, toward the bluff. The line was deployed at right angles to the general direction of the river, and skirmishing commenced at once.

The Indian scouts had disappeared so Hare and I rode to the line, and I reported to my company commander, Moylan. When I had been there for ten or fifteen minutes, I heard some of the men calling out that Company G was going to charge the village through the woods, or something to that effect. I rode to the middle of the timber and found a little glade or opening from which I could see the river. Reno was there, deploying G Company. I rode over to him, and he said, "I wish you would go back to the line and see how things are going and come back and report to me." On my way to the line I met Hodgson who had just come from there, and I asked him to tell Reno how things were. When I got to the line, it had fallen back to the edge of the timber. I could not see all the men.

Moylan called to me that Indians were circling to the left into the timber. He said something must be done or our horses and ammunition would be cut off. I told him I would bring up the horses. I rode through the timber to the left of the line and called for Company A to follow with their horses. I guess all the others followed. We went to the rear of Moylan's company. I had dismounted and returned to the line when I heard Moylan say that he was out of ammunition and had ordered every alternate man back to get ammunition from the saddlebags.

I met Girard and Reynolds at the right end of the line and talked with them for about three minutes. Then we heard cries of, "Charge, charge, we are going to charge!" There was a lot of confusion. I jumped up and started through the woods. I grabbed my horse. Everybody was mounted. I heard no orders. Then men passed, and I followed them out letting my horse race to the head of the column which was then halfway to where we crossed the river soon after. When I came out of the timber, there were a great many Indians with Winchester rifles across their saddles, riding next to the column and firing into it. A large number were in the bend next to the river. When I got to the head of the column, those in front had run off. I saw fifteen or twenty to our left, and others were near some clumps of bushes. Several bodies were found there. I supposed that the column had met some Indians and wheeled and started for them with no officer in command. I yelled to them to stop. Then I saw Reno and Moylan at the head of the column. They went on to the crossing, but my orderly was shot, and I stopped to help him so I do not know what happened at the head of the column.

As the command rode out and across, the men were using revolvers. They had to jump the horses into the river. It was a straight bank four or five feet high. The other side was a little better. The water was about four and one-half feet deep. The crossing was not covered.

The retreat from the woods was hasty, and the rear of the column disorganized. It was a movement to get out of there and onto higher ground. When I reached the prairie, they were getting away from the Indians as fast as they could. When the command retreated from the timber, no rally point was designated that I know of. We stopped about four hundred yards from the point we had crossed in retreat, up a steep bank at the top of a hill. I found several wounded there.

Everybody I saw on the hill was considerably excited. They were excited when they went in, for that matter. The command was demoralized to a certain degree. They had left a great many behind; the organization was not as good as when it went in; a great many men were missing. I don't know how the command felt when we got to the hill, but I personally thought we had been licked badly.

A few minutes later, a column of troops was sighted coming toward us. We waited ten or fifteen minutes until they came up. It was Benteen and his three companies. McDougall's company and the packs were not yet in sight, and Hare started back to hurry them up. The packs arrived about forty-five minutes later.

The position in the timber was as good as any place on the left bank, but I don't think we had enough men to hold it and keep the Indians out. The front was good, but I don't know about the rear. Of course, the position threatened the village to some extent and kept a containing force of Indians there, but it was not a very safe place. At the time the move was made, a great many bullets were dropping into the woods from the rear. I did not see any Indians there, and whether the bullets came from the bluffs above or from below, I don't know. Up to the time we left, I know of only two casualties, the first sergeant of my company and my orderly.

It is almost impossible to estimate the number of mounted Indians. Soon after the command dismounted, there was a large force circling around and passing to the left and rear. The heaviest force was toward the right of the line, as that covered the village. There they came within three or four hundred yards. I think the main force was against us when we dismounted, but I don't think the entire force attacked us, because we could see parties a long way off after we got on the hill.

I don't think there were less than three or four hundred Indians in Reno's immediate front, and there may have been a great many more. I cannot say how many were actually firing. They maintained a heavy fire, and up the valley the whole country seemed covered with them. It is impossible to estimate how many the dust concealed. As a rule they fired from their horses, scampering around and pumping their Winchesters into us. The heavy dust was eight hundred to one thousand yards away. I would estimate that the fight lasted half an hour before the command went into the woods.

I don't know whether Benteen could have joined Reno in the timber or not if the Indians had seen him. It would depend on how much they opposed him. They might have driven him into the timber and prevented him from joining us. As it turned out he could have joined us when the Indians turned back and left us and went the other way.

As to Reno's conduct, I have nothing to say against him and nothing in particular for him, either one way or another. Certainly there was no sign of cowardice, or anything of that sort and nothing special the other way. I didn't see anything special to say on either side.

Cross-examination: I do not see how Reno could have depended on Benteen or McDougall. I don't know whether he knew or could have known what orders they had. I do not know if he knew the plan of the fight. I did not.

If Reno thought he could not hold the timber and saw no troops coming, it was for him to use his own judgment and leave it for a place he could better defend. Benteen united with Reno twenty to twenty-five minutes after Reno left the timber.

Re-direct examination: I do not think the Winchester will shoot accurately over six hundred yards. The Springfield carbine is accurate at one thousand yards. Indians would not be likely to charge mounted into the timber. They would take advantage of cover and crawl up on the line. I saw no Indians in the timber. Many casualties must have occurred at the rear of the column as it left the timber. The majority of ours were killed and wounded in the retreat from the woods to the bluff. I do not consider Reno's retreat a disorganized rout insofar as the head of the column was concerned, but the rear I think was. Column of fours was a good formation to use in going through the Indians. Platoons would have caused delay. There was no danger of enfilading fire as Indians would ride the flanks. I do not know whether any wounded were left in the woods. There were men left there, and they were dead when we saw them. If a man was so disabled he could not mount, he would be left and probably killed at once.

Re-cross examination: Indians are individual fighters. Each one has his own way of doing it. It would make no difference whether a ford was narrow or wide insofar as a troop formation was concerned. In such a movement the troops must be kept well closed up, and if there is any delay in crossing, some disposition must be made to cover it.

Dr. H. R. Porter

Direct examination: I was assistant surgeon under Custer on June 26. I heard the adjutant give an order to Reno about 1 P.M. on June 25. The adjutant told Reno that Indians were just ahead, and Custer directed him to charge them. Reno asked whether Custer was going to support him, and the adjutant answered that Custer would support him. Reno asked if the general was coming along, and Cook said, "Yes, the general will support you." I heard no other order. This was by the tepee with the dead Indian in it, about one and one-half miles from the crossing of the Little Big Horn.

Reno started down to the crossing at a trot. He asked me if I didn't want his gun because he had a fiery horse that was difficult to manage, and the gun was in his way. I said, "No." After we crossed, I heard him command, "Forward!" and we went on down to the woods, about two miles, at a lope or trot.

I saw a few Indians and a great many ponies. They seemed to be driving the ponies down the river. There was no opposition. When we got to the woods, the men dismounted and formed a skirmish line. I was right where I could see them. The horses were led into the woods. I watched the fight a few minutes and then led my horse into the woods, looking for my orderly who had the bandages and medicines. I had been there only a few minutes when the men on the left and right came in, and I heard Reno say that we would have to get out of there and charge the Indians. He rode out. One man had been wounded up to that time.

When Reno moved out, the men followed from all directions. They had a great deal of trouble finding their horses, but as soon as they mounted, they went out. I stayed a few minutes with the wounded man, and when I got out the men were all running and the Indians too. I went out expecting to see the command charging the Indians, but instead the Indians were charging the command. They were all on the run. I let my horse out and got to the edge of the river, and he jumped in and crossed with the rest.

There was a great deal of dust, hallooing, and confusion. The wounded man was left in the timber.

The first officer I saw on the bluffs was Varnum. He had his hat off and was saying, "For God's sake, men, don't run. There are a good many officers and men killed and wounded, and we've got to go back and get them." When I saw Reno, I said to him, "Major, the men were pretty well demoralized, weren't they?" He replied, "No, that was a charge, sir." The command was demoralized. They seemed to think they had been whipped. In a few minutes I saw some troops coming, and some of the men shouted, "Here comes Custer," but it was Benteen and his battalion. Then the command felt pretty good. They thought they were going to have some help.

No wounded were brought from the bottom, but I know that some were left there. Seven or eight, however, had hung on to their horses and dropped off when they got to the hilltop. It was about 1 P.M. when Reno got his order. I am just guessing at the time, as I did not look at my watch. It took ten or fifteen minutes to get to the crossing, five or ten more to cross and re-form, and fifteen or twenty more to go to the place the command halted. The Indians were then eight or nine hundred yards away. It was hard to reach them with the guns at that time.

I do not remember any firing until the men dismounted. Then a few shots were fired. The Indians were circling back and forth and coming nearer in squads, firing more rapidly as they came. I did not see the village until I was in the woods. I would judge there were about one thousand lodges. The nearest tepee was one-quarter of a mile away.

Only about fifty Indians were engaging Reno when he halted. They increased to seventy-five or one hundred. There were many more down the river, but I could not see how many. Reno's command, while in the timber, heard no bugle calls at any time. I knew the command was leaving because I heard Reno say, "We've got to get out of here. We've got to charge them."

When I got to the river, I saw a dozen cavalrymen in the water, and the Indians on the right bank were firing at them. I don't remember seeing an officer until I got across. There was no order in the rear of the column. Every man seemed to be running on his own hook. I judge it was fifteen or twenty minutes from their deployment until they left the woods, possibly longer. I don't think the run to the hills lasted over four or five minutes. It was between a half mile and a mile.

The river was forty to fifty feet wide, and the water was up to the saddle pockets. The left bank was straight, four or five feet high, but after some of the horses had caved it in, it made a pretty good crossing. On the other side it was about the same. When I got there everybody was rushing in, trying to get across as fast as possible, and the Indians were firing at them. It was every man for himself.

About an hour after Reno left Custer, Benteen joined Reno. The packs came in a half hour to an hour later.

I saw nothing in the conduct of Reno particularly heroic or the reverse. I think he was a little embarrassed and flurried. The bullets were coming thick and fast, and he did not know whether it was best to stay there or leave. That was my impression at the time.

Cross-examination: I was at Reno's side when he conversed with the adjutant. We were at the head of his command. I think Hodgson was there, but I do not remember seeing Wallace or Girard. I was within speaking distance of Reno until we reached the woods where the command dismounted. I left him there and went into the timber. After the horses were taken into the woods, I rode out and met Girard and others. After a minute or so, I rode back into the woods and stayed there. I was moderately cool during the fight, a little excited — nearly all were — but not so that my judgment was much out of the way. While on the run I was frightened. I found that I was alone, and I let my horse go. I think there were two hundred or three hundred Indians mixed in with the troops to the right and rear during the run to the river. Reno knew as well as I did that there were officers and men killed in that stampede. Everybody knew it.

CAPTAIN MYLES MOYLAN

Direct examination: I was in command of Company A. I believe that Reno's column was discovered before it crossed the Little Big Horn. The village was lower than the place where the troops crossed the river, and if the Indians didn't see the command, they saw the dust it raised. Whether Custer followed us on the trail toward the crossing, I don't know. Reno's adjutant told me that Custer was supposed to support Reno. I saw no movement of Indians toward us before we crossed or during the time we galloped down the valley. The distance was about a mile and a half and took us about ten minutes. I think that when we dismounted, enough Indians were within five hundred yards to warrant Reno's halting. About four hundred Indians were from two hundred to four hundred yards away. The skirmish line advanced about a hundred yards after being deployed. The engagement commenced before the deployment. Indians fired on us before we halted, but there were no casualties at this time. The Indian fire was scattering, and the companies commenced as soon as they were deployed. The scouts were already firing and had been for some time at long range. Some of the men were new, and it was impossible to regulate their fire, but the fire of the majority was well regulated. The right of our line was 150 to 200 yards from the river. There was timber with heavy underbrush about 30 yards wide next to the river, and the rest had only a tree here and there with scattered underbrush.

After about ten minutes, I understood that Reno had information that the Indians were turning his right by coming up the left bank of the river and were threatening the horses. The greater portion of Company G was withdrawn and taken into the woods, leaving an open space between the right of my company, which had been in the center, and the timber. I extended to the right to cover that.

We remained there from twenty-five to thirty minutes under heavy fire until the Indians seemed to be withdrawing from our front and working around to the left. I called Reno's attention to this, and he ordered the line withdrawn. The movement was executed by a flank movement to the right. The flank as a whole was never placed in the timber, which was about thirty feet higher than the bottom and the banks of which were precipitous in places. No less than two hundred Indians had turned our flank before it was withdrawn.

A few minutes later the command was given to mount. Up to that time I had one killed and two wounded in my company, and another man was wounded as we were going out. The men had fired forty to fifty rounds apiece, while dismounted, which would have taken about forty minutes. I think two-thirds had been expended judiciously.

Being mounted and unable to form in the timber, I ordered my men to move out and form outside. When half of them were mounted, I went out and formed them in a column of fours. Company M came up soon and formed on my left. Company G did not mount so soon nor get up as fast, but they were in the column before it reached the river. Reno was on his horse overlooking the formation. He asked my opinion as to the point to which we should retreat. It was evident that we would be entirely on the defensive because of the large force of Indians in sight. He designated a high point on the opposite side where we could go to establish ourselves and await developments. The command moved forward at the trot and then at the gallop. At gallop, the head of the companies were almost in line, and the Indians closed in on both flanks and fired into the column. The Indians who had turned our flank had advanced to within five hundred or six hundred yards. None were at the front of the column but a good many were on our right and rear, and the firing on the rear of the column was severe. The Indians passed along the banks of the stream, and thirty or forty fired on us as we crossed. I had one man wounded there. I do not know how many Indians were in the timber. I saw forty or fifty, but there may have been several times that many. I saw only six hundred or seven hundred Indians while in the valley.

When I reached the river, I found it full of horses and men. I stopped at the head of my people and tried to get them together. Many were missing, nine or ten wounded and four or five killed. Then we rode to the top of the hill and dismounted. It was rumored that Custer's command had passed that way. My own idea was that Custer was to our rear and coming to our assistance. I did not know much about Benteen's command, but when someone said cavalry was approaching, I assumed it must be Benteen because of the direction from which it was coming.

If we had stayed thirty minutes longer in the timber, unsupported, I doubt whether we would have gotten out with as many as we did. If we reached the other bank, there was a possibility of aid coming up. We could not have successfully resisted the force of Indians if they had followed us across the river because we did not have sufficient ammunition. The command was not actually driven from the timber, but virtually so, and would have been actually, in a very short time.

There were no trumpet calls, either during the advance or the retreat. Some men, including De Rudio, were left behind in the timber, and there were twelve enlisted men who came out and joined the command about one hour later. Several were killed and wounded at the crossing, among them Hodgson. The crossing was not covered.

The men were not demoralized or despondent when they reached the hill. Neither were they exultant with success. A skirmish line was thrown out in a few minutes. I think Reno rode in the interval between two companies at the head of the column during the retreat. I do not know whether any officer was charged with looking after the rear of the column.

Reno gave his orders during the advance in the bottom as coolly as any man could under the circumstances. He was in front of the command all the time. I saw nothing during the afternoon that indicated cowardice.

Cross-examination: During the advance to the ford and after crossing, the companies were in a column of fours, the heads of the columns separated by an interval of fifteen to twenty-five yards until they were formed in line. Reno's order was, "Companies form left front into line." He was in front. The skirmish line was deployed by his command. He ordered the men to leave the woods and form on the plateau.

Dr. Porter rode at my side on the way out of the timber and up to the plain where my company was being formed. He has told me since that he never was so scared in his life.

In my judgment, if Reno had continued to charge down the valley, he would be there still. The purpose of leaving the timber was to save the command, which, in my judgment, would have been annihilated there unless it had been reinforced. If the Indians had followed and closed in on the retreat to the bluffs, the same result would have followed.

The Indians first became visible in force about the time the companies were formed in line, about half a mile from the crossing. There was a very large, dense cloud of dust. You could not see through it.

I have never heard anyone claim that the retreat to the hill was in the nature of a triumph. I would rather be dejected on the top of a hill than dead in the timber, or anywhere else.

Re-direct examination: Dr. Porter did his duty on the hill in a superb manner. Excitement was a pretty general thing that day, and being frightened at a time of great danger did not imply cowardice. I think everybody was a bit shaken up.

Q. Would it not have been better as a soldier to have been dead in the timber than dishonored on the hill?

A. I don't know that that is a proper question to put to me. Very few men but would prefer to die in the timber than to be on the hill degraded.

Re-cross examination: While the command was in the timber I remember having a conversation with Wallace. He asked me if I could not send word back to Custer of the facts. There was a half-breed Indian scout by the name of Jackson present, and I asked him if he would take a message back. He looked around before he replied, and then sweeping his hand in the manner of Indians to the left and rear, he said, "No one man could get through there alive."

George Herendeen

Direct examination: I was a civilian scout and courier assigned to the Seventh Cavalry Regiment on June 25. About a mile and a half from the village, I heard Custer tell Reno to lead out and he would be with him. Those are about the words I understood him to use. We were next to an Indian lodge. It was about three-quarters of a mile from the river. Custer added, "Take the Indian scouts with you, too." We started at a lope and went to the Little Big Horn. As we advanced down the valley, there was some firing from the timber. The command halted and formed a skirmish line near a little point of timber that came out on the prairie. I did not see any Indians oppose the advance, and I was in front. They were sitting still on their horses and seemed to be waiting for our approach. They did not move until we dismounted. They then rode back and forth and fired at us. I was about one hundred yards to the left of the column. When the soldiers deployed, I went to the left and rear, in a little swale. I was between the troops and the bluff to the left, about on a line with them. Reynolds and Girard were with me. We dismounted and sat down, watching the fire of the troops for a few minutes. We could see some Indians on the hills, but they were too far away for us to shoot at. The troops fired rapidly. At that time I could not see any Indians close to the line. A little while after, the Indians in the valley came up to within three hundred or four hundred yards.

After watching for a few minutes, we took our horses into the timber and tied them there. In coming out I became separated from Reynolds and Girard and was alone after that. I saw Indians circling around through the hills and coming closer to us. I could not see the troops because I was facing away from them. [The skirmish line had apparently been withdrawn to the edge of the timber by this time, and Herendeen must have been beyond the left end of the line.] Presently the soldiers ceased firing, and the Indians came to within forty or fifty steps of me. As there was no firing on the line, they came closer and ran into the timber. I fired at twenty or twenty-five, and more were coming. They were not firing at the troops. They fired three or four shots at me. Ten men could have checked them from getting into the timber at that point. I was there six or seven minutes and fired seven or eight shots. I got in some nice shots and then went to see what the soldiers were doing.

I found all the horses gone but mine. I mounted and rode through into a little park or glade in the timber. There I saw some troops, probably a company, mounted and drawn up in a line with their left toward the river. Reno was sitting on his horse in the park. I heard him order, "Dismount." Then a volley was fired by the Indians. An Indian scout called Bloody Knife was standing about eight feet in front of Reno, and he and another soldier were hit. As Reno gave the order to dismount, the soldier cried out, "Oh, my God, I've got it." The soldiers had just touched the ground when he gave the order to mount, and then everybody left the timber on the run.

On the twenty-sixth or twenty-seventh I was near Reno and asked him if he remembered Bloody Knife being killed. He said, "Yes, and his blood and brains splattered over me." I thought at the time that it demoralized him when Bloody Knife was killed and the soldier cried out. The Indians were not over thirty feet away from us when they fired that volley. Reno mounted, and his horse jumped as if the spurs had been put to him. I always judged, and still do, that the volley and the killing of that man were what made Reno start, and were what stampeded the command.

They got out at any place they could find. There was dense underbrush, and not more than one man could pass at a time, so they had to go single file on a trail that had been made by buffalo or some other animals. I followed and got to the edge of the timber. The men were going as fast as spurs will make a horse go. The dust was dense, and I could not see where I was going. I got about 150 yards when my horse went down, and I fell off. Men were passing me all the time, and everybody was running for his life. About 20 Indians almost ran over me as I fell. I got up and ran back into the timber.

As I got near the timber, men were still coming out, and from the other side of the timber, I could hear an officer trying to halt his men. I think he said, "Company A men, halt! Let us fight. For God's sake, don't run."

I saw no shots fired by the men as they ran. I saw one man throw his gun away as he left the timber. He was left behind, and I don't suppose he knew what he was doing. I found eleven enlisted men in the timber, three of them wounded. We stayed there about two hours and were not troubled by the Indians. Then we rejoined Reno's command on the hill across the river. He was not under attack at the time we joined him, and we saw only a handful of Indians with whom we exchanged a single shot. Varnum and four or five men came out to meet us. The pack train had just come up as I arrived.

In my judgment one hundred men with six or seven thousand rounds of ammunition could have held that timber against the Indians. If they had water and provisions, the Indians couldn't have gotten them out of there at all.

Cross-examination: I was at the side of the dead warrior lodge when Custer gave the order to Reno. I had helped to cut it open to see what was inside. Custer was within fifteen feet of me, coming up, and Reno was right in front of me as I heard the words spoken. I rode within ten feet of Reno until my horse stumbled three or four hundred yards from the ford, at which point I dropped behind. Reno received no other orders from Custer or Custer's adjutant that I know of.

I think the soldiers I saw in the clearing were from more than one company. I was at the edge of the park and could see into it and into the timber, and also onto the hill on the other side. Reno left the glade on a run, and the men started in no order at all. That was what fixed it in my mind that they were running. When I got out a minute later, the troops were running across the prairie, but I could not see the head of the column because of the dust. They were running as fast as they could. There would not have been time to form outside of the timber. I am not saying that Reno is a coward. He was under my observation for not more than a minute. I did not know of the two men who say they were left in the timber at the time I left it. I did not see Girard there either. The skirmish line was deployed for about fifteen minutes before it was withdrawn.

Re-direct examination: Cook might have given an order to Reno without my knowledge. I judge it was about twenty minutes from the time Reno halted and deployed before he left the timber.

Lieutenant L. R. Hare

Direct examination: I was on duty with the scouts on June 25. The scouts called my attention to some Indians ahead, and I spoke to Custer about them. He told me to take the Indian scouts and go ahead, and he would follow. The Indians refused to go, and Custer ordered them dismounted. He turned to adjutant Cook and told him that since the Indians would not go, to order Reno ahead with his battalion. Reno started forward immediately at a fast trot. He took twenty to twenty-five minutes to reach the river. On the other side the command formed into a column by trumpet call and moved down the valley to within a short distance of the point of timber. There it dismounted and formed a skirmish line. Up to this time there were probably forty or fifty Indians riding around and firing. After the command dismounted, four or five hundred came out of a coulee about four hundred yards in front of us, and moved to our left and rear. Reno could not have seen the Indians in this coulee until after he halted and deployed. I was in a better position than he, and I saw nothing until we were deployed.

When the command halted, the Indians, who had been riding back and forth stirring up dust, were about two or three hundred yards away. As fast as they came out of the coulee they would fire from their horses. They were riding to the left, going out in the foothills and coming down again. During the time we were in the bottom, there were always Indians in our front, downstream, two hundred constantly, maybe more. I did not hear Reno give any orders in the bottom. The first I knew that we were going to leave was when my man brought me my horse and told me they were leaving. The left of the skirmish line was thrown back near the timber.

There were probably one thousand Indians opposing Reno on the bottom. The constant firing came from only a part of them, probably two hundred. The command left the timber about thirty to forty minutes after the skirmish line was formed. When I rode onto the beach, the three companies were individually together, well closed up, and seemed to be moving independently of each other. They formed three angles of a triangle and were going at a fast gallop. I first thought it was a charge, but I soon saw that they were making for the bluffs on the other side. I caught up at the crossing where there was considerable confusion, and for that reason I went below and jumped my horse off a bank six or eight feet high. During the retreat, all the Indians were on our right flank, fifty to one hundred yards away and firing into the column. I did not think the movement from the timber was a run, but it was a pretty fast retreat. I heard no bugle calls in the timber. The crossing was not covered, and no effort was made to hold the Indians back. After I got on the hill, I looked back. Not a great many Indians — perhaps one hundred — remained in the bottom. The command was scattered but not demoralized. They rallied and formed promptly.

Before I got to the top of the hill, I heard Varnum calling to the men to halt, and when I got there, Moylan was forming a skirmish line. Reno was in a position from which he could supervise. If the Indians had followed us in force to the hilltop, they would have wiped us out, though not before Benteen came up. The hill position was much better than the timber. I think the difference in the positions more than balanced the loss sustained in getting there. If the Indians had charged us in the timber, we could not have stood it more than a few minutes, but Indians don't do that. We could have stood them off for perhaps thirty minutes by using our ammunition judiciously.

The men's firing was continuous from the time they dismounted until they left the timber. They probably expended forty rounds per man. By judicious use, the ammunition might have lasted an hour longer, though that would have depended on the action of the Indians.

Benteen joined us on the hill about fifteen minutes after we got there. That was about an hour and a half after Reno left Custer at the tepee.

The timber position contained very few large trees. It was mostly underbrush. There is a cut bank downstream and a bend on the other side, continuing to where the river makes this cut bank. In this there is a little park about two hundred yards wide and four or five hundred yards long. The bench around the plain runs into the river downstream. I don't know how it was upstream. The village was not visible from the bottom. On the bank you might have seen the tops of the tepees. We were about six hundred yards from the first tepee. The village extended down the river for three or four miles. The timber position threatened it, but I don't think it would have held the bulk of the Indians there. It did not do so, as a matter of fact, for at no time were there more than one thousand Indians around us. It was a very good defensive position. The bench, or second table, was five or six feet above the level of the park and ran entirely around it, so that men inside were protected by the edge of the bluffs. I think Benteen could have joined us there, but not McDougall. In either case they would have had to charge through to get there, and McDougall could not have charged with the pack train. He had the bulk of the ammunition, twenty-four thousand rounds, besides what his men carried. One hundred and forty mules were in the train.

I don't think that if Benteen had joined Reno, it would have made any difference as to McDougall. The Indians would have closed around again. McDougall could have come along the bluffs on the other side, but he could not have gotten down to the timber. Twenty Indians could have kept him back, or else have killed his mules.

Reno stayed in the timber until all hope of rear support from Custer had vanished. I think the reason we left was because if we had stayed much longer, say twenty minutes, we could not have gotten out at all. Of course, as soon as the command got to the top of the hill, all but one hundred or one hundred and fifty Indians went downstream. Those that stayed in the bottom were taking care of their dead and wounded. They were too far away for us to tell if they were warriors or old men and women.

My impression of the retreat from the timber was that Reno thought we would be shot up there, and the best way to get out was to charge out. At the time, I did not think it was absolutely necessary. If the command had been pursued by the one thousand Indians who were about us, we would have all been killed. It would not have lasted ten minutes.

I know one instance of gallantry on Reno's part, and none of cowardice. When Benteen joined, Reno turned and said in a very inspiring way to his men, "We have assistance now, and we will go and avenge the loss of our comrades." I can only estimate his conduct by the way it turned out. I think his action saved what was left of the regiment. His conduct was always good. He seemed to be very cool at all times.

Cross-examination: I do not know what orders Benteen received nor whether Reno knew what those orders were. From the timber one could see all the way back to the place where Reno had crossed the river. Benteen's column was not in sight when Reno left the timber. The disposition of the troops in the timber was a very good one. I saw no evidence of fear among the men. As to the retreat from the timber, there is certainly always more or less disorder about a cavalry column moving at a fast gait, but I don't think that command was particularly demoralized because when I got on the hill, the men were halted in column and moving to a skirmish line without any difficulty.

LIEUTENANT CHARLES DE RUDIO

Direct examination: I was attached to Company A. I did not hear any orders given to or by Reno, nor any bugle calls on the afternoon of June 25. When the skirmish line was engaging the Indians, their bullets were reaching the troops, but the troops' fire was falling short. I was in the timber investigating the approach of Indians on the other side of the river when the troops retreated, and I was left behind. I spent the first night with Girard and Jackson but was later separated from them. I returned to Reno's command about 3 A.M. on the twenty-seventh.

The Indians followed closely when Reno left the timber, but some of them yelled when they got near the river. I looked up and saw Benteen's column approaching the ford where we had first crossed the Little Big Horn. Before reaching it, however, they turned and disappeared to the right.

Cross-examination: About two hundred Indians were on our right when we were in the timber. I don't know about the left. I was with the skirmish line all the time, and I withdrew to the woods at the same time it did. I saw no indication of cowardice on Reno's part, nor any want of skill in the handling and disposition of the men. When he halted and dismounted, I said to myself, "Good for you," because I thought that if we went five hundred yards further we would be butchered. Some of the shells I found were Winchester, which were used by the Indians. The cavalry used the .45-caliber Springfield carbine.

While in the timber, Girard said it served him right to get in such a position for not having stayed with the pack train. He said that he was not employed to fight.

Re-direct examination: Reno could have held his position in the timber three or four hours by careful use of ammunition. The men on our line fired rapidly; those in the woods, slowly and deliberately. I noticed that when the men on the line fired fast, they overheated their rifles and had to use knives to extract shells after firing eight or ten rounds.

Insofar as I know, it is not the duty of an interpreter to fight.

SERGEANT EDWARD DAVERN

Direct examination: I was Reno's orderly on June 25. I heard Cook tell Reno, "Girard comes back and reports the Indian village three miles ahead and moving. The general directs you to take your three companies and drive everything before you. Captain Benteen will be on your left and will have the same instructions." Those, I believe, were the exact words. This was near a tepee which we passed about a mile and a half or two miles from the river.

[Davern corroborated the testimony of other witnesses regarding the nature of the advance and the skirmishing. He said there was much confusion when the troops left the timber. He learned of the retreat by seeing other men run for their horses.]

When I got out, I saw the command running as fast as it could. The horses were going on a run. I think that some of the men didn't get their horses because they were so mixed up and demoralized. All the men that did get their horses got out. I saw two dismounted men from Company G overtaken and killed by mounted Indians.

Cross-examination: I saw no evidence of cowardice at any time on the part of Reno.

SERGEANT F. A. CULBERTSON

Direct examination: I was assigned to Company A. There were about two hundred and fifty Indians riding back and forth in front of the command at the time it halted, and a few had crossed to the bluffs on the left. The Indians were about five hundred yards away and firing at us when we halted. I heard no firing from the command until we halted and deployed. I was at the extreme left of the line; the right rested near the woods. The skirmish line was about two hundred and fifty yards long. We had remained on the line for a time, some of the new men firing very fast, when the command was given to move by the right flank. Every man moved off by the right flank toward the timber. I stopped when I arrived at the timber with three other men. The balance went into the woods. One man had been wounded on the skirmish line and others were wounded after they got into the woods. We were on the line about thirty-five minutes. We fired three or four shots from the edge of the woods, and then someone called to get our horses. I heard no order to charge and no bugle calls. I don't know where the order came from.

[Culbertson corroborated earlier testimony regarding the confusion during the retreat.]

Cross-examination: If the line had not been retired within three minutes from the time it was, I don't think anyone would have gotten off the line. I don't think Reno could have held the timber but a very few minutes. My estimate of the number of Indians about his position on the skirmish line and in the timber is one thousand to twelve hundred. I always knelt before I fired, but most of the men were new and had never been under fire before. They tended to fire at random. I fired twenty-one shots, but one of the new men told me he had fired sixty.

Girard told me, the night of the twenty-sixth, that he had lost his watch and that he threw his rifle into the river trying to get away.

I saw no evidence of cowardice on the part of Reno at any time.

Major M. A. Reno

Direct examination: About 10 A.M. on the twenty-fifth, Cook came to me and said, "The General directs that you take specific command of Companies A, G, and M." I turned and said, "Is that all?" He replied, "Yes." I made no further inquiry, but moved with my column to the second ridge. Between myself and Custer's column there was a small ravine which developed into a tributary of the Little Big Horn. I moved parallel to General Custer for some time. Previous to that, Benteen had started to the left up a hill. I had no instruction about him, and asked him where he was going and what he was going to do. His reply was to the effect that he was to drive everything before him on the hill. This was all that passed between us. He had Companies D, H, and K. He went over the hills and was soon out of sight. The two other columns continued moving on opposite banks of the stream until we came in sight of the tepee which has been referred to. Custer then beckoned to me with his hat to cross to the bank he was on. When I got there, the battalion was somewhat scattered, and I was about opposite the rear of his column. There I received an order from Cook to move my command to the front. When I got up there, a tumult was going on among the Indian scouts. They were stripping themselves and preparing to fight. I understood that they had refused to go forward, and that Custer had ordered them to give up their guns and horses. I moved forward to the head of the column and shortly after, Cook came to me and said, "General Custer directs you to take as rapid a gait as you think prudent and charge the village afterward, and you will be supported by the whole outfit."

Hodgson was on my left and Wallace was on his left at this time. Wallace had come up laughing and said he was going as volunteer aide. He was not at the time on company duty.

I took a trot and proceeded to carry out my orders. I crossed the creek and formed my battalion with two companies in line and one in reserve. I have been in Indian country a good deal and was convinced that they were present in overwhelming numbers. I sent back word twice; first, by a man named McIlargy, my striker, to say that the Indians were in front of me in strong force. Receiving no instructions, I sent a second man, Mitchell, a cook. They were the nearest men I could get hold of quick. That was some minutes after I had sent McIlargy, and I was convinced that my opinion was correct. I still heard nothing to guide my movement and so proceeded down the valley to carry out my orders.

My first thought was to make a charge with two companies and to hold the third as a rallying point, but when I saw the number of Indians, I sent my adjutant to bring the third company on the line. I was in front near the center and to the right. The Indian scouts had run away, except three or four, and we did not see them again until we got to the Powder River, ninety miles away.

We were then at a gallop, and I was about forty paces in advance. I could see a disposition on the part of the Indians to lead us on, and that idea was confirmed when, upon advancing a little further, I could see them coming out of a ravine in which they had hidden. The ravine was eight or nine hundred yards ahead on what are called the foothills on the left bank. There were also straggling parties of Indians making around to my rear. I saw that I could not successfully make an offensive charge; their numbers had thrown me on the defensive. The village was stretched along the bank to the front and right. There were times going down when I could not see it at all.

I dismounted by giving the order to the company officers. Hodgson gave it to Company G and myself to M and A. I gave the order to dismount and prepare to fight on foot and to shelter the horses in the point of timber.

I had an idea of the number of Indians from their trails, and I saw five or six hundred of them with my own eyes. The dust on the trail I followed was four to six inches deep, and there were several other trails showing that numbers of animals had gone there.

We were in the skirmish line under hot fire for fifteen or twenty minutes. I was on the line near Moylan when word came to me that the Indians were turning my right. I left Hodgson to bring me word of what happened on the line, and I went with Company G to the banks of the river. I suppose there were forty men in the company. When I got there, I had a good view of the tepees and could see many scattered ones. It was plain that the Indians were using the woods as much as I was, sheltering themselves and creeping up on me. I then rode out on the plain. Hodgson came to me and told me they were passing to the left and rear, and I told him to bring the line in around the horses. After going down to the river and seeing the situation, I knew that I could not stay there unless I stayed forever. The regiment evidently was scattered, or someone would have brought me an order or aid. In order to effect a union of the regiment, which I thought absolutely necessary, I moved to the hill where I could be seen, and where I thought I could dispose the men so that they could hold out until assistance came. The men had one hundred rounds each — fifty in their belts and fifty in their saddlebags. Their firing for twenty minutes was what I call quick fire.

While in the timber, I had not the remotest idea where either the pack train or Benteen's column were. No plan was communicated to us. If one existed, the subordinate commanders did not know of it.

I left the timber, sending Hodgson to give the order to French, and giving it myself to Moylan and McIntosh, to mount their men and bring them to the edge of the timber and form in column of fours. I had no other means of accomplishing the formation.

When Bloody Knife was shot, I stood for about ten minutes while the formation was going on. I had nothing to do with it. They had their orders to form the men in column of fours out of the timber. I had made up my mind to go through those people and get to the hill for the purpose of getting the regiment together, so as to have a chance to save those who got through. There was no use of staying in the timber when I could assist no one and create no diversion. I acted on my best judgment, and I think events proved me right.

The Indians were increasing, particularly on the right bank, skipping from tree to tree, keeping themselves as much under shelter as possible. They were much more cunning in woodcraft than the soldiers.

The Indians are peculiar in their manner of fighting. They don't go in line or bodies, but in parties of 5 to 40. You see them scattering in all directions. My opinion is that 600 or 700 Indians were there, and I had but 112 men. I thought it my duty to give those men the best chance I could to save themselves as it was impossible to have a victory over the Indians. I thought it my duty as a military movement, and I took the responsibility.

The column was formed to go through the Indians on that side. I felt sure that some us would go up. We were bound to. Some would get hit, and I would lose part of my command. I was willing to risk that in order to save the lives of the others from the desperate position we were in.

I saw Bloody Knife shot and also a man of Company M, to whom the attention of the doctor was at once directed. Bloody Knife was within a few feet of me. I was trying to get information about the Indians' activity from him by signs. I did not immediately leave the glade and the timber and go on a gallop to the river. I had given orders for the formation, and I went through the timber and up on the plain to satisfy myself about the Indians there. Moylan was at my side. Before Bloody Knife was killed, the formation was being made to leave the timber. The column was formed, A in front, G in the center, and M at the rear. I was at the head of the column, and the gait was a rapid one. I thought it my duty to be there, to see about the direction of the column and to observe the ford and the hill on the other side. I would be on the hill to rally and re-form the men. I stopped at the river a moment. The men crossed hurriedly, and it threw the rear into confusion. They were exposed to heavy fire, and I lost many there. The Indians had Winchester rifles, and the column made a big target. They were pumping bullets into it. I did not regard the movement as a triumphant march, nor did I regard it as a retreat. When I reached the hill, after a glance about, I thought it as good a position as I could get in the time I had. I immediately put the command in skirmish line through the company commanders.

At the time I left the timber, I did not see Benteen's column, nor had I the remotest reason to expect him to unite with me. But in a short time after reaching the hill I saw him not far off and rode out to meet him. I told him what I had done. He moved his battalion to where mine was.

My motive in leaving the timber was that we had an immense force against us, and nobody came to our assistance. I was not certain that anybody knew where I was, unless directed by the firing. The position, in my judgment, was not tenable, and I thought that by placing my command on the hill, the scattered portions of the regiment could get together. It was my opinion that that was the only possible means of getting anybody away alive.

I never had any intimation that Benteen was to support me in my attack on the bottom. I did not even know where he was.

I received no communication from Girard at the place we crossed the river. He had no right to speak to me officially. I had had trouble with Girard and discharged him because I thought he was stealing from the government.

The only expectation of support I had from the order I received was from the rear. I do not feel that I failed in my duty, and I think the results of the day justify me.

Cross-examination: When I said that no plan was communicated to us I meant to the regiment. I do not think there was any plan.

I had no reason to believe that Custer would support me in any other way than from the rear. In my opinion there was no other way. An attack on the flank would not have been a support under the circumstances, though I may have stated in my first report that he intended to do so. I did not know where Benteen was. He might have gone to the mouth of the Rosebud for all I knew.

My relations with Custer were friendly enough, and if my own brothers had been in his column, I could not have done any more than I did.

Q. The question is, did you go into that fight with feelings of confidence or distrust?

A. My feelings toward Custer were friendly.

Q. I insist that the question shall be answered.

A. Well, sir, I had known Custer a long time, and I had no confidence in his ability as a soldier. I had known him all through the war.

I suppose from six to nine hundred Indians were on my left and rear when I left the timber, and plenty were in front, between me and the village. And they were in force on the other side of the river, in sheltered places, within close range, less than one hundred yards away.

My casualties, before I decided to get out of there, were one scout killed and three or four soldiers wounded. The smallest number of men who could have held that timber was six or seven hundred, and they would have had to hold the edge of the timber all around or the Indians would have crept up and infiltrated the timber. I think the regiment could have done it, but not one hundred and twenty men — and I did not have one hundred and twenty. To cover the necessary space, that number of men would have been beyond speaking distance apart, and their fire would have been no support at all.

I suppose the Indians killed the wounded left in the timber. I could make no effort to take them out, and none was made. I do not know what became of the wounded left on the plain. The Indians would not permit me to take care of them.

I received no communication from Girard at the crossing. I would not have believed it if I had. I should have listened to him, but I repeat, I should not have believed him.

I consider that the results of the battle justified my every act, and with the knowledge I then had, I would again do the same thing under the same circumstances. I believe that I obeyed orders. I did not charge into the village, but I went far enough to discover that it was impossible. Of course, ten men could be ordered to charge a million; a brilliant illustration is the battle of Balaklava. I knew nothing then about the topography, but it afterward developed that had I gone 300 yards further, the command would have been thrown into a ditch ten yards wide and three or four feet deep. The Indians were in it, and the command would never have gotten that far. By the time they had got within a few yards, most of the saddles would have been emptied and the horses killed.

I was responsible for the union of my battalion with the rest of the regiment, and I believed I would find them on the other side of the river. I knew they were not on my side.

Re-direct examination: I had 112 soldiers and officers when I crossed the river going to the attack, and about 27 Indian scouts who didn't remain with me long. I did everything I could to assist and co-operate with Custer as much as if he were my own brother. Never in my life did I feel more interest in the success of an engagement because the Seventh was essentially my own regiment. I feel that I did everything possible short of sacrificing my command.

The principle which actuated me in returning to the hill was that of reuniting with Custer, not leaving him unsupported. I went out of there as much to aid him as to secure aid.

When I said in my report that Custer meant to support me by a flank attack, it was a conviction formed after the fight. I expected my support to come from the direction I had crossed. I did not see how it was possible, on account of the high banks on the other side, for support to come down from the flanks. I didn't think it was practicable to get down below me.

The number of wounded had nothing to do with my action in the timber. I should have done the same thing if no man had been hit.

Examination by the Court: When I retreated from the bottom, I had no idea where Custer was. I knew he was not on the side where the village was, and if there was any chance for him to see me it was on this hill. I had no doubt that I could explain the retreat from my position, but I did not give it a thought. I never thought it would be questioned.